RIVERSIDE WOMEN CREATING CHANGE

Riverside Women Creating Change:
Stories and Inspiration

ISBN: 978-1-955969-29-1 (paperback)
ISBN: 978-1-955969-30-7 (ebook)

Permissions
Inlandia Institute
4178 Chestnut Street
Riverside, CA 92501

Executive Director: Cati Porter
Publications Coordinator & editor: Laura Villareal
Editor: Nicolette Rohr
Book layout & design: Mark Givens

Library of Congress Control Number: 2024945699

Printed and bound in the United States
Distributed by Ingram

RIVERSIDE WOMEN CREATING CHANGE

Stories and Inspiration

A project of

The Riverside Women Creating Change Collaborative

AN INLANDIA INSTITUTE PUBLICATION

RIVERSIDE, CALIFORNIA

Every moment is an organizing opportunity,
Every person a potential activist, and
Every minute a chance to change the world.

Dolores Huerta

No one does anything alone.

Jane Block

Contents

Introduction 11

Ancestors 17

A note on the interviews 19

Daisy Ocampo
On Cahuilla lands, on Serrano lands 21

Nancy Melendez
"Grassroots preservationists" 27

Mary Figueroa
"A voice for the community" 33

Chani Beeman
"Healing work" 41

The Group: Rose Mayes, Ola Faye Stephens, Jennifer Vaughn-Blakely
"Speak out and speak up" 49

Deborah Wong
"We agreed to stay at it" 57

Linda Dunn
"The secret is listening" 65

Marilyn Sequoia
"Peace is…" 69

Rose Y. Monge
"Always peacebuilding" 77

Andrea Briggs
The next step 83

Judith Auth
"Being a librarian is a radical act" 89

Joan Donahue
"Speaking from a well-informed perspective" 97

Nancy Takano
"Another good trouble" 101

Jane Block
"No enemies, just people who need more information" 107

Connie Ransom
"Sometimes you have to be the one to do it" 115

Sarah Wright Garibay
"Be that person that shows up" 123

Sue Mitchell
"Leverage yourself" 127

Patricia Lock Dawson
"Go get it done" 133

Ofelia Valdez-Yeager
Connecting people 141

Marisa V. Yeager
Team player 147

Lecia Elzig
"Focus on the mission" 153

Donatella Galella
Righteous anger, generative action 159

Rabbi Suzanne Singer
"Don't let them erase you" 167

Vonya Quarles
"We co-power" 173

Maribel Nuñez
Help create different spaces 179

Yolanda Esquivel
"Think about the lives that are touched" 185

Elizabeth Ayala
"Train the community to speak for itself" 191

Penny Newman
"We were dismissed as hysterical housewives" 199

Thomi Clinton
"Everything's a process" 207

Connie Confer
"The gay people to talk to" 211

Erin Edwards
Love and Riverside 217

Gaby Plascencia
The first 225

Clarissa Cervantes
Planting seeds 229

Riverside Resistance Revival Chorus: Kris Lovekin, Jerri Mendivel, Dawn Pia
A ripple effect 233

Sherry Mackay
Building community 241

Selin Yildiz Nielsen
"Everywhere can be home" 249

Friba Dawar
"The education of women" 257

Paulette Brown-Hinds
"Behind the scenes, below the surface" 263

M. Rosalind Sagara
The power of place 269

Carol Park
"Be tenacious" 277

Precious Pipeloluwa Fasakin
"Be the archivist of your own life" 283

Rose Mayes
"Then pass the torch" 289

Women's History Timeline 297

Acknowledgments 301

About Riverside Women Creating Change 303

Index 305

About Inlandia Institute 309

Inlandia Books 310

Introduction

Like many other projects in Riverside, this book was Jane Block's idea. Jane envisioned a kind of "how-to" manual for would-be women-identifying activists. Here, you will find stories of exceptional women who have contributed to the Riverside community alongside examples of what they have done and some practical, useful ideas and advice to inspire you to make your own contributions—excerpted from interviews with the activists themselves.

Jane first shared her idea with Connie Ransom. Connie talked to Cati Porter, Executive Director of the Inlandia Institute, as well as Catherine Gudis and Christine Gailey from UC Riverside, who, along with Paulette Brown-Hinds of *Black Voice News*, attended early meetings and affirmed this idea with their interest in collecting and sharing stories of Riverside women. Cati invited Nicolette Rohr, a historian who had worked with Inlandia on another story of Riverside women. Then someone had the brilliant idea to invite Deborah Wong, professor of ethnomusicology at UCR, who moved the project forward with enthusiasm and led us to Andrea Decker, who transcribed the interviews and offered valuable insights. Catherine Gudis introduced us to Katherinne Reinoza-Zaldana, an undergraduate at UCR, who contributed to the transcription as part of their studies. Kris Lovekin helped gather materials. We – Jane, Connie, Cati, Deborah, Nicolette, Andrea – became the working group, which we called "Riverside Women Creating Change," meeting regularly. Our model is one of collaboration, sharing the labor, with each of us taking on different roles to make something out of this idea.

Our earliest meetings were at Jammin' Bread, Cellar Door Books, or Simple Simon's, all iconic Riverside spots that have been incubators for change. We thought out loud, listened, and made lists of women we might interview. We talked about how a book might look. Then, shortly after meeting on March 13, 2020, everything changed. The pandemic began, and we moved our meetings to Zoom. Our conversations started to include finding toilet paper, shopping for groceries, wearing masks, supporting our treasured local businesses, and the new routines of our pandemic lives.

In the midst of it, we dove in. Together, we interviewed Jane and Connie. By now, we all knew each other but learned so much more from asking questions and listening. Who to interview next? We put out a call on Facebook and created an online form for recommendations of women to interview. Cati introduced our project to readers of *The Press-Enterprise* in Inlandia's weekly column. We gathered more local women – still on Zoom! – to tell them about the project and collect ideas. Deborah and Nicolette started interviewing. Our Zoom interviews – although missing some of the comfort and connection of being in person – proved easy to record and were welcome hours in the isolation of the pandemic. What a gift to talk with so many remarkable women!

The "Riverside women" included in this book were interviewed in 2020 and 2021, and a few in 2022. We know they have many peers and that we all have many ancestors.

Riverside sits on Cahuilla, Tongva, Serrano, and Luiseño land, Indigenous peoples who first called this place home. In the time of the Californios, the women of Agua Mansa, whose descendants we interviewed for this project, made homes on this land. Some of them, like Mercedes Alvarado Jensen, left traces we still see today. Later in the nineteenth century, English immigrants sought to establish a colony on this land. Eliza Tibbets is well known in the city of Riverside's founding story for planting the parent navel orange tree that helped birth the citrus industry, as well as being an advocate for women's suffrage and abolition. Immigrants from China, Japan, Korea, Mexico, and elsewhere picked and packed the citrus that made Riverside flourish. Alice Miller Richardson of Riverside's Mission Inn contributed to Riverside's growth through her hospitality. Women's labor was essential to both the Inn and to the citrus groves, and women built community – this community – in the neighborhoods, churches, and schools that became part of Riverside. When the predominantly Mexican American neighborhood of Casa Blanca petitioned for a neighborhood school, it was two women who walked miles across town to successfully present their argument to the school board. Those women, known then only as *Las Adelitas* but now identified as Ysabel S. Olvera and her *comadre* Margarita Salcedo Solorio, are our ancestors. In the 1960s, when many of the stories in this book begin, Sue Strickland and Woodie Rucker-Hughes were part of the integration of Riverside schools and pillars of the community for many years. Ruth Anderson Wilson, Martha McClean, and Kay Black founded the Tri-County Conservation League in 1966 and worked to save the Santa Ana River. Beverly Wingate Maloof helped save the Mission Inn and Heritage House and organized Riverside's inventory of historic homes. Mothers of Jurupa Valley, then part of Riverside, fought tirelessly to raise awareness about the Stringfellow Acid Pits and the harm done to their families, laying a strong foundation for environmental justice organizing.

Oral interviews are at the core of this project, therefore this book features only women we were able to interview, but we acknowledge our ancestors in telling the history of women in organizing in Riverside. Some of these ancestors are acknowledged at the beginning of the book. Many of their names – Sumi Harada, Woodie Rucker-Hughes, Kay Smith, Mary Lou Morales – are brought up in these interviews. Ruth Anderson Wilson and Sue Strickland died while we were working on this project. We had the privilege of interviewing Nancy Takano, Jennifer Vaughn-Blakely, and Ofelia Valdez-Yeager before they joined the ancestors. Their passing affirmed the need to keep collecting and sharing stories.

There are, of course, many women we did not interview for a range of reasons, not least of them time. There are those we tried to contact but never reached or who declined to be interviewed. There are also some who were interviewed for this project but whose interviews are not included here due to space constraints and other considerations. Their interviews, along with the full transcripts of those excerpted in this book, will find their home in the local history archives at the Riverside Public Library and throughout California on Calisphere and will, hopefully, provide both information and inspiration for researchers and Riversiders of the future, and others who may wish to use this project as a model and blueprint for their own like-minded projects.

We knew from the beginning we could not interview all of the women creating change in this community. The women we interviewed represent a range of ages, interests, and involvement. The oldest was in her early nineties at the time of the interview, and the youngest was in her early twenties. Many were born in Riverside, and many were not. Some had spouses and partners, some did not. Some did not have children, and of those who did, only some had access to child care. Noticing this, some of these women worked to expand child care resources. Some of them were drawn to activism early in their lives, and others much later. Some women had ready access to funding, while others encountered more material barriers. Some own or owned businesses, some were or are educators, many worked in both blue-collar and white-collar sectors, some never worked, and nearly all volunteered their time. Some have served in elected office, some have worked to elect others, and many have fought with or beside elected officials at one time or another. All contributed to the making of this community. Some are also connected to national movements and campaigns.

Many of the women interviewed were reluctant to call themselves activists. We chose to conceive of activism and organizing broadly and include a range of experiences. All of these women share commitments to social justice and community – whether through equality, the environment, cultural heritage, historic preservation, the arts, education, or any number of other causes.

"Community" has been central to each part of this project. The influence, inspiration, and support of others are clear in each interview. "No one does anything alone," Jane often says. Pride and appreciation for this community are clear as well. In many ways, these interviews are in community—they give us glimpses into how women navigated their lives and their lives in Riverside, the barriers they faced, and the issues that activated them. They remind us that people build and experience community differently. The interviews offer different advice about attitudes, approaches, and outcomes. The experiences often reflect varying access to resources and ideas about money. We are mindful of the role of privilege and the real barriers many women face. We present these interviews with attention to these distinctions and a belief that recognizing them helps contribute to understanding in and of our community.

We hope, therefore, that along with the stories of these individual women and the advice and inspiration they offer, this book also helps tell stories of Riverside, especially those individual stories that are in danger of being forgotten or may not have yet been told or told often enough. At its core, this is a local history – it takes place on the Eastside and in the Wood Streets; at UC Riverside and Riverside City College; the Riverside Art Museum and the Mission Inn; First Congregational Church and Temple Beth El; and often at Simple Simon's and Zacatecas.

These interviews also document the histories of national and global events and movements as they looked here: consciousness-raising, conservation, domestic violence, gun violence, police violence, police reform, marriage equality, Black Lives Matter, the Women's March, the March for

Our Lives. Hopefully, some of these stories offer a glimpse of how these movements looked in Riverside. Memories of Bobby Kennedy and Cesar Chavez visiting the Eastside. Jesse Jackson and Al Sharpton marching with the people of Riverside following the murder of Tyisha Miller. Nancy Takano chatting with Nancy Pelosi. These are all reminders of the connections between the local and far beyond.

This book includes a timeline that is also available on the website of the Inlandia Institute and can be used in classrooms, along with excerpts of the interviews themselves. The website also includes a map of places named for women in Riverside – there are not many, but we are hopeful there will be more to come.

Part of Jane's original idea was to offer advice for others, both practical ideas and philosophical inspiration. We are well aware that there are more stories to tell. The partial nature of our knowledge underscores the importance of these interviews and the need to listen. Here, in profiles of these women, snapshots of this community, stories amount to wisdom. We hope they offer an appreciation for the work that has been done and inspiration for the work ahead.

—Riverside Women Creating Change collaborative

Ancestors

Lulamae Clemons

Deenaz P. Coachbuilder

Melba Dunlap

Nati Fuentes

Eleanor Jean Grier

Sumi Harada

Sylvia Martin James

Martha McClean

Tyisha Miller

Marion Mitchell-Wilson

Mary Lou Morales

Margarita Salceda Solorio

Miné Okubo

Ysabel Solorio Olvera

Woodie Rucker-Hughes

Kay Smith

Sue Strickland

Nancy Takano

Eliza Tibbets

Ofelia Valdez-Yeager

Jennifer Vaughn-Blakely

Ruth Anderson Wilson

A note on the interviews

Each woman was asked a common set of questions: When and where they were born, and how they came to Riverside; how they were called to activism; what they believe are their most significant contributions; who their role models are; and what advice they would give to would-be activists. Their responses are organized into five categories: *roots, call to activism, contributions, inspiration, and advice.*

These oral interviews were significantly longer conversations with one or more interviewers. The interviews were transcribed for archival purposes. Each interview comes verbatim from the subject, though for purposes of this book, all have been edited for length and clarity, and ellipses have been removed for readability. Some explanatory brackets have been added, but only when necessary.

All of the interviewees gave their consent to be interviewed. Those included here also gave their permission for their interviews to be shared and published in this way. We are deeply grateful to all these women for sharing their stories with us and with you.

On Cahuilla lands, on Serrano lands

Daisy Ocampo

Roots

I was born in 1987 in L.A. I grew up in an area called Mid-City, and then later on we moved to the Crenshaw area of South Central L.A. My parents took us back home to my dad's hometown in Mexico very often, to our small community of about three hundred people, so my upbringing was always in two different places. I always had this awareness of home being elsewhere. Home for me is our small community outside of Juchipila, in the Caxcan region. My experience growing up in L.A. was layered by different identities. I was born here, so I was American, but I was in such a bubble within my community that I was often out of the loop of popular shows and all. I grew up with like-minded kids, cousins, and peers with very similar experiences, and very similar experiences as our parents. We had multi-generational households. We were very protected by our own cultural space.

I came to Riverside for college, like a lot of folks. I came to UCR for undergrad and I stayed for my graduate program, which included my MA and my PhD. As an eighteen-year-old, I came here thinking I was just going to go to UCR, but as the years went, I started meeting more people, and I was welcomed by my family here, and I'm thankful for that.

Call to activism

Back home we have our creation mountain, Tlachialoyantepec. In Spanish it's called Cerro de las Ventanas. There are a lot of issues surrounding it, with Native people and tourism and dispossession and needing to access our sacred places for ceremonies and culturally specific dances. We are people of this place, we came from this place, from this mountain, and our stories narrate how and why that mountain is there and how we came to be. INAH [Instituto Nacional de Antropología e Historia, or National Institute of Anthropology and History] had a really hard time understanding that and why we oppose the way they're handling the remains of our ancestors. I was called to activism because I was asked to produce a historical accounting of our tribe's relationship to this mountain. My work and my call to activism was through my graduate program because my community needed proof that this is a sacred place for our people and that we should therefore have some bargaining power in the way the place is presented and programmed and accessed, ultimately. I did archival research. I conducted ethnographic interviews with community members. **Activism needs to meet a community need, and that's how I saw some of my work, engaging with a need that was there.** They needed a PhD to say the same things that we had been arguing for decades.

When I think of Riverside as a place, I know a lot of folks see this place as "The City of Riverside," but I think of my role as a guest on Cahuilla lands, as a guest on Serrano lands, and that kind of reorients things for me so that my place here in Riverside and as a guest is really to think about the ways that I can support California Indian communities here in the Inland Empire and how I can help. That has meant starting a tribal college. That has meant doing a virtual exhibit for Sherman Indian Museum. It's about making sure that my position is of service for communities here in the area. That's how I was called into activism, and I always think of my work in conversation with activism because it is always meeting community needs, and I don't think anything I engage in is ever divorced from that reality. I like working with people. I like understanding the nuances of the needs. I work really hard to be thorough in my thinking and listening to folks about what's needed, and making sure that I'm not projecting what I think is needed. I did public history at UCR, and that can mean a lot of different things to different people, but for me, it was always driven by community, and community approaches can be different than public approaches to history. With my community, our community needs look very different from what INAH hoped would be this publicly accessible archaeological site. I look at that thread of conversation with my people and also the Chemehuevi people here in the East Mojave Desert and their sacred place, which is Mamápukaib, or the Old Woman Mountain.

Contributions

My projects are very long-term. I've come to terms with that; as a person, I like very long-term, visionary work. Years ago, it was so hard to break through meetings to be heard or even have a platform to speak about needs and our own unique approaches to community and place and culture. When I got to Riverside, where there was limited institutional infrastructure around Native people, and fast forward seventeen years, I'm always at meetings with Land Acknowledgment. Everyone's trying to understand how to engage with Native people. Just to be able to witness that growth and trajectory is very exciting. We've seen it in higher education, we've seen it in a lot of city planning. I was asked to work with the water board on stewardship and Native partnership. These are things that would not have been possible even ten years ago.

I'm absolutely excited that I got to witness the California Indian Nations College. It is located in Palm Desert. The goal was really to develop a stepping stone that was missing within higher education in the area, which is a two-year college, so when someone graduates high school and they didn't have the best grades, like a lot of us, and want to go to college, there's this community college step. We always give credit to Theresa Mike from the Twenty-Nine Palms Band of Mission Indians. We were at the Museum of Riverside at one of these UCR meetings about what tribes need, and she just stood up and said, "I don't want to keep coming to these meetings; we need a two-year college. We have students that are interested in accessing higher education but we keep losing them in the community college systems because they need that cultural grounding." She asked us to meet one day, and we did, and we kind of stayed along for the ride. I helped in its establishment and founding, but she's really the visionary, and I learned a lot from her. Theresa's vision to bring us together and keep us together was to me very inspirational. We've worked with College of the Desert, and the college is still going and growing and because it caught this momentum it's finally receiving support and resources.

I teach at Cal State San Bernardino now, and I believe they hired me for what I do. I've never felt like I had to do anything different than what I'm already doing. I've been lucky enough that my work and their interest to keep growing partnerships with tribes aligned.

Inspiration

In terms of organizers, I would credit my community and how they're able to organize across borders. It's amazing to keep that level of engagement and communication and project-oriented work, on both sides of the border. They just do it because it's part of the thing you do. I have always admired their work and how they're able to operate that way.

I admire Theresa Mike. She reminds me a lot of my grandmother. She has a very subtle and direct way of asking for what she needs. She's very calm. She doesn't speak much, so when she does, it's always a moment of pause. While I'm not necessarily that person, I admire that there's different leadership styles and that not everyone is an MLK or Dolores Huerta. **People have different ways of participating and of creating that momentum and movement towards life with integrity and purpose.** Odilia Romero is an administrator for an organization called CIELO [Comunidades Indígenas en liderazgo], a Native migrant grassroots organization in L.A. to help advocate for Native immigrant experiences and rights, especially when dealing in court and hospitals. Odilia developed this platform when no one really cared for it, and she grew the organization and it has expanded and developed and bloomed. I admire people that are able to carry a vision when no one believes in it and see it when it blooms.

Advice

Let me think of what I needed to hear growing up. I think what I needed to hear, and young women still need to hear, is to find your voice. That gets said and tossed around so much, but now as I'm older, I understand that finding your voice is finding that part of yourself that has kind of managed to peel all these external projections of what a woman is supposed to be and who you are supposed to be and what the world wants from you. I think to be able to find you outside of all of that is extremely difficult, and it takes many of us our entire lives trying to do a lot of unlearning. As a mother, one of my goals is to reduce the amount of things that my daughter is going to have to unlearn in the future. But in there is your voice, the thing that you can identify as what you like, what you do, what moves you, where your imagination drifts when you're by yourself. My advice would be to connect to those spaces more and more and then somehow build community around that. One, you're yourself, and two, you're not alone. Those are two critical things in life, but especially in activism. You're trying to find like-minded people who are trying to find new liberatory paradigms. People are just trying to taste freedom a little bit more, you know?

"Grassroots preservationists"

Nancy Melendez

Roots

I was born in St. Bernadine's Hospital in San Bernardino. I lived for my first four years in Colton with my grandparents, and then we moved to Highgrove, just across the county line into Riverside. I went to Highgrove Elementary School, University Heights Junior High, North High School, RCC, and then graduated from Cal Poly Pomona. My dad and my mom were kind of a 1950s Romeo and Juliet story. My dad was Latino, my mother was a white girl from a very prominent family in our town—Barbara Best of the Best and Krieger family. At the time in Riverside, we were still pretty segregated, and my mother was not afforded the support that she needed, so she gave me to my grandparents. My dad was always in my life, as was my mother. She came to visit, and I got to meet my half-siblings. I was happy living with my grandparents and being raised by the Baca side of the family. So it was all well and good.

We've been here a long time. The earliest community in this area, La Placita de los Trujillos, started in the 1840s, prior to statehood and thirty years prior to the city of Riverside. It was a small community of around eighty-five families, so the marriage pool was limited, and cousins abounded. In the 1840s, Lorenzo Trujillo, who was a Genízaro, a Native American raised in a Spanish household in northern New Mexico, led several travel expeditions across the Old Spanish Trail from Abiquiu (near Santa Fe), with the ultimate destination of Los Angeles and Mission San Gabriel. He did that for people that we know well in history, like Louis Rubidoux and like Benjamin Wilson, mayor of Los Angeles in the 1850s. He knew the Lugo brothers of Rancho San Bernardino, who enlisted Lorenzo to bring families west to settle there. In 1842, Lorenzo set out with ten families, walking across the Old Spanish Trail, twelve hundred miles, walking. They settled in what we know as Inland Center. They were there for about eighteen months, and there was some issue with the land being transferred from the San Bernardino land grant to the settlers from New Mexico, and they were quite distressed after walking three months to get here to start a new life. They contemplated going back to New Mexico, but Juan Bandini came forward and deeded them land in today's Northside and South Colton. They began community-building. They built the first church, San Salvador de Jurupa, in 1852. Lorenzo and these Genízaro families from New Mexico wanted to own land, that's the American dream, so they came here and started La Placita. It was the largest non-native community along the Old Spanish Trail between 1842 and 1848, and then, with statehood, it continued to grow until the flood of 1862 totally decimated the over one hundred family dwellings that were in the area. No lives were lost, but all the homes were lost and the area that was so very fertile at the beginning was not so fertile because of the feet of silt that was deposited. We always grew up with that proud heritage. After the Mexican-American War and statehood in 1850, the majority of our community embraced the United States. We were Americans. We were here first. We didn't cross the border, the border crossed us. We were very Americanized. Schools were not equipped to teach children who didn't speak English, and I recall in elementary school that some of my friends who spoke mostly Spanish were seated in the back of the classroom, so they were segregated within the classroom because the teacher didn't have the capability to communicate. My grandparents knew that, so they encouraged me not to speak Spanish, which was a big detriment in adult life.

Call to activism

I grew up in the sixties, a time of social revolution, and you were supposed to make it better. You wanted to make your community a better place to live, not only for yourself but for your neighbors. I'm just a child of the sixties. We've been labeled the generation that wants to fix everything, and here we are, trying to share this history and let people know that it's important and that we should all share stories of history.

Contributions

I went to work for the Chamber of Commerce in 2000. I was a member of the Chamber at the time, and the director of the Keep Riverside Clean and Beautiful program stood up and said she was leaving and they were looking for a replacement. She kind of read off her job duties, and I went, "They pay you to do that?" Because I did all this stuff for free as a volunteer in the community. I was lucky enough to get that job and worked with various departments and programs—seven years in litter reduction, graffiti prevention, beautification, tree planting. Then I went to the Riverside Community College District Foundation, where I got to work with students and make wonderful connections in the education community.

When Darlene Trujillo Elliot was working in Mayor Ron Loveridge's office, and I was working in the Chamber, the first time I came into the Mayor's office, Darlene said, "Are we cousins?" And yes, we are! In 2011, we received notice of an activity at the Agua Mansa cemetery, where another cousin, Lenny Trujillo, had been working with the San Bernardino County Museum to recognize Lorenzo's role in forming the community. By that point, the Agua Mansa cemetery had been closed and vandalized and we couldn't identify where Lorenzo's grave was, so Lenny wanted to commemorate his significant role in creating this community with a sculpture. So we met at this event, and folks from Highgrove, La Placita, Northside, South Colton were there. I met a third cousin, Suzanne Armas, and we looked around and we saw these wonderful people that we'd known as children who were now aging adults, and we thought, "Gosh, they've done a great job trying to keep this story alive, but someone's got to take up the mantle and run with this." Truthfully it was something I had always wanted to do. I had grown up with the stories of La Placita through my grandparents, and I wanted to do something, but life gets in the way. You get married, you have children, you get a job. So at this point in 2011 we decided the three of us were going to do something. We tried to figure out how we could reach the largest amount of people at one time and get the message out, because no one knew about the story of this early settlement prior to cityhood and prior to statehood except a few historians who really dug in and knew the story, and those of us who heard some bits of the story growing up. So we thought, in our families, whenever we want to tell somebody something, we gather everybody, we feed them, and then we give them the news—good, bad, or ugly. We decided to have a tamale festival. We had about two thousand people there, which we thought was a glorious success. We had a family connections booth to share the story, where people could come and talk to descendants of Lorenzo, see pictures, see mementos, check their DNA. We got up and shared the story to the public assembled. In the meantime, we went about gathering support from our local electeds. We started sharing the story in that way and growing the festival. It went from two thousand to five thousand to about fifteen thousand the third year. We filled the street all the way down Ninth Street from the gate of White Park. It was our way of getting the word out. We get together, we eat, and we share the story.

We call ourselves grassroots preservationists, because we are in no way professionals. We have been learning as we go. We all heard those stories, because when our elders would gather, usually the girls were kept inside with the women and the boys went out to play. My cousin Sharon Trujillo Kasner would hide under the coffee table and just listen to everything that was said, so Sharon has a rich background of all the inside stories of the family and knows who's related to whom and who married whom, and has a wonderful collection of wedding photos throughout the years. I didn't know about the Old Spanish Trail until I got involved with Lenny Trujillo, who introduced me to Alex King, who is the Baca descendant, and I'm a Baca descendant, so we started talking. He was involved with the Old Spanish Trail Association. We started a chapter here in town, and it now is one of the larger chapters in the Old Spanish Trail Association that spans six different states: New Mexico, Colorado, Utah, Arizona, Nevada, and California, all the states the trail goes through. We went to Genealogical Society of Hispanic America conferences and Old Spanish Trail Association conferences. We started reading old historical documents, we started talking to the Riverside Historical Society, looking at everything we could to learn what actually happened here in our little city. As we go along and we learn new things every day, we have uncovered this treasure trove of history that we want to share. We even discovered that in Riverside Unified School District's curriculum, there's an optional curriculum for third graders about the Trujillo Adobe. We have been sending out notices to teachers to say if you want an optional curriculum for your city and county history, here's this. We're right now working with the Riverside Art Museum on their Art-to-Go program. We're hoping to have the new school that's being built in Highgrove be named after Lorenzo Trujillo. We just worked with the Mayor's office to ceremonially rename Orange Street from Columbia to Center Street Spanish Town Road. When Riverside started in the 1870s, our community of La Placita de Los Trujillos was still a thriving community, and so the road from the Mile Square to La Placita was dubbed Spanish Town Road. It was a derogatory name. We decided we'd take that name and go with it, and that's how we came up with the name for our foundation as well. All these things that we've been doing are little bits of telling the story. We just submitted an application to the National Park Service to have the Adobe recognized. It's already recognized along the Old Spanish Trail as a site of high potential, but with the certification of the site, it will be on the GIS app for National Park Service, so that when people are in town, they can ask, "Are there any National Park Service sites in town?" it will lead them to the Adobe, and we did that for the Agua Mansa Cemetery as well. The Trujillo Adobe was recently named to the "Eleven Most Endangered Places" list [of the National Trust for Historic Preservation]. These are all Riverside stories, and we should learn them all along with John North and Sam Evans and all the histories that we learn in school. It should be a rich tapestry of all these things. This is what made Riverside what it is today. Because we celebrate ourselves as a community of diversity and inclusion, so now we need to prove it.

I never professed to be a writer or a storyteller, but I can talk a lot. People will ask, "You've been pretty successful, what's your secret?" And I say, "Well, we don't stop talking." I think a lot of people do things just to make us go away. Inlandia was a draw because I love working with people who have this talent to write and create. I don't think I have that talent, so I want to be around them and to support them and to help them share their story, because in some way that helps me share our story. I particularly love when Sharon and I go to the schools to share this story with third graders and then we tell them the names of the ten families that first came over in 1842–43, and their faces light up, the eyes get big, the hands shoot up in the air, and they say, "That's my name! That's my cousin's name! That's my aunt's name!" And they know. It's that sense of empowerment and belonging. And to see that in those children's faces, and I see that in my sons' faces now that they know that this is our family history and that we are definitely part of this community.

I think in community-based organizing you have to determine who you want to communicate with and share your story with and then make your plans to do so. If it means you have to join a few different groups to do that, then that's what you do. We ran into having to do some organizing in our preservation efforts because of the heavily commercial area the Adobe sits in. We were involved in the battle over the warehouses in our city, and so it led to a lot of communications and community events to share the importance and significance and why we need to take another look at the Northside, a neighborhood that has received relatively little attention. Our ultimate vision has always been to see the area preserved and to have an interpretive center and have it open as a park, like an Old Town Riverside where people could come and learn the history.

Inspiration

I look up to our local leaders, Ofelia Valdez-Yeager, Rose Mayes, Jennifer Vaughn-Blakely, Woodie Rucker-Hughes, all great Riverside legends. These are the people who got things done.

Advice

Be yourself. Don't let anyone intimidate you or tell you you can't do what you want to do. That is something that people tell women all the time - you can't do that - and we have to remember *sí se puede*, you can do it. Be kind, but get your job done and move forward. Sometimes it's so difficult, you just don't want to do it again, but like we tell our kids, you get up, you dust yourself off, and you go again. I probably learned that from my family as well. Listen to other people's perspectives. Listen to everyone. **Hear everyone's stories.**

"A voice for the community"

Mary Figueroa

Roots

I was born and raised in Riverside. I've lived here my whole entire life. We lived within a probably four-block radius, almost my entire childhood. We moved several times, but it was always within that four-block radius. It was an extended family. I spent a short time as part of a career with the DA's office in the Indio area, and I did have an apartment down there for part of that time, but I still stayed in Riverside.

Call to activism

It was my religious upbringing. I'm Catholic, I'm very faithful to my religion, and I've always believed that we're supposed to help people and help the community.

The community work that I do started out because as a senior in high school, I started volunteering in the community. When I was at North High School in my junior year, there was a man that came to our government class. He was running for City Council in Riverside at the time. Our government teacher had him come in, and if you volunteered for two hours, you got extra credit in the government class. His name was Eric Haley, and when he was up front of the class, he basically said to us, "I need your help and if you help me, I can win, but if you don't help me, I may not be able to win." I'm sitting there thinking to myself, "Who's this person who's telling this sixteen-year-old classroom that we have to help him or he's not going to win this seat?" That was so interesting to me. Well, all he was asking for was two hours, so I went ahead and signed up. I was really intrigued by him. It was supposed to only be two hours. It turned out to be like six or seven months! It just turned into that because I enjoyed it so much. I enjoyed the interaction, I enjoyed the people. That's how my community service started.

I graduated from UCR in 1979. During the time that I was at UCR, I was working in the community. Because [Eric Haley] ended up on the City Council, I really started keeping track of what was happening in the city. One of the things that we were dealing with back then was a lot of tension between the police department and the community, between Casa Blanca and the Eastside. As a result of that, we would have meetings all the time with the police department, we would be having dance nights to keep the young people occupied, and we partnered with the police department on some of that stuff. That's the kind of work that I started with back in the late seventies.

I went on with the Rape Crisis Center. I ended up getting awards for being the advocate that put the most amount of time into the volunteer work, because I would get phone calls in the middle of the night from the police department, or from the hospitals, because they had a victim at the hospital. So I would respond to the hospital and I would be there with her, and I would help her understand what was going to happen to her, the medical exam, the interview with the police department. I was with her throughout the whole thing. I did that for five or six years. Eventually, I knew that it was time that I needed to leave it because I had done it enough, and so I did. I ended up on the Board of Directors. I did a lot of community stuff, a lot of youth-involved activity, the Riverside Youth

Council, a lot of stuff with the American Diabetes Association. At that time, they were just trying to get out into the Latino community because of the diabetes numbers, and so we helped.

Because I was involved in the community all those years, once I got into my twenties and graduated from UCR, I decided, "You know what? We're always working in the community, and we're always having to go to City Council in order to ask for anything." I thought to myself, "We know what we need. We've been working in the community, we know what the community needs, we need to be sitting at the table where everybody needs to go to ask for help because they're the ones that control the money." I decided, "You know what? I'm going to run for City Council." So, that's what I did. I ran for the Riverside City Council Ward 4. I was at a reception at UCR and a friend was there, and he came up to me and said, "So let me ask you a question. Who told you that you could run for City Council?" And I looked at him, and I said, "You know what, I haven't had to ask permission to do something in a long time. I didn't even ask my mother if I could do this." But the bottom line was, it was because I was a female, and I had not gone to them in order to ask their permission to make a decision like running for the City Council seat. It totally floored me. I've always remembered that. I ended up running, and I came in second out of the four. Everybody thought I would not get that high up. I thought to myself, "Yeah, but you guys don't know how much contact I have in the community." That's what they were not recognizing. It was the community connections that I had that put me in that second place. Because I ended up running so well in second place, about a year later a group came to me and said that they wanted me to consider running for RCC [Board of Trustees], because they had seen that I had done so well in the City Council race. I had never considered running for RCC. I told them no at first. But then they came back to me again, and I said, "Well, let me think if I have something to add to this position that would benefit the community." And what I came up with was I knew the value of my education. I knew, having been the first one in my family to finish high school and graduate, the first one in my family to actually attend a college, and then the first one in my family to, lo and behold, graduate from UCR. I figured, I do have something I could add to running for the Board of Trustees. I can add the value and the difference that an education makes in somebody's life. That's how I ended up running for RCC in 1995. Everybody, again, thought that I was not going to get it. **Again, they underestimated me**, because like I said, I had been working in the community for a long time, and people know me just because of the community work.

Contributions

The Eastside Think Tank has been my greatest contribution, without any funding, without any formal structure, but with the need in the community. All of those years of violence in the community—the homicides, the shootings, the officer-involved shootings—all of those things that happened have continued to happen for decades. They happened when I was a little kid, they happened before I was born. But things kind of come up and get created, and then they function for a little while and then they disappear. But the Think Tank has lasted longer than any other grassroots organization in the city that deals with this issue other than the Community Action Group in Casa Blanca. We've got an organization, a grassroots community organization, that has been the voice for the community.

The Latino Network came about because years ago, before I ever thought about RCC, before Jane Carney got onto the RCC board, there was a vacant position. There had not been a Hispanic on the RCC board since Joey Aguilar back in the late sixties. When the board seat came up, there was a push from some people, Latino leaders in the community, to get together so that we could push the agenda of having somebody that was a Latino on the board. At that time, we started meeting. We met next to City Hall at this little café that's next to the alleyway that used to be called My Brother's Place. We would meet there for breakfast, and we would start strategizing. They decided that they wanted to put Andy Soto up for the position of the RCC board member that was supposed to be appointed. That's how Latino Network came about, because all of us came together, we even pulled people from San Bernardino to come in and be part of the group. We would meet, and we'd strategize, and we would get in touch with different people, and we did whatever we thought was necessary in order to get Andy appointed to the RCC board seat vacancy. At that time, we were told that it would happen. And it didn't. Well, that didn't sit well, we felt betrayed, and so we decided as a group, we're going to continue meeting. Latino Network didn't have the name at the time, it was just a group that met on a regular basis to talk about what was happening in Riverside, to talk about the Latino issues that were happening in the community and how we could help, what we could do, how we could move the agenda forward to assist the Latino community.

Whenever we would go to the city and ask them for additional training for the police officers, when we would ask them for alternative means of restraint, like non-lethal weapons, the city always came back to us and said there was no money. They didn't have money, and it took too much money to put the officers through training, because once they get out on the street, it takes too much money to take them off the street, and replaced, and whatever. Once Tyisha Miller happened, all of a sudden now the scrutiny was coming from not us as a community, but now the scrutiny was coming from the Attorney General's office. Once [Bill] Lockyer did the investigation and made the recommendations, I was on the Mayor's Use of Force [Panel]. Jack Clarke was the Chair. We ended up making those [recommendations], the city accepted them, but then the consent decree came, and the city had no choice whatsoever but to now finally follow through on the request that the community had been saying for so long. So, I remember going in front of the City Council at one time, and I ended up saying to them at that time, I said, "We have come to you for years asking for these very same recommendations that are coming down from the Attorney General's office. And now, here's the difference. You told us, we can't do it, we don't have money. Now, to the AG's office, you're not allowed to do that. Now you're gonna have to find the money. But this is exactly what we've been talking about. The training that needs to happen, the additional officers on the street, the additional supervision on the street." All of those things that the city had gotten away with by saying that they didn't have the money, now, guess what? They found the money.

I sit on the Air Quality Management District's Environmental Justice group. I've been sitting on that for several years, and that is another thing that is totally eye-opening, because so many of the communities of color are the ones that are impacted the most with the environmental issues of water and air. I'm asthmatic, and it was diagnosed when I was in high school, so it's not a childhood onset, which sometimes tends to go away, but it was more of an adult onset. I really do believe, now that I have more information that part of that was my environment—because of the fact that I lived on the Eastside.

I was able to help with the medical school [at UC Riverside], with getting it off the ground. I ended up working on a grant with them for two years in the community, doing outreach to the Latino community. The medical school needs a research connection to the community. I have always told them, if they do not have the connection to the community when they need the research stuff that they're going to need, they're going to be hard-pressed to make it, because they've never made the connection. That was my whole thing, they need to make a connection to the community so that the community understands that the university is not just there to have them as guinea pigs, but is actually there to partner with them and do something that will help them overall with the health of the community and the health of the families. We got a grant, and the grant let us do outreach into the community in order to figure out how to partner up with the medical school. My first comment was, "The first thing you do not do is you do not tell the community to come to you." That will not go anywhere. We have to go out to the community. What I came up with was basically in-home meetings. We identified people in the community, and then we went out and we set up meetings in the community. Not even at the community centers, but in peoples' homes, because people will go to other peoples' homes. If you really want to start talking to them about health issues like mental health, about diabetes, about personal stuff, and this is personal stuff, you need to get them into an environment where they're comfortable. Do you remember the Tupperware parties? That's the kind of stuff you need. Host a meeting at a person's house. Make it enjoyable. Everybody used to go to the Tupperware parties, not so much because we needed Tupperware, but because we wanted to be there and they were going to have drinks, and they were going to have appetizers, and we would socialize, and we would have fun, and then we would buy Tupperware. That's what you need to do, only this time you're not making them buy anything; you're giving them information. So we hosted these in-home meetings. It ended up being so successful. As a result, there's a book that UCR put together, and inside the book, my name is there, because we were the ones that came up with the in-home meetings, and then in-home meetings came up with exactly the information that we needed to come back from the community to the medical school. That was another avenue of making sure that the community stays connected to the benefits that it needs to take advantage.

Inspiration

Eric Haley is the reason that I'm in the situation I'm in right now. I was sixteen years old, and Eric Haley was the one that sent me in the path of having become politically involved. Diana Webster, who was the campaign manager for Eric back then, is the other one.

Advice

It's a cliché, but get involved and do stuff that you enjoy. Because then, if you do it that way, you don't see it like work. You're doing what you enjoy and what you like doing.

"Healing work"

Chani Beeman

Roots

I was born here, so **I grew where I was planted**! My grandparents came to L.A. from Nebraska, and they settled in Riverside in the very early fifties. My father was in the Navy at the time, and when he got out of the Navy he came to stay with his parents and did his education at Riverside City College, and then UCR, and when he was at City College, he met my mom. He was in the second graduating class at UCR. We have very deep connections to Riverside. [My mom] was Miss Citrus in maybe '51 or '52. She was a stay-at-home working mom, so she raised five kids, of which I was one, and we had that benefit, having mom home.

Call to activism

I've always regarded activism, or at least my activism, as healing work. It is work that is done to try and address something that's not working, perhaps, or to enhance something that is working and make it stronger. So I would say my first call to action was as a grad student at Cal State San Bernardino with issues around the presence of the ROTC program. As a branch of the military at that time, they had policies that would exclude lesbian and gay officers. You could take the classes, but you couldn't be an officer. I think that was the first time where I was translating a lot of the information and thought, the product of this critical thinking in my education, and began applying it to how I thought things could be better in the world, how things could be better around where I'm planted and the people around me. So we did some activism around that and more activism around campus, and then that just expanded into community activism.

Working with the union [at Cal State San Bernardino] gave me such tremendous skills and knowledge and experience that really led me, ultimately, to my career of choice. Information technology was the career of need, but then having the opportunity to develop skills and knowledge and experience that was available around me allowed me to make different choices according to what I really wanted to be doing.

Contributions

One of the projects that I'm most proud to be associated with was a group called Women Enraged, which was a grassroots organization of women dealing with violence against women. It came as a result of the rape and murder of a very dear friend of ours—she was very much an activist around women's issues—and the need to continue her work and advance it, dealing with domestic violence and rape, and really getting better attention to the need for services and support. I think a lot of people forget that even just twenty, thirty years ago, a lot of services, a lot of what we take for granted now, were hard fought a few decades ago.

Prior to the shooting of Tyisha Miller, there had been another incident that some of us were aware of. It involved three RPD officers picking up a Hispanic man who was not an English speaker. He was walking, and he was drunk, and the police picked him up, beat him up, handcuffed him, and threw him in the lake here in Fairmount Park. And it took about a week for him and his family to get the police to pay attention to what he was trying to tell them. This is a documented event. The officers didn't continue with RPD. None of them did. But one of them got immunity for turning testimony over on the other two. We were very concerned about it, but we couldn't quite get traction. We knew there were issues in our police department, but we couldn't quite get traction on getting attention. And then the Tyisha Miller shooting happened, and that was just so clearly over the top. At every stage in the aftermath of that—"Oh, she shot her gun," well, then it turned out the gun was dysfunctional. "Oh, she was on drugs," well, that was inconclusive. The police officer's urine test disappeared, didn't make it to Sacramento. It seemed like daily and weekly, and then monthly, there was something that came out that just kept pointing to problems in our police department. But right after the shooting there was a community forum that was held, and people were talking about establishing a police accountability citizen oversight [committee]. I went to a New Year's Eve party, and there was a law enforcement officer there. He spoke very frankly about Riverside officers having a reputation of being cowboys, even within law enforcement. That hit me very personally. I just thought, "This is my police department!" So I put the word out in this network of activists and said, "You know, I think we really need to think about this, continue it," and we ended up having a meeting of about ten to fifteen people in my living room, and we just kept on from there and ultimately educated ourselves—that's the key—educated ourselves about police accountability, and pulled the community together. There was so much going on in that aftermath, and we felt like we maintained a collaborative work approach that arrayed our focus, and this was the contribution that this group could make while supporting the other efforts. We just stayed with it, and we were able to get a police accountability oversight commission established. It's not as strong as we wanted, and it's been beat up a little bit, but I think we're in a moment of resurgence. I feel like we had a step up and a real advantage to other communities that were like, "What? What do we do here?" [in the aftermath of the murder of George Floyd]. Even at the time, and still to this day, we get a lot of phone calls asking, "How did that happen? What did it take? What did it do?" And you know, we can give our experience, but again, I really believe you grow where you're planted, and it's going to be different in each community. You can't just say, "Oh, let's transplant this structure into this community."

I think one of the reasons this mattered for me was that it went to the heart of fairness and being able to trust law enforcement, to trust that justice is real, that we can depend on it. If we can't depend on that, what can we depend on, really? So I think it was kind of a core principle for me. You'd open your paper, and say, "Really? That happened?" I really had a sense of wanting to make this core element to our social fabric meet the expectations that we had for them. In my twenty-plus years of working in this area, I now have family members in law enforcement. My oldest son and his wife are both law enforcement officers with Riverside Police Department, so we have very interesting conversations. I think one of the things that attracted me is it's one of these issues where there is so much more in between the polars. We want law enforcement. We pass laws, and we want people to adhere to those laws, and we want our law enforcement to be done fairly and justly and humanely. There is so much in that middle that we need to work through. I am not anti-police. I'm not, never have been. I'm pro good policing. It's a community responsibility, and the more I started working in that issue, the more I recognized that part of how we got into the situation we got into with our department is we ignored them. We don't do ourselves or the police or community members who come in contact with the police any service by ignoring them. It really became a moral obligation for me. Ultimately, I was on the Police Review Commission, and I served on the Chief's Advisory Committee, because I felt like with my own personal experience with law enforcement in my family, I could really see these issues from multiple perspectives, and I thought that was an important perspective. I could sit in a room and listen to someone who has had horrible experiences with the police, and/or, historically, as a community, have really horrible relationships with the police, and I can hear, believe, and trust that that is the truth, and also know that there's a way through all of that, and we just need to come together and work on it together as a community. We need to listen to each other. We have a compulsion to make things better, and I'm proud to be part of that in Riverside. But I also recognize that I'm privileged. I could talk about police accountability because I was a middle-aged white woman. I recognize that my siblings of color have been saying these things for a very, very long time and had been living a life that was completely different than mine because of the color of their skin. And so I try to be very mindful of that and recognize that my speaking up is different than the speaking up of people who have life experiences different than mine. **As important as it is for me to speak up, it is equally important for me to make space for others to speak up.**

In the aftermath of the 2016 election, I, like so many people, were just like, "What has happened? Where do we go from here?" We were traveling, and I was on Facebook, and someone made the comment, "Chani, aren't you the one that usually helps us find what's next?" And I thought, "Oh yeah, I guess it is one of the things that I try and do." So, in response, I talked with Sue Mitchell, and I said, "Look, why don't we host a gathering at my house? We'll get a handful of people, we can figure out where we go from there." So, we just started putting the word out to people that we knew. We started to activate this network. We had over fifty people show up, in the pouring rain, which doesn't usually happen in Riverside. I put my big purple board up on my wall in my dining room, and it's that sticky wall, and I made sheets of paper, a little 5x7, and said, "Put your idea on the wall." And then together we moved them around. What's related, what isn't. It really started that sort of inward focus from "I can't go on," to "what's the next thing?" We were working on that when Linda [Sherman] up at the bookstore [Cellar Door Books] and Connie [Ransom], they came to us and said, "We want to do a Women's March." So blending the ideas that we were already putting in focus and saying, "Okay, let's do the Women's March" and then have this larger meeting. The whole point of Rise Up was to bring people together and begin getting that focus of "we've got a lot of work to do in four years, and really, how are we going to do that here in Riverside? What is our work to do?" From there, it evolved to Indivisible 41 because it felt like local work is really important, but it needs to be connected to the larger state. The marches are important, and those kind of direct actions are important, but I want people writing postcards to voters. Going out on the street and then coming back and sitting on my sofa drinking tea isn't going to get things done. It raises awareness, and it raises profile, but I think more and more I have felt in these past four years that it really is about connecting our efforts in ways that aren't just about awareness but about the change that we need to make and helping people feel empowered to do that.

I'm proud to say I'm part of this network that when someone has a question or wants to talk through an idea or a concern, I think I'm one of those people that I look to turn to. And if I don't know, I say, "That's a good question, let's figure it out!" So I like to think that I'm part of that really important and effective network of activists in the community. Certainly what I do is not done alone, **none of this is done alone.** It is this network that pulls experienced people together but then also makes the effort to draw in new folks. You never know what's going to catch someone's interest. All of a sudden there's a George Floyd situation, and someone who's never been active before goes, "This is enough." They've reached their own watermark. Prior to the first Women's March, I think our high watermark for march participation had been the Orlando Pulse nightclub shooting. We had about five hundred people show up, and I thought, "Wow." We'd had hundreds before, but five hundred was a pretty high watermark. For the 2017 Women's March, very late in January, it was decided to have a march in Riverside. Over six thousand people showed up. We were just like, "What?" So, so many of those folks were saying "This is the first time I've ever done anything like this." The follow-up to that march was to try and find ways for those folks, who had never been activated, to become activated. I think we did a pretty good job. Riverside is one of those communities that, no matter what the issue, we've got action going on, and for our size, I'm pretty proud of that.

Inspiration

I think back on my mom [Shirley Ray Blatchford], saying, "I'm gonna write a letter, I'm gonna raise my voice on this." I think about Marge Jackson, who was a neighbor who petitioned the city of Riverside to make the Islander, which was closing as a private club, a public pool. I spent every summer there from the time I was born to the time I went to college. These were people who saw a need in their community and started speaking up. My mom was a big supporter of Cesar Chavez and the grape boycott, and we missed grapes for many, many summers. We all understood why we were boycotting grapes. When I was in high school, I was walking home from North High School up Linden Avenue with my friend Elaine Hernandez, who lived in the family student housing [at UC Riverside]. We stopped at her house and I came inside to get a glass of water for the rest of my trek home, and Cesar Chavez was there speaking with students. So, there was a very personal connection to things that we were seeing happening on a national level, on a broader stage, and it felt very personal. It wasn't remote. It was right there in Elaine Hernandez's living room. I didn't know Cesar Chavez or MLK, but I felt like they were in my living room a lot and were completely inspirational.

When I was an undergraduate and then a graduate student, I had so many professors who were tremendous role models for me. Susan and Tom Meisenhelder really are my activist godparents. Tom Moody was a philosophy professor who did so much to help me be able to think through issues, and even the professor who did statistical research taught me you can open stuff up and say, "Who measured this?" Or, "Why aren't we measuring this?"

I also think of people like Mother Jones who didn't get active until her 50s, because I was a later-in-life activist.

Advice

Every effort that I get involved with, a golden thread that goes through is a keen awareness of how important it is to listen to the new activists, to recognize that that flow into activism helps us grow and get stronger. Hearing the questions that are being raised, the education and the questions, and the understanding that's emerging is such an important part of making sure you're not doing the same thing expecting different results. Especially for women, we have to pass the ball. We're not all going to be the ones standing up and speaking. In fact, I prefer not to be. One of the things that would bother me the most is someone would say, "Oh, you know, Chani's group." No. I want it to be, "You know that Riverside Police Coalition." It's this group of people who are doing things. My advice is, especially as you get more experienced, keep listening to those who are coming into the process. If you're first coming into the process, speak up! You have a valuable and important part of the conversation to contribute.

Probably most important is to support one another, to recognize that sometimes we stagger down the path. It's not a straight line, and we shouldn't expect it to be a straight line, because for each of those staggers, we're learning something else, and we're making that course correction that is so important. I'm learning more and more in my reading about antiracism that going from point A to point B is such a white supremacist proposition. If we're going to be genuine in making sure we're incorporating as many voices and perspectives as possible, we're not going from point A to point B. We're going to make our way and stay in conversation and in relationship with one another to get the job done and make the adjustments that we need to make along the way. And that's not failure. We can't measure ourselves by the way things have always been done.

"Speak out and speak up"

The Group: Rose Mayes, Ola Faye Stephens, Jennifer Vaughn-Blakely

Roots

OLA FAYE STEPHENS: I was born in Terrell, Texas, in 1937, and moved to Dallas when I was three weeks old. I've lived in Riverside since 1960.

ROSE MAYES: I was born in Melville, Louisiana, in 1943. We moved to Houston, Texas, in 1955, and then I relocated to Riverside in 1979. I've been here ever since.

JENNIFER VAUGHN-BLAKELY: I was born in 1948. I came to Riverside in 1973, right after I got married. My husband Tony worked for the Greater Riverside Chamber of Commerce, and Art Pick told him one day, "Don't you think if you're going to promote Riverside, it would be a good idea if you lived here?" And so, we moved. We love Riverside.

Call to activism

JENNIFER VAUGHN-BLAKELY: I first became involved in community activities in Riverside through the National Council of Negro Women. I trusted Ola Faye, and I have been hanging onto Ola Faye ever since. I met Rose when I worked for Riverside County Community Development, and I went to a meeting in her community in Mead Valley. It was one of the wildest meetings I'd ever been to. There were a bunch of old Black men who knew everything in the world, and Rose stood up to them and challenged them. They were shocked, but she didn't back down. Rose took them on, the county supervisor, and the whole room, practically. The rest is history because it was through those things that I became involved. We've worked together on community issues and public policy issues. And every once in a while, we do something just for fun.

OLA FAYE STEPHENS: I came from an era that was segregated, where everything that I attended or went to was Black-owned, and I was taught real early that if I owned the water fountain I could control the flow. My mother and her friends were very active as I was growing up. My first situation with having to be active, so to speak, was in the early sixties when my son was due to start kindergarten at Emerson, and they wanted to bus sixteen kids including my son. I rebelled, so, out of sixteen families, mine was the only one that was not bussed. The situation with the school district was number one as to why I became active, because I wanted to control my own destiny and my son's.

ROSE MAYES: Coming from the South, when you live in a family of fourteen, you knew what you had to do to survive. My father worked at the sawmill. My mother was a homemaker. However, they took a lot of pride in making sure that we went to school and that we would get a good education, even though it was a segregated school. They made sure that there was food on the table, and there was lots of love. The values that were instilled would eventually pay off, the value of hard work, how to value one another, to look out for one another. My brother was put in jail because he was accused of stealing a rifle that had gone missing. I will never forget that, and it still runs true in my heart and soul and my mind right now, how he stayed in jail for one year. My brother at that time was seventeen, eighteen years old, and he was beaten. We weren't able to see him, but eventually the shotgun was found—another friend was using it—and so they eventually let him out of jail. He said at that time, "I'm going to leave this little town, and I'll never come back. I'm going to bring my family because it's not right what they do to us." He joined the military, and when he got out of the military, he moved to Houston, Texas, and we migrated, slowly but surely. He had gotten a place that would house all of us. That's how we got out of that little town. At that time, I was in high school, and I worked as a waitress. When the civil rights workers and the sit-in demonstration people would come in, I would see that they got their water, their hamburgers, their hot dogs. I used to listen to them speak and talk about what was going on. Some of them would have food in their hair and on their clothes, they were wet all over. I would listen to their stories, and I decided that I wanted to do something about it, but my mother would not allow me to get involved. But **I knew from that point on that I would be the type of person that would speak out and speak up for justice.**

JENNIFER VAUGHN-BLAKELY: My greatest trauma regarding a young Black person was Emmett Till, and in my family, they did not talk about it. However, my grandfather, who was a wonderful man, subscribed to the *Chicago Defender*, and in Mississippi, you got it in the mail wrapped up in brown paper. I remember him laying that paper on the front step the day Emmett Till's mother had him buried the way they killed him. He never said a word, but I never forgot that. Growing up and when I went to college in California, I remember my family and my uncle, whom I lived with in San Bernardino, said, "You came here to get an education. You didn't come here to be in no messes." And by that, he meant marches and all of that.

Contributions

OLA FAYE STEPHENS: We had never had a Black person on the Riverside City Council. We were being defeated each time because so many people were running for the same position. So the time came when we had to have a meeting and ask ourselves if we really wanted to win, and if so, we were going to have to leave the ego at the door and choose one person who was electable. That happened to be Jack Clarke, so everybody went behind Jack Clarke, Sr. That's a time I can remember where we came together.

JENNIFER VAUGHN-BLAKELY: After Tyisha Miller was killed, everywhere you turned, there was news about what had happened, about her being killed. All the faces talking on the TV were nationally known people, for the most part, like Jesse Jackson. But there was no organized Riverside effort. I think a group of us were at either Rose Mayes's home or Rose Oliver's home.

ROSE MAYES: That's when the organizing started.

OLA FAYE STEPHENS: I think a group of us had been meeting before that…

JENNIFER VAUGHN-BLAKELY: We then started going to council meetings, vigils, and we would really go to whatever and wherever they were talking about this young girl who was killed. I grew up in Mississippi and came to California when I was sixteen and had never felt anything or witnessed anything of that magnitude.

OLA FAYE STEPHENS: You had different groups who were working on different issues that concerned all of us. So, in order to be effective, we needed to come together.

JENNIFER VAUGHN-BLAKELY: That was sort of organic. Nobody was competing. We all worked together, and just sort of grew in the groups we were already in, and just kept moving forward together. I don't remember anybody or any group trying to take control or run the agenda.

ROSE MAYES: In 1998–99, I was the chairperson of the [Riverside] Human Relations Commission, and I was called by Chani Beeman and asked, "What are you going to do about that?" I said, "I'm going to put it on the agenda. We're going to talk about it." And she said, "You're gonna do more than talk about it, y'all gonna do something about it." It was through that that we had a meeting in the [Mayor's] Ceremonial Room at City Hall. I'll never forget that. I was invited, Jack Clarke, Jr. was invited, Norm Martin was invited, Rose Oliver was invited, and there were a whole lot of local ministers invited. There was a room full of nothing but ministers from all over Southern California saying, "What are you going to do, Mayor Loveridge?" There were a couple of city council people there along with staff. Norm Martin said, "Don't worry, we'll take care of this, and we're going to get something done, and we'll meet with you." Some of those ministers said, "No, we're going to do something now, we're going to start marching." I remember Norm said, "Do what you have to do, but meanwhile, we're going to get organized."

Rose Oliver came to my office after that and said, "We got to have a party at your house, a Christmas party, we've got to organize, because we've got to start speaking up for what's going on to have control in our community, because we've got people coming from Los Angeles, they're coming from Rialto, they're coming from San Bernardino, and if we don't have something to say in this, then they are going to speak for us." It was then that The Group came into existence. Dr. Lulamae Clemons and the Griers were there, and they got very upset. They said, "We didn't know we were coming to an organizing committee here to fight the police department." We said, "No, this is not that, but we need to come together to start discussing it." Dr. Jackie Mills was the first chairperson, and then Jackie moved away, and Jennifer stepped in. We met at churches, we met at restaurants, we met at wherever we could. We were meeting at seven o'clock, and someone asked us, "Why do y'all meet so early?" I said, "If you were committed, you would come. You would come to that meeting early in the morning." It was very, very effective, because we talked about issues and concerns impacting our community as a whole.

JENNIFER VAUGHN-BLAKELY: It was primarily women who were sitting and talking about the need. There was Rose Oliver. There was Woodie [Rucker-Hughes]. These were women who were already doing things.

ROSE MAYES: I recognized at that time that we have a small percentage of African Americans in Riverside. And most of the men were working out of town, and the women were mostly working in town. I surmised that's the reason that we women were getting together, working so hard and speaking out.

OLA FAYE STEPHENS: Another thing I think was good that The Group did was to provide a forum where the political candidates could come. People who would normally not know what was going on would attend The Group meetings and find out about the candidates.

ROSE MAYES: The Group was able to receive various speakers and to ask questions, and at the same time be able to let you voice your opinion without feeling like you were being too radical in any way. You had the right to voice your opinion, and that was an outlet for people who wanted to articulate some of their views. We were not judgmental on that.

JENNIFER VAUGHN-BLAKELY: There was a meeting that the Irvine Foundation had when Irvine was trying to become better known in the I.E. The representative from the Irvine Foundation asked us something like, "What can you do?" and we were, "Almost anything!" And then, the woman said, "Well, what would you do if we gave you some money?" We don't know. Afterwards, I think we went from that meeting to Rose's office to start putting the Foundation format together.

ROSE MAYES: They said, "Well, you don't have a 501c3, so we can't give you the money!"

JENNIFER VAUGHN-BLAKELY: Okay, no problem, we can find one!

ROSE MAYES: We got the Riverside African American Historical Society. They were doing work, and that's when we used that 501c3 and have been using it ever since.

JENNIFER VAUGHN-BLAKELY: I think we blew two myths. One: People of color can work together very well and be successful. There's a myth out there that they can't, they'll have a fight. And that has never happened with us.

OLA FAYE STEPHENS: No. If we did, we left and went and had a drink.

JENNIFER VAUGHN-BLAKELY: And we don't allow ourselves as individuals or as a group to get bogged down in nonsense. **We do what needs to be done, and we're not into, "Oh, they didn't recognize me." You'll get yours in heaven or somewhere.**

Advice

OLA FAYE STEPHENS: You have to have patience. Whatever you embark on, it will take time. You have to be serious and committed to what you want to do. You need to look at the whole picture, listen to all sides, and you should be confident in whatever you are attempting to do. **You have to think about the feelings of others, because if you don't, you're not going to find people that want to work with you.** You need to be well-versed on the issues affecting their community. And don't just go along to get along.

ROSE MAYES: Find your passion. Find your mission in life. Everyone was put on this earth to do certain things, and once you find out what that is, do it to the best of your ability and be true to yourself. Don't do something just because you see another person do it because you will not have the energy or whatever it takes to stick to that. You will be going from one thing to another. That's where it goes back to find your mission. And the next thing is to do something that will help the next generation of young people. Pass it along. I've always said that, and be responsible and accountable and stay in your lane.

JENNIFER VAUGHN-BLAKELY: I think being bold but being respectful is real important. It doesn't matter how much you know if you're not committed to it. If people can't feel it, you are closed in dealing with people. People need to know that you're genuine, that they can count on you to tell them the truth and to be there for them and with them. One thing about The Group: We don't always agree on everything, but we have respect for one another.

ROSE MAYES: That's it in a nutshell. And not only that, because we always know it's not what you say, it's what you do and how you treat others with dignity and respect.

JENNIFER VAUGHN-BLAKELY: The other thing that The Group does, when people come to our meetings, we don't have a hospitality committee. However, we do treat people in a—and this is a Southern thing—in a hospitable way. We welcome people.

ROSE MAYES: There's a value system that we share, and we'll correct each other, because Jennifer will tell you in a minute that you know your mother did not teach you that. In a minute.

JENNIFER VAUGHN-BLAKELY: And I can only do that because I know, as my mother would say, people who've been raised, you know better. You have a value system. And we need to instill that wherever we are. And I think we've established a reputation in the community that people know that we're going to show up. If we tell you something, we're going to do it. We will also tell you things you may not be ready for. But we'll hang in there until you either get it or we've decided we have done all we can do.

"We agreed to stay at it"

Deborah Wong

Roots

I was born in New York City in 1959. I lived on the East Coast through college—New Jersey, my father worked at Rutgers University. High school years in Richmond, Virginia, college and a few years after that in Philadelphia, grad school at the University of Michigan, and a couple of teaching jobs that eventually took me to UCR in 1996. I moved to Riverside in July of 1996, when it was hot. I was thrilled to be here! I was really excited about being in California, period, and especially SoCal, because at that point I was pretty deeply into research on Asian American performance. And although there are Asian Americans everywhere in the United States, there's no question that there's a real critical mass out here on the West Coast. So for me to come out here was just like moving from the backyard to the front yard of Asian America. No disrespect to the East Coast communities, but I wanted to be in a part of the country where there was a really vibrant Asian American scene. I was pretty thrilled to be out here.

My earlier research was in Thailand. I'm an ethnomusicologist. I'm an anthropologist who does research on music. That means I treat music as culture, not just as notes on a page that can be analyzed. I'm mostly interested in how people think about music and use music, how music is part of people's lives and usually carries enormous symbolic and actual weight in any given culture.

Call to activism

I have these extraordinary parents. They were both from Buffalo, New York. My mother was white, my father was Chinese American. When they got together in the early 1950s and then got married in 1955, those kinds of cross-racial marriages or relationships were simply not common, and when they did happen, they often weren't supported, as was the case for both my parents. My parents were already kind of unusual people and were not only thinking outside the box but were willing to step outside the box, my mother in particular. She was a feminist before that word was being commonly used, and then definitely after it was. I learned a lot about what it meant to be engaged in the world, in a community, through my parents, and especially through my mother. I also grew up during the 1960s. I was a child in public school during the 1960s, so it was impossible not to be aware of not only politics but activism. The civil rights movement was in high gear, the anti-war movement was in high gear. I vividly remember in fourth grade the principal bursting into our classroom and saying that Dr. Martin Luther King, Jr. had been killed. So there was not only an awareness of a big world of politics and tumult out there for me as a child, but also a sense that things were not as they should be or even could be, and that things needed to change, and that there are people out there who had ideas about how to get us there. All of that was part of the foundation for the way I think about the world.

For me personally, it was a gradual start. I did quite a bit of volunteer work as an options counselor for several different women's healthcare clinics, first in Philadelphia, then in Ann Arbor. I spent some years doing that kind of work of advising women who had just received the results of a pregnancy test, advising them on their options. That was also part of my entry level to activist work. I'm an ethnographer—the most important work takes place at ground level, person to person. I believe quite deeply that a lot of change happens right there.

The other big thing that happened was when I got a job interview at Pomona College. I went out and spent two or three intense days in the music department. I went back to my hotel room, pretty wrung out as you are after an interview, and was watching television, and was watching this footage being shown over and over and over again. A Black man named Rodney King had been beaten by four Los Angeles Police Department officers. I was watching this, and I found myself completely pulled into it, not realizing that it was actually national news, not just local SoCal news. I was already wanting to be out here to think about race and to work on Asian American community and culture, but seeing that footage was pretty formative.

I got the job, I moved out to Claremont, and at the end of my first year of teaching in that position, in April of 1992, the Rodney King trials had been spinning out for that entire year, and the results broke in April, and in a matter of hours, once the officers were acquitted in that first set of trials, L.A. began to burn. I was not the only person who was deeply affected by watching this. At that point I had hooked up with an incredible, dynamic circle of Asian American Studies scholars at the Claremont Colleges, and all of us spent those four or five days glued to the TV, thinking deeply about, "What can we do?" What can anyone do about the urgent need for better models, both in terms of Asian and African American relationships and also in terms of law enforcement. At that point I was addressing it only through Asian American Studies and my research. But then, a few years after that, I had moved to Riverside in '96, and in December of 1998—I'd only lived here for a little bit over a year at that point, not quite two years—during winter break, I got up on the morning of December 29th and read in the newspaper that Tyisha Miller had been shot and killed, again by four police officers. **And everything changed for me at that point.** I was thrilled to be at UCR, because even then, we were the UC campus with the highest proportion of students of color. So, in seeing that Tyisha Miller was a 19-year-old African American woman, my first response was, honestly, that she could have been any one of my students. That was the moment when it no longer became just something that was happening out there but began to feel personal.

Contributions

Tyisha Miller was killed on December 28, 1998. In a matter of days, I personally swung into action and organized an on-campus roundtable and invited a number of people to come speak about law enforcement and the local need for what we were at that point calling a civilian review board, which Riverside did not have. I thought that roundtable would go on for about an hour, and after three and a half hours, people were still there, and more people wanted to speak, and there was clearly a very pressing community need. It wasn't only campus people that were there of course. So, when that, almost four hours later, began to break up, and people were still not wanting to leave, were still talking, were planning, were trying to think about how to proceed, Maggie Hawkins walked up to me. And I knew her a little bit, but not super well. We had both been on the Committee on the Status of Women for UCR. She was the director of the Women's Resource Center at that point at UCR. She walked up and she said, "Hey! You need to know about this community member named Chani Beeman, who just last week held a meeting at her home to begin to talk about exactly these same issues and the possibility for community review for the Riverside Police Department." So I was like, "Okay!" Not realizing that, basically, I had found my people. So I went to the next meeting, and what followed was an incredible year. It took a while for everything to get organized, but that was the formation of the Riverside Coalition for Police Accountability [RCPA]. Chani and a treasured friend who has passed on named Ray Lewis were the founding co-chairs of the RCPA. 1999 was an incredible year. We were meeting once, sometimes twice a week. Sometimes there were more than fifty people at those meetings. There were also demonstrations going on constantly in the community. Jesse Jackson, Al Sharpton, a lot of folks came to town to call for justice for Tyisha Miller. We did a lot of things in the RCPA. There was us, there was the Tyisha Miller Steering Committee, which was a group of mostly African American men, mostly pastors. The Group came together that year. Jennifer Vaughn-Blakely, Katie Green, Rose Mayes…we were not by any means the only people organizing and working and moving forward.

We decided that our focus would be to call for a community review board for the Riverside Police Department. We simultaneously got a lot of things in motion. For one thing, we did a lot of homework. We had to learn—what are the models? There was no such thing in our entire region! We had to do a lot of reading, a lot of writing. We brought in outside experts, like Eileen Luna, who had worked with the Albuquerque police commission. We learned about the different models. We learned that some are strong, and some are weak. We learned that there are hybrid models, where we could try and split the difference. Meanwhile, we were working as much as we could with city officials. Mayor Ron Loveridge formed a task force, the Mayor's Use of Force Panel, which was headed up by Jack Clark, Jr., so a lot of these things were all going on at the same time, and as much as possible we worked, we collaborated, we kept in touch, we strategized together as much as was possible across all these groups, and by the end of 1999, it was very clear that the community wanted community review for the Riverside Police Department. It was also clear that a consent decree was on its way, because all of this had attracted the attention of Bill Lockyer, who was the California State Attorney General. So, by the year 2000, that had been put in place as well. It was called a stipulated judgment, it was a five-year arrangement, an official, legal relationship between the Department of Justice and the Riverside Police Department. And so, by hook or by crook, the city of Riverside, by the year 2000, created the Community Police Review Commission. It had nine members, it still does, all of them—as is true for all city boards and commissions—all volunteers, and the founding chair of that commission was Bill Howe, who has become a very dear friend. He's African American, he's the former chief of the UCR Police Department, also the Corona Police Department, a pretty amazing guy who knows law enforcement from the inside out, but is also Black and knows from the inside the problems that most law enforcement has with race. So these are some of the remarkable people I was meeting. It was not only scrappy feet-on-the-ground activists, but it was these amazing folks who were deeply established in the very systems that are sometimes the problem.

The RCPA has met pretty much continuously since then. Chani and Ray were co-chairs for quite a while. Eventually, it became me. I became co-chair of the RCPA with Michael Dunn, who remains my dearest friend and someone I've learned so much from over many years. So, the group remained active, but I have now learned that work on police violence and police brutality never keeps going at a steady state of intensity and need. People's interest drops off after a certain amount of time, because these are old stories, that people of color get killed by police disproportionately. This is not news to communities of color. Communities are generally only able to maintain a certain level of attention and demand before they need to go back to their lives, as it were. So the work of the RCPA, we realized after a certain point, we got down to the point where there was a core group of about fifteen, and we agreed to stay at it. We had learned from experts on accountability that the only thing that makes it possible for community police review commissions to succeed is if the political will of the community remains in place. Once the community stops paying attention, things tend to go off the rails, studies have shown. **We basically agreed to stay at it. We agreed to keep paying attention.** One thing I've learned is that when there are moments of crisis, which almost always in terms of this kind of work, means that another person of color has been killed by the police somewhere, these moments are awful, repeated wake-up calls, but they are also moments of opportunity, where ideally some important changes can be put in place more quickly than would otherwise be possible. So what we've been working on since June [2020, following the murder of George Floyd] has been really looking at other models for law enforcement at this point. What is going on right now at the community level is talking about what it would mean to really dedicate more positions to social workers and to other first and second responders, who could take care of some of the things that by default have now become part of the work of the police, things that frankly are not appropriately part of the work of the police. So, we have a new city council in place, at least there are four new city councilmembers who are pretty amazing. They're open to these ideas, and already there's the new Chief of Police—there's a lot of newness at the moment. I'm hoping this is just the beginning. What are the shifts in thinking, what are the structural changes that may be taking place before our eyes? That's what I'm interested in.

What happens is that collectivities emerge, connections lead to relationships lead to partnerships. That's how change occurs. A lot of the things I'm proudest of are the people and organizations I've learned from and worked with. The fact that the RCPA is a **coalition is not just a word, it's an actual strategy and model for organizing.** I learned this from Chani Beeman. A coalition comes together when it becomes clear that there's a need, that there is an issue that needs to be addressed. And you get together different stakeholders, whether they're people as individuals or organizations. And you come to an explicit agreement that you are going to remain different organizations, but you generate a list of what Chani calls points of unity, where you agree that these are the things we can work on together, these are the things we agree need attention, and that we can work on together. We can continue to be different from one another in lots of other significant ways. Nobody has to agree on everything. But these are the points we are going to work on together. The RCPA has long been a coalition. There have been a number of amazing community partners, organizations from the Riverside NAACP to The Group, at times the Latino Network, and so on and so forth. All of this happened fairly quickly after I arrived in Riverside, so this is how I've learned about Riverside. This is the Riverside I know, through those people, those organizations, those thought leaders.

I care about Asian American history and living presence, and Riverside has one of the last remaining archeological sites for a Chinatown. Most of them up and down the West Coast have long since been destroyed, developed, overbuilt, but the one in Riverside is still here, two blocks from where I live. In 2008, a local developer was about to buy the land and build a huge medical office building on top of it, which would have destroyed the site. A bunch of concerned community members came together and met and met and met and talked and talked and talked and organized, and, long story short, managed to get that project taken elsewhere. Big struggles, huge struggles. We had to bring in a lawyer to get there, it was a four-year struggle. We succeeded. There's still a lot to be done. It needs to become a park, it needs to become protected land, but that's the next stage of struggle.

Inspiration

I've had a number of role models, some of them directly, one-to-one, and others somewhat more distantly. I learn from Yuri Kochiyama, an amazing Japanese American activist whom I didn't know personally. But more locally, definitely Chani, who remains a friend, a role model. We're like the same age, but it's not about age or seniority as much as it is we learn from people who know how to do what we most need and want. The members of The Group, I can't acknowledge them enough. Beyond Riverside, there's a Canadian ethnomusicologist named Beverley Diamond who has been a big influence and role model for me. Nobuko Miyamoto, who is a Sansei activist-artist based in L.A., who I've been following for years, learning from for years, and for the past five years or so have been working very directly with her to get her memoir published, and to get a double album of hers to come out through the Smithsonian. I've learned so much from her. I want other people to learn from her, too.

Advice

I really think it's true that a lot of the work we do is about showing up, and then to **keep showing up**, you know? You can't come once and then figure the job has been done. You have to keep showing up.

Always be thinking two steps ahead of wherever you are now to the extent that that's possible. Think ahead of the curve of whatever you're in the middle of.

Get mentors. Never assume that it's up to you to figure it out by yourself. **Get mentors and make that plural.** And surround yourself with inspiring people, whatever that may mean to you, and do everything you can to ensure that those people are both younger and older than yourself. Reach into different generations, reach into difference of all sorts as much as you possibly can, because **we need to have our minds blown**. We can't know a world outside of ourselves unless we step outside of our own worlds.

"The secret is listening"

Linda Dunn

Roots

I was born September 1, 1939, the very day that World War II began. I was born in Grand Junction, Colorado. My father was a large animal vet, and going on calls with him was very formative for me because of the wonderful way he treated the farmers and the family members on the little farms—people going through very difficult times—and the way he treated me with stories and respect and involvement.

We came to Riverside in 1970 when my husband Michael joined the Biochemistry Department at UC Riverside.

Call to activism

When we were in Eugene, Oregon, we had friends that had adopted some children, and they were helping to place children from Korea. We were at a party at their house, and it was kind of a big old house and when I went to the bathroom, I saw the floor was kind of rotting out, and you could actually see the ground through their floor. And I thought, "If they can adopt, so can we," because of the realization it wasn't how much money you had or your stature in the community. We adopted one child, and had three born to us, and then had a foster daughter join our family when she was a teenager.

Contributions

We formed an adoptive parent group in Riverside, and it became a member of the North American Council on Adoptable Children, which was recently formed at that time. I was the first president. I testified before government task forces on adoption of special needs children and the need for changes to laws that created obstacles in the adoption of these children. NACAC was very successful in facilitating the transformation of the face of adoption across North America.

I stepped down in 1982 and entered the School of Business at UCR. I completed a master's degree in 1984 and joined the staff of a health agency, then the program was defunded by the Reagan administration. I then became the director of what we renamed Inland Agency, and I went to work securing grant funding for health through education and violence prevention among youth. The program was called People Reaching Out, and it brought a lot of funding to the Eastside, a federally designated Pocket of Poverty. I retired in 2003.

In the meantime, Michael and I were involved in the Sanctuary movement, helping refugees from Central America. There was a big organization in L.A. that helped a lot of people, and they had people who needed a place to stay, and they would stay at our house. I remember picking up some people at a ranch, just at the other side of the station where cars would be stopped and searched. We heard of a few who had arrangements and a need to move on up north to Canada. We worked with people who were in touch with them to figure out a date and a way to go and get them. We had a car that had a big trunk in it, and Mike agreed to get in the trunk, and I'd drive around a while and see if he got exhaust. Somebody had to do it! I drove around a little bit, and then I stopped and went in the back and lifted the lid, and, bless his heart, he just laid really still. We went home and told the people that we were working with in L.A. that we were ready. So ours was a house on the railroad, the underground railroad still alive and well. Those were the days where you used telephone booths sometimes, when it got to the point where you didn't use your home phone anymore. So we got that all arranged, and we needed to have a reason to be driving back from the beach, so we had our kids, we put three of our kids in the car, our own kids. They agreed, they knew what they were doing. So, we went there, and we had agreed to take two of the men through the check station between the ocean and Riverside. We went to get food for everybody, and as it became known that's what we were going to do, more and more of these young men came out of the orchards where they worked and where they stayed until we had about twelve of them. So, we went to get food from a fast food place. We went in and ordered about nineteen hamburgers. And the guy looked at us, and then looked out there and looked in the car, and he said, "Was that nineteen?" And I said, "Yeah, nineteen hamburgers!" So we bought nineteen hamburgers and went back, and everybody ate, and our two young guys got in the trunk of the car, and we had enough people in the front of the car that we didn't look funny going all the way. So we got past that station and they got home with us. It was kind of late, but we were all wound up, and Mike turned the TV on, and there was James Bond. The next morning I fixed breakfast and went out in the driveway to see there was one young man with the hood up, and he was blessing the engine of the car that they would take on the next part of their trip.

We were involved in the Riverside Coalition for Police Accountability after Tyisha Miller was killed. There were so many people: Black, white, old, young, from churches and Quaker meetings and a marvelous mix of people that you just knew you were on the right track. There were a whole lot of people to follow. When the RCPA organized the 20th anniversary vigil for Tyisha Miller in 2018, I had a job handing out flashlights, and I was proud to do that job.

Prior to these involvements, I was one of several founders of the local Inland Communities chapter of the Fellowship of Reconciliation—a national and international hundred year-old peace and nonviolence nonprofit. Our ICFOR chapter still exists today—20 years later.

Inspiration

My mother for her work in the community, and my father—as a large animal vet—for his teaching of the family's children. Eleanor Roosevelt, NACAC, David Hartsough, Jim Sommers, Betty Figeroa (Quaker), Jane Block, the Inland Agency staff, Juliann Anderson, and the Wadoffles who were Jews from Germany who lived in Grand Junction after World War II. I admired the way they went on living after the war. I also respect many Quakers who played their active parts in working for social justice and peace so willingly over the years.

Advice

Beyond a healthy discipline, be gentle with yourself. There are opportunities that will enrich your life, but in order to find those opportunities, you need to be aware of people, be aware of what's going on in the world, and seek the place that you can serve. That's not an easy thing to do. You can't always make something happen. All you can do is be ready. And sometimes that's the hard thing to do. But there's so many times in my life where an opening came and somehow I had the capacity to recognize it. **I think the secret is listening. There's usually something that you're supposed to hear, but you've got to listen to find out.**

"Peace is..."

Marilyn Sequoia

Roots

I was born during World War II in Cleveland, Ohio. I was the oldest of seven children. There was a span of twenty-two years between us. After college, I came out to California for a couple years, and then I went back to Ohio, but I had to come back to California. I got to Riverside in the fall of 1967. As soon as I got here, I got a job two weeks before school started at Norte Vista High School in the Alvord School District. Eventually I moved over to Riverside Unified School District a couple years later. I had one semester at Central Junior High, and then I went to Poly, and I was there for seventeen years, then I transferred over to North High School to become a counselor. I later went back to the classroom and I ended up being a consulting teacher for the district.

Call to activism

I haven't really called myself an activist, but the preparation for creating change and doing things to help began back in Ohio with my family. I have a large extended family, a Bohemian, Czech, Polish, Catholic family, and the Catholic part was very important. It was the hub around which our whole life revolved. We went to church every Sunday, and with the large family, we were always going to first communions and confirmations and weddings and funerals. We had carnivals in the church parking lot, and my dad always had to stay after to count the money because he was an accountant, and that was one of his contributions to the church. He was an usher at mass on Sunday, and he belonged to a Catholic men's club. I watched him participate in the community. I feel that my father was my role model. I didn't seem to take that much to homemaking parts of things. I was more interested in what I was doing in school and admiring my dad. He even served on the city council for a short period of time, and my grandfather was very supportive and political. I found out later that he had been writing letters to the Cleveland *Plain Dealer*, and one of his letters I found later on was a letter having to do with Social Security that said, "It's not socialism, it's Christianity." That puts in a nutshell, to me, what this background that I come from is all about. My dad's motto to us children was "love one another." I learned from him that "love one another" was in the family, but it was also beyond the family. This is definitely the basis of my activism.

Contributions

My choice of career as a teacher is one of my key contributions, because as teachers we work together on the common goal of educating and socializing the next generation. I think because it's a job, we don't think of it as "activism" as such, but I think for many teachers, we are participating in the community and making a major contribution in that way.

The man that I married in 1968 got drafted into the Vietnam War. We'd been going to demonstrations here in Riverside, and there was a lot of stuff going on once he got drafted. We even talked about moving to Canada. But he did go off to Vietnam, and I was back in Riverside, and the psychology teacher at Poly was retiring. This was just the beginning of the Encounter Group movement, and all kinds of things were happening in the psychology world. I was very attracted to this, and I started working on a master's equivalency to be able to teach psychology. I took over the job, and it turned out that my students loved that class so much that they got a petition and signatures they turned into the office saying that they wanted a second semester of psychology. I was so honored. In those days, there was a lot of freedom, so I had the opportunity to make a class. I decided to call it "Personal Growth." There was no textbook. It was based on experience and reflection and activities and speakers and projects. We led these rap groups. I had a big rug in the middle of the group, and sometimes we'd all sit on the floor. It was a blast. I want to claim that as my primary contribution to the citizens and the children and teenagers of Riverside, because I had tremendous feedback from that class. I think it was right where those kids were and trying to figure out who they are and be listened to and talk to each other.

Rose Monge and I met at Poly High School in 1970. When I was at North, we got the idea to start a peer helper program at our respective schools. The students are trained in listening skills and resource-finding skills so that students in need, who might be afraid to come talk to a counselor or teacher, would talk to each other, and then they would consult with us and with the resources we were providing. That was another activism thing in the teaching realm, creating change and creating something that hadn't existed before.

I retired in 2003. 9/11 had happened, and we were going to war in Iraq, and I was very upset about that. I harkened back to the days when I had been in demonstrations as a way to make change. I saw this little tiny ad in the newspaper from the artist Don O'Neill that said "I'm going to be walking against the war on Sunday at ten o'clock if you want to join me." So, I got my nerve up, and I went. We started downtown. I thought there'd be big crowds, and there were like ten or fifteen people there. But something wonderful happened—we didn't stop the war or anything, but I met Linda Dunn. I found out there were Quakers in Riverside, then she also told me about this organization called the [Inland Communities] Fellowship of Reconciliation and invited me to their meetings. **I said, "Linda,**

I just want to do something." Say that to Linda, and then that's it for the rest of your life. She's got stuff for you to do. The Fellowship of Reconciliation had just started a couple years before, when there were a lot of demonstrations happening in Riverside and some of the people were very militant about stopping the war. The Quakers tried to negotiate, and some people said "No, we're not willing to agree to use only nonviolence in our protests." That made a schism between two groups, and one group formed a chapter of the Fellowship of Reconciliation here in Riverside. Pretty soon they were looking for new co-chairs. Madelyn MacKay and I hit it off like gangbusters, and we just really went for it.

We continued holding the candlelight vigil for peace, in the season of peace—at Christmas time. We were in front of the library on the sidewalk, next to the Festival of Lights at the Mission Inn. I learned about First Amendment rights, and where you can stand, and what you can do ,and so forth. I knew a teacher over at Norte Vista, Vanessa Segura, and she got very interested and started bringing her students to the candlelight vigil. They would come and hold the signs and pass out flyers, and they started making these huge signs. My husband, Jeffrey Laird, would talk with me and listen to me and ask really deepening questions all the time. So after a few years of doing the candlelight vigil with "Peace on Earth Now" signs that we were using, he said, "What do you think those people think you mean by peace?" We started trying to define what we mean by peace and what the people who saw the signs could do towards peace themselves. We came up with this long list of "Peace is…" and then Jeffrey designed these signs. My favorite one is "Peace is Hospitality." Peace is Compassion. Peace is Civility. Peace is Disarmament. Peace is Fairness, Equality, Forgiveness, Generosity, Integrity, Humility, Knowledge, all these things that the people walking by could say, "Hey, you know, I can do that, or I could do that better."

After September 11, there were a lot of commemorations throughout the city. We discovered a book by Michael Nagler about Gandhi, and we discovered that September 11 in 1906 was Gandhi's first nonviolent action in India. The subtitle of this book is "The Other 9/11," so we decided that we would meet at the Gandhi statue on September 11, and we would hold an event called "The Other 9/11." We used the opportunity to teach about nonviolence. We had speakers, we had poetry readings, we had prayers, we had music, we had different groups that sang there. The Why Nots sang there, the Mission Bells sang there, and we tried to involve other groups in the community as collaborators and supporters and return our support back to them too.

The Dunns found out about this organization called the Nonviolent Peaceforce, and they brought that information to Riverside. ICFOR [Inland Communities Fellowship of Reconciliation] held a fundraising dinner at Jane Block's house to support this organization. The Why Nots sang at that event, and Mayor Loveridge was there because his wife was in the Why Nots. Soon afterwards, we had a speaker named Hindolo Pokawa come out from Minnesota. He was from Sierra Leone, and he was going to talk about Nonviolent Peaceforce and the work they were doing in Sri Lanka. Rose Monge and I used our contacts, and we got Hindolo Pakawa to talk to a whole theater of students about nonviolence, and at Poly, a group of students started their own little club called Nonviolent Peaceforce as a result of that. The next thing you knew, Madelyn and Rose and I were learning about these nonviolent techniques and practices, and we used the manual that they used to train their people. We adjusted it for local teaching to students and we started teaching nonviolent conflict intervention classes. We went to the religious studies classes at UCR. I made two complete Saturday elective classes at RCC, and then we spent a whole semester at La Sierra going once a week, and we would teach these nonviolent skills there. This was, I think, one of the best things that we did. Madelyn and I then got invited to go to Tucson, Arizona, to take the show on the road, and we did a weekend training with a group there called No More Tears that worked around border issues.

We've done the commemoration of the United Nations Day of Peace for ten years, mostly at the Ben Franklin stage downtown. We usually use the theme that comes out from the United Nations that is the worldwide theme. We participated in Juneteenth celebrations. We had an activity booth. We sponsored an interfaith forum at RCC, and that was the seed for the Riverside Interfaith Council that was started by Ajene Wilcoxson and Robert Earl Bogan. We did tabling all over the place, we hired interns, we paid for some kids to go to a conference in Washington, and we collaborated and supported many groups of people. We have a long list of people that we've collaborated with, either by them helping in our activities, or we with them. The most recent one is the Mission Inn Foundation. Our collaboration started a couple years ago on a project called Toward

Peace. Theresa Hanley has been coming to our meetings ever since. I think we are trying to build awareness, trying to keep alive this idea of peace and nonviolence, and to educate the people in Riverside that there are other ways to solve problems.

Inspiration

They are long ago and far away and close. I will start with Jesus's teachings that I learned as a child, and which follow me throughout my life. "Love one another," from my father. Gandhi and Martin Luther King, and I just feel like we're so blessed to have those statues right in our city. Then the Quakers: Linda Dunn, Michael Dunn, Trudy Freidel, Sue Scott, Jane O'Shields Hayner, Bill Hayner. Then Robert Earl Bogan and Dr. Ajene Wilcoxson, Tom Schultz, now deceased, Andrea Briggs, Nicolette Rohr, who was in my seventh grade English class by the way, Mike Kinsman, Kevin and Margie Akin, Deborah Wong, Rose Monge, Madelyn McKay, Rabbi Singer, Connie Confer, Jerri Mendivel, Kris Lovekin, and my dear friends from before, Linda Missouri and Nelly Darby. I include role models and supporters. I want to acknowledge the need for support. My husband Jeffrey wasn't in these organizations, but he loved talking with me about them and thinking about them. He's so great at asking these deepening questions and helping me when I started having doubts. He would help me talk through those things quite a bit. And then when I needed physical help he would make things and carry things and drive me. That has been important.

Advice

Follow your nose, as my mother would say, for wherever your nose goes, so goes the eyes, the focus, the hands, the warmth, the food, the heart. Notice what you're looking at. What are you paying attention to, and what do you want to know about that? The main thing is to reflect upon your values and also upon the price of activating them. Then take a first step. If it's right, things will magically start opening up to you. That's the most amazing thing I remember from the follow your bliss idea, that the universe starts supporting that. It's magical. It starts happening, you just find all these things that you never knew. After a while, during your work, take time for reflection and don't be afraid to ask the hard questions, like, "Why am I doing this? And is this work doing any good? How could it be more effective? Do I still want to be involved in this way? Do I still want to be leading? How might I be honest with myself and my colleagues?" Find and use support for yourself and your work. Take care of yourself along the way. Be grateful for these leadings, the questions and answers and opportunities to serve, and thank God. Finally, thank God.

"Always peacebuilding"

Rose Y. Monge

Roots

I was born in Agua Prieta, Sonora, Mexico, and the family lived there for a while until we immigrated in the mid-1950s. My dad was concerned about the fact that he could not provide for his children, and he wanted a better life for us, and so we settled into the unincorporated area in San Bernardino and Riverside, in the Etiwanda area. I have lived in the Riverside area for about 65 years, and I consider myself a native Riverside person, with my roots in Mexico. We did have relatives in Rubidoux. It was my grandmother's sister who married an American gentleman, and when we first crossed over, when we first immigrated, we stayed there for about two months until my dad got a job while working in the vineyards in Etiwanda. We were migrant workers. We worked in the summer, we picked grapes, we picked cotton, we went from Riverside all the way to Sacramento, Colusa and Marysville, and we didn't buy our first home until I was in high school. I have a lot of respect for my parents for taking that leap of faith and hope that they could provide a better life for us.

I transferred from RCC and then to UCR, and the last two years at UCR I worked in the Extension office. I was a typist because I prepared myself to be a business major as I was doing college prep courses at Rubidoux [High School], so I was able to be hired as a secretary. The validation that I got from the staff members there was just amazing to me. It puts tears in my eyes. There weren't that many Hispanic students, in fact there weren't any Hispanic students in the French Department, and that was my major, so I felt kind of special that I was able to break the mold. I felt very welcomed at UCR.

Call to activism

I was kind of at the periphery of the Student Nonviolent Coordinating Committee [at UC Riverside]. These students were actually going out there and confronting the status quo. I go, "Wow, these students are doing something!" But I just didn't have time to do what they were doing. Then Vietnam was major in my lifetime, particularly for young people, particularly if you believed in nonviolence. Several of my classmates that graduated from Rubidoux went to Vietnam, and we lost quite a few of them. I had to find a way of making peace in my head. I did not support the war, but I needed to support the young men that were going out there. One of the first things I did when I started teaching was that I joined the USO. We basically met the servicemen that were stationed at March Air Force Base and Norton Air Force Base, and we provided support and letters and the like. **My interest was always peacebuilding.** The USO kind of provided me an opportunity to support the young men, not necessarily because I believed in war, which I don't.

I graduated from UCR in '67. I'm the first college graduate in my family. I took a real quick course at LaVerne University to get my partial teaching credentials because I needed a job. Everybody wanted me to teach Spanish, but my major was in French, and I graduated with a French degree from UCR. I accepted a job when school started at University Heights [Middle School], and I was there for three years before I got transferred to Poly [High School]. The principal at University Heights, Horace Jackson, approached me about possibly going to a conference at UC Berkeley, because of the situation that was happening in the schools in terms of the unrest, and the walkouts in L.A., the call for Ethnic Studies, Chicano Studies, and Black Studies. So I went to that conference, and I got to meet some of the leaders of the UFW [United Farm Workers, the early labor movement, and I got to meet the first Chicano publishing house, El Quinto Sol. I was surprised that he wanted me to go, because I never saw myself as doing that. My main goal when I graduated from UCR was to teach French, but that was my first experience meeting others that had an interest in learning about Ethnic Studies as well as social movements.

When I got transferred to Poly, my assignment was to develop a Chicano Studies program curriculum. I thought, "Oh my goodness, how am I going to do this?" I also got my wish, I was able to teach advanced French classes, plus they gave me the assignment of being a counselor for the Hispanic kids. Irma Sutton taught Black history and was counseling the Black students, and she was doing the lower-level French. It was so interesting to me that there were the minority teachers teaching French. Let me tell you, that first year, I do not remember a thing. It's almost like a lost year for me in terms of what I was doing. I felt overwhelmed, and that I did not have the credentials to do a good job. We were not welcome at Poly because they thought that we did not have the credentials to do the job. Irma and I went to LaVerne and got our PPS [Pupil Personnel Service] credentials, I guess to quiet the naysayers. Eventually we were able to get a regular counseling assignment. I graduated from Rubidoux High School, and my experience with counselors was rare. I remember going to a counseling office, where the counselor called me in. I was kind of surprised, because you think you're in trouble if you go to the office, and the only thing he said, which really shocked me, was, "How are you dealing with the boys?" And I go, "What?" Not, "How're you doing in school?" or "How are your grades?" or "Is there anything I can do to help you?" So, I think my counseling style is what I would have liked my counselor to do for me. And so that was my guiding light, was, what should the counselor do?

Contributions

After the Columbine incident in '99, I created the Stop the Violence program, and then later on I created the Peer Tutor Program and the Peer Helpers. I'm very proud to say that I listened to the kids and addressed a need. I think a lot of what I did in my professional life was also a type of activism.

In a way, my interest in peace went back to when I was in high school and opposed the Vietnam War. Much later, I knew Marilyn Sequoia at Poly when I first started teaching, and then she got involved with the Inland Communities Fellowship of Reconciliation through Linda Dunn and Mike Dunn who were both Quakers. In the later years I was at Poly, she was looking for students to participate in the candlelight vigil and other activities, like Gandhi's birthday. I got my Stop the Violence kids involved with the group and we participated in those events. For me, it was kind of a perfect fit for the students who were opposed to violence to be part of this group. Once I retired, I didn't have the connection in terms of getting the kids involved, and I felt badly because youth need to be involved in peacemaking. They're our hope for the future. We branched out and I formed a bond with Norte Vista kids to start participating in our events through one of their counselors, Vanessa Segura. We have a peace essay contest every year in the springtime, and we award scholarships to the students. Back in 2009-2010, ICFOR joined forces with the Nonviolent Peace Force, and Madelyn MacKay was one of the directors and got us involved. I created a curriculum for the Nonviolent Conflict Intervention (NCI) workshops, and we did trainings at RCC, UCR, and La Sierra.

I started being involved with the Multicultural Council of the Riverside Museum Associates in 2015. My first foray in that was for the Family Village Festival. Since 2016, I have been the chair or co-chair of the Day of Inclusion. I decided if Multicultural Council is part of the museum, why don't I apply to become a museum board member? So I became a museum board member in late 2016, and guess what happened afterwards? The museum got shuttered. Since I've been a board member, the museum has been shuttered, which is really kind of distressing.

I have been a memoir facilitator since retirement. Getting those stories from the seniors at the Goeske Center has been another blessing in my life. Once again, with no formal training, I just said, "I want to write my memoir." I signed up for a short class at RCC in the summer after I retired, and then the class got canceled, so I took it upon myself to be the facilitator. The stories are going to be archived and they're going to be historic. I'm glad that I'm at least part of that process, to collect stories.

Inspiration

I've been influenced by the people around me. In terms of a national person that has totally consumed me, Cesar Chavez was a major influence for me. I only got to see him, I never really met him, but in terms of his educational message, I espoused that change can occur with an educated constituency. I have to give him a shout out, as well as Dolores Huerta, in terms of the first role models. My other role models have been tidbits of seeing people in the community doing things. Madelyn MacKay with ICFOR, and I consider Irma Sutton a role model as well.

Advice

I don't think you're born an activist, or, I never considered myself one, but I think the term itself is action-related. You cannot be an activist until you espouse a change of some sort. It has to be tempered by what's going around you and your experience of what change you want to see. It cannot exist in a vacuum. You have to be willing to see something that needs change. Even one small change can get you started. It's a first step into a wider picture of how else you can be involved. You just cannot do it by yourself. **You have to have a collection of kindred spirits.** You have to surround yourself with those cheerleaders that also want the same change to happen. Listen to your mentors and your elders. Keep your ears open, have an open mind. Sometimes you may be asked to modify your way of thinking; don't be stodgy in terms of putting your foot planted on cement. There has to be an opportunity for change.

The next step

Andrea Briggs

Roots

I was born in Cincinnati, Ohio, and consider myself a Midwesterner. I moved around a bit for school, went further east and then further west, and met the guy who became my husband in Chicago. We migrated from Chicago to Kansas to California for his work, and I got to California in 1980, pregnant with our first child. I didn't have any connections in Riverside. I studied religion and psychology and was working on a PhD at the University of Chicago and thought that I was headed toward a profession as an academic. After our firstborn was about a month or two old, I was climbing the walls and the Avon lady was my best friend, because she was the only person I had to talk to. Out of some stroke of genius, I called up June O'Connor in the UCR Religious Studies Department and asked if I could come and meet her. I said, "I'm bored, I'm lonely, I need work and I need a friend." She arranged for me to be an assistant in the class that she was teaching the following term. The position to be ombuds at UCR came up and required prior UCR experience, and I had an inside track by about two weeks at that point, so I fit the guidelines. I was hired as a university ombudsman in 1981 and retired from that position in 2007. That job was an enormously good fit for me. It was before ombuds work was particularly well defined, and I kind of grew up with it as the position grew up. We were evolving it as a profession, as something that was recognized with a name and a particular set of guidelines for how it was done. It was very satisfying.

Call to activism

I think that I've had a heart for the underdog since forever. If somebody's getting the short end of the stick, there's part of me that is enraged that someone would take advantage in that way.

My grandmother didn't follow the rules. She made her own path, she did what she wanted to do and she had a sense of personal integrity. I think I inherited that. Her influence, either genetic or taught, was that it's okay to find another way that calls to me.

My freshman year in college was the year that the U.S. bombed Cambodia. That was so clearly wrong to me. I could see no justification for it. I discovered at that point that I was a pacifist. There was no question about it. I knocked on the door of a church in the town where the college was, Swarthmore outside of Philadelphia, and said, "Can I talk to one of your adult study groups, bible groups, about pacifism?" I went in and started teaching. "Here's what Jesus says;" it is right here in the book! It was a very naïve, youthful thing to do, but they opened the door and let me in.

Later, the church became a lot less meaningful to me. I was still studying the history of Christianity as a graduate student, but I wasn't engaged in it personally. I had no faith community. I wasn't attending church. John and I were married in a church, the chapel at the University of Chicago, and that was about as close as I got. I began pursuing other faiths with a great deal of interest and learned a lot about Hinduism and the meditation practices of Hindus and the paths of devotion to a deity, or knowledge as a path to enlightenment. It probably was in the middle '90s when it started to occur to me that spirituality was extremely important to me, and that I had gone as far as I could in my own solitary practice. I needed one, and so I started looking around for one. I looked at my husband and said, "I think I want to go to church, and I think we might want to do this together, because it might take up a lot of my time." So we went church shopping and ended up at All Saints Episcopal Church in 2002. I got involved really quickly in leadership roles at the church. I went to seminary for three years. That didn't have the outcome I was expecting, and I came back to All Saints and basically said, "I need something to do." The clergy person at that time said, "Well, we're going to give you a title and then figure out what it is you want to do." What a wonderful carte blanche. I think I've been able to make good on that offer.

Contributions

The way that I most value being an agent of change, being an activist, is person to person, and I think I've been doing that for a long time. The way that I can be most useful in making change in my community is by empowering other people, by activating other people as agents of change, by teaching and modeling how agency is so very important. We all can do something.

The Riverside Concert Across America to End Gun Violence [2016] may have been my debut in terms of a big splash among a very small number of people. I'm a more recent addition to the Riverside Coalition for Police Accountability. It's another situation where things that are so clearly wrong are happening, and we can do them better. It's just important to say that. The Riverside Interfaith Council is where I get to know folks. The Fellowship of Reconciliation and their mission was just so right for me, because it was both pacifist and faith-based. I learned so much from that organization and from watching and imitating people there, and got on their board of directors. I haven't been able to be as involved in the local chapter here as I would like, but it's a really important influence for me. I went to Iran with the Fellowship of Reconciliation as a citizen ambassador. The model is that when the top level of diplomacy between nations is not working, you just send people who are willing to walk on the streets and say, "Hello." "Where are you from, I'm American." These of course were only the Iranians who spoke English, because I couldn't do anything with Farsi, but we heard with amazing consistency, "Americans are fine, it's your government I don't like." The two most important institutions in my life are the Fellowship of Reconciliation and the Episcopal Church.

I've had the opportunity to lead and arrange small worship services at All Saints. I was looking around for a church to be in on New Year's Eve. So the idea was, well, let's just have one! I've had such a wonderful response from the clergy leadership at All Saints. I propose these things, and they say sure! The way that I've pitched these things ever since is, "I want to be in church on New Year's Eve. And if you'd like to come too, that'd be great." And so it's happened New Year's Eve, it's happened at Thanksgiving, then we did an Inauguration Day service [2017]. I wasn't going to be watching TV and I didn't want to just spend the morning crying, so we arranged a worship service in the morning of that day. People from other churches came. We did a prayer vigil all day on Election Day this year [2020], which was something that meant a whole lot to me. That's what I wanted to do, and so I make the space open and available and say, "You can come." My idea, my hope has been that this is a community event. I haven't been able to quite get it to be an interfaith event. It's not easy to lead an interfaith anything, but it's just so important to me that we have such opportunities. I'm still working on making an interfaith event one of those opportunities for something we do together. I do the marquee at All Saints too. What an opportunity that is—right there on Magnolia with who knows how many thousand cars going by to declare who All Saints Church is and what our take on Christianity would say to the rest of the world.

The Food Share started in June of 2020, a few months into the pandemic. St. Michael's Episcopal Church in Riverside had access to the USDA Farmers to Families programs. USDA was paying for packed up boxes of milk and meat and cheese and produce, and it was such a simple thing. You go pick up the boxes, they're on the back of a truck, you put them in people's cars. It was a no-contact exchange. People didn't need to get out of their cars and they didn't get exposed to the volunteers and vice versa. It was very simple and straightforward. We thought we could do it at the other end of town at All Saints as well. We picked up about sixty boxes and served maybe fifty families. It was a pickup truck in the All Saints parking lot, and half a dozen volunteers. And it grew. The contract for the boxes ran out, and they had bulk produce instead, pallets of onions or potatoes or jicama or chili peppers, and we'd develop an assembly line and put them all in bags and boxes and put those in the trunks of people's cars. It got to the point where we were moving four hundred of the boxes when we could get them, or five pickup trucks of produce, and we had twenty-five volunteers at a time. We had the idea that we were doing a short project for the pandemic, that with people out of work, they needed food, and so when this is over, we'll be done, but our volunteers didn't want to stop, and we found more food. We thought, "Has there always been a food shortage in Riverside? And was this just exacerbated by pandemic, but not caused by it?" We picked up something that fit a particular need, and if it's going to change into something else we figure out how to sustain it or we change it or stop doing it.

Part of what I think of as my own activism is that there's the world that needs to be changed, but there's me that needs to be changed, and **I'm not going to be much good to the world if I haven't done my own work first,** if I haven't engaged in enough reflection to know myself well and to discover where I could be doing better. That is a foundation for how I go out into the world, with kindness and love and respect and compassion and forgiveness and all those good things. They have to come from inside. They can't be just manufactured at the moment. And it takes a while.

Inspiration

My grandmother was one. June O'Connor was another. There are people that encouraged me and gave me an opportunity and put me in places that I wouldn't have necessarily gone without a push. Linda Dunn got me on the Inland Agency Board of Directors, an opportunity to take a formal leadership role early on. The people that I notice, whom I want to imitate, seem to be the ones who just do what they do because that's what they do. What was most important to June showed in the way she lived and the way she went about the job that was hers to do. It's like the phrase, "Bloom where you're planted." Within this realm where I have some influence, I can do these things, and I can show you how I engage with the things that are the very most important to me. I love watching the folks who can lead rallies and give speeches and demand this change or that change, and I'm just not one of them. It's just not the way I roll. I think I'd like to be, but I probably wouldn't enjoy it, and I might not even be very effective.

My oldest daughter is a role model, too, because she's so deeply engaged in anti-racist activism in Arlington, Virginia. How'd she do that? I'm so proud of her.

Advice

I'm not good at advising anybody, but here is what I did. What I did was work on myself first, and I found that very valuable. You've got to work on yourself first. Not exclusively, that gets to be some kind of self-preoccupation, but first, and then go out and do your work, and then go back and do some more work on yourself.

Do what the next obvious step is. **Take the next small step**, the one that's in front of you. It can be a small one, and it's okay to go slow.

I've got to listen way more than I talk. I'm a slow processor, it takes me a long time to figure out what I think and what I need to do. Listening to people I agree with as well as people I disagree with is where I learn the most about what I'm going to do next.

"Being a librarian is a radical act"

Judith Auth

Roots

I was born in 1943 in Upland, California, and I lived in Upland until I married, and with my husband and son I moved to Riverside in 1971.

Call to activism

My mother was an inspiration. She was a housewife in the 1950s. She had been credentialed as a teacher, but when children came, she stayed at home. She invited the new mothers, all with spanking-clean houses, and their children, to come to coffee, and it became a weekly event. But it wasn't just tea and cookies, it was talking about community issues, and at one point, it was focusing on a house that had become a drug house, and taking action to see that the proper authorities were called in and changes were made. She also was instrumental in forming the first girls' home in Upland. It began with the Upland Presbyterian Church, but the county of San Bernardino took it over. Living with her and her outreach to other women in the community was a primary inspiration. But even that was preceded by my grandmother, who was actually an ordained minister who started her own church in Ontario, California, a church that I grew up in. It was kind of a radical little group called the Church of God. She became quite well-known as a preacher and a thinker and a healer.

I was in Girl Scouts all the way through to high school. June Lewis was the leader, who had had polio, and who could not hike or do those kinds of things, but she taught us how to be independent and to appreciate the influence that a group of well-intentioned people can have.

Contributions

I worked for the Riverside Public Library for thirty-five years. I started at the Marcy branch as the children's librarian. Then, I was promoted to the librarian in the main library's children's room. From there, I moved into the children's services coordinator role. Then, as a senior librarian, I was eligible to transfer to a branch manager position, which I did, and then I was invited back to the main library as the head of the central library and did a turn as the interim director of technical services during one of the early upgrades of the automated systems. Then Linda Wood selected me to be assistant librarian, and when she left, I interviewed for her position and was appointed director. It was a remarkable opportunity to start out as an entry-level librarian and to move into the directorship. **Just being a librarian is, in my opinion, a radical act,** because you are trying to provide a service without partisanship and without prejudice. At one point in a public meeting, I was called Robin Hood, because the speaker said I stole from the rich to give to the poor, because in the library world, we try to equalize the resources that we delivered. We took in the tax money, and we bought the materials, and then we distributed them through the library branches.

One of the challenges I had was to redesign the city library when the board of library trustees released the county from their partnership, which had been in place for over eighty years as the city and county library. As the city librarian then, the first thing we did to reinvent, as it were, the city library, was to form the library foundation [the Riverside Public Library Foundation]. Marion Mitchell-Wilson was my staff person who took the lead on that. Now, being an activist and being a leader aren't always the same thing, but I think that leadership is finding people who have the ideas and the talent and the will to carry projects through, and they deserve the credit when they succeed. So Marion Mitchell-Wilson got the library foundation running. Its goal was to enhance the excellence of the library. Soon after that, we embarked on outreach to the young people on the Eastside. At the time, the digital divide was increasingly severe with the poorer children having no access to computers, and so we formed the project the Eastside Cybrary, which ended up being funded with community block grant money and Library Services and Construction Act funds. Sharon Duffy at UCR worked with us, and her students served as mentors for the young people at the Eastside Cybrary. This was the nucleus of what became the Eastside branch of the public library.

In 2000, we decided to go for a tax measure. There hadn't been a successful municipal tax measure in Riverside since the 1960s. Our campaign committee met on September 11, 2001. It was very sobering, and we all agreed that if there was ever a time when libraries were needed, it was now. We went forward [with Measure C] in 2002, and it was passed with 68% [of the vote], and we got our $19 per parcel library fee. That brought in several million dollars more to the library. This was a real shot in the arm until the economy in 2008 took a dive, and then the city decided that that money had to be used to backfill some of the costs that they could no longer take from the general fund. So it's been a struggle to sell the library tax, but it was renewed in 2012, and it will come up again in 2022, and I hope that a new committee can sell it again, because nineteen dollars per parcel is not a whole lot of money when you consider the value of having access to the libraries and the programs and the services that are offered. Dawn Hassett was our campaign manager from Geographics, Inc., and Vic Miceli was our campaign chairperson, and that was how I got roped into Evergreen, because Vic won us the library parcel tax then turned to me and said, "Now you've got to help me."

I had gone to the City Council in 1988 as a librarian and told the City Council that the cemetery really was an open-air museum that needed to be better cared for. And I was coming to that from work on the Eastside with an artist named Leer Larkins. One of the activities that we sponsored was taking young people through the teen youth employment program and introducing them to various aspects of the city, especially children from the Eastside. Some had never been in restaurants, some had never been in City Hall, some had never been in a public library, and none of them had ever been to the cemetery, so Leer had as a project that we would go and photograph the stones at Evergreen cemetery. His goal in doing this was to let them know that this cemetery and the names on those stones were part of their community. John North, they went to John North High School, so here is John North's gravesite. Here is Prince Edwards, whose family was still living on the Eastside, and some of these young people knew the descendants. In this way, we were able to, in a small way, convey to them that they were part of this larger city and that they had reason to invest in it. Then my interests sort of lay dormant. Leer had taken over five hundred photographs of the standing stones, thinking that the photographs were all that were going to be left, because the place had been neglected so severely.

I'm not really a scholar, but I am a storyteller, and I do enjoy finding out the details of other people's lives and understanding the choices that they made that resulted in success or failure or disappointment or whatever. So, I began small. My husband worked with me, and we put together a walking tour of Evergreen Cemetery, and we identified the most well-known names of persons buried there. There was Eliza Tibbetts and there was John North, and I had to find out something about them for this walking tour, and as our interests moved beyond the, as it were, movers and shakers, we became more aware of the contributions made by other parts of the community. At one point, we had the African American Historical Society raise a monument to the families on the Eastside who were buried at Evergreen. Just this last year, I discovered that the monument that has Korean writing to a Mr. Kim, actually an important person in the Koreatown development that Edward Chang writes about in the recent [2020] Historical Society sesquicentennial edition of Riverside history. It's a web, and you travel along one thread and it connects up with another thread and another thread, and you eventually begin to see a kind of design emerging. And for me, the design of the cemetery is the design of a unique group of people who wanted to make a different kind of community. They weren't looking just to get rich, they were looking to be a cooperative, well-educated group of people taking care of their families and their community. And wanting to share that idea with, particularly, young people, to convince them that they had reason to be proud of their history here in the city of Riverside, and proud of the efforts that had been made to create the institutions that we now benefit from.

Judge Miceli was a wonderful arm twister, and he had a group of people from the city, private enterprise, that were willing to work with him on the rehabilitation of the cemetery. That was not my thing. And yet he also recognized that in order to gain widespread community support, we needed to have a compelling story to tell.

My predecessor Linda Wood was a very political animal. She had worked very successfully with the elected officials, the county board of supervisors, city managers in the city county system, to put in place plans that allowed the library system to weather the cutbacks from Prop 13, which was devastating for libraries. She had told me, as a young librarian, that I should join the League of Women Voters, because I needed to know what the civic issues were in the local area. And so, at her suggestion, I joined the League, and I met some of the dynamic people that were involved, but I was very much a working woman, and I didn't have the same amount of time that some of the women in the League had to devote to the current issues. They did wonderful things about the public utilities and wonderful studies of the Santa Ana River. I admired their work, but it wasn't until after my retirement that I joined the board and was willing to serve as secretary to the Riverside chapter of the League. I got elected president and went to a conference in San Diego, which was a real eye-opener. I was really proud to be part of the group. I came back with a renewed enthusiasm for the work that the League does, which is quietly, behind the scenes, working with rule makers and legislators to understand complex situations. The process by which they take a position is quite lengthy. Start with local level, asking people what are their concerns. Then it goes to the state level, and those concerns are investigated, and then at the state convention they are presented as possible areas of study. And then, when they are adopted as an area of study, like right now they're working on a homelessness taskforce, they're working on a taskforce for the climate change, and when a position is finally agreed on, then every League member can speak about that position to elected officials, to the public, as a member of the League. But, until that position is taken, we cannot speak on the issue as League members. But we do work as individuals to frame those issues. The most important thing about the League is that it does not take a partisan role. It does not endorse candidates, and instead we conduct what are called candidate forums, where the candidates are invited to a meeting where they are asked questions by a League member in a public setting, and they are given a certain amount of time to answer, and we have been able, through technology, to put those forums now online, so not only the fifty people who show up to hear the candidates for the council office or the mayor, now it can be seen by a wider swath of the general public. I have been fortunate to be a moderator for some of those candidate forums, and I really admire the way the League asks the question and lets the candidate respond, and does not take a position and say, "This is the right position or that's the wrong candidate or this is the right candidate, that's the wrong candidate." But, by asking questions, enables the public to hear the position that the candidate holds.

I also did work with Linda Dunn, who was the executive director of the Inland Agency, which started out as a health agency promoting health programs. And eventually I was president of the board of the Inland Agency, when we were working on a project called "Promoting Peace on the Eastside." It was a time of gang violence, and we had marches up and down Park Avenue, and we conducted discussion groups, and we tried to frame gun violence as a public health issue, and to look at the spread of gang violence as an epidemic. We're dealing with another kind of epidemic right now [COVID-19], but at the time, that was an odd term to put to violence. Brady has picked up some of those same points and is carrying that forward. "Promoting Peace on the Eastside" was not successful in stopping gang violence. It was not successful in getting rid of guns. But it was a real education for me on how the disadvantaged families cope in what looked like an affluent city. I think that all of these things do accumulate. What has happened now on the Eastside under Andy Melendrez as city councilman are good things, that there's new energy and new investment. It doesn't help people who were there thirty years ago, but it promises a different future for those living there now.

Inspiration

Jane Block is just my star role model, because when Jane gets a bee in her bonnet, she just brings in everybody who had anything to do with that subject until she's got enough mass to move it forward. I worked with her in several of the YWCA Women Supporting Women conferences, and at one of them I gave the keynote address, which was entitled "To Dwell in Possibility." And if there is a motto for me, it is Emily Dickinson's poem "To Dwell in Possibility." To live in the possibility.

Joan Donahue is really a skilled leader, and I admire her care in putting together a strategic approach to problem solving. She carried this amendment to the charter through the charter review committee and the ballot, and now it is in place. Sue Struthers, who was hired as a children's librarian when I was at the library and is now part of the Riverside Food Co-op, is another important innovator. She recognized the opportunity to provide local, fresh food to people who were willing to pay a little bit and has built this Riverside Food Co-op as a viable organization. They're now reaching out, working with the county schools, working with local growers, and ideally moving toward a storefront that sells local produce. And again, she had a passion and she did her research and she formed the group of people who would share her enthusiasm and move forward. What Cati Porter has done with Inlandia is truly remarkable. I sat at the table where Malcolm Margolin first proposed to us at the library that there be an anthology of writings about Riverside County or the Inland area. At that time, we had a list of local authors that included some very interesting people, but there was no real sense that there was a literary culture in the Inland Empire. We began with programs featuring our authors, and then this with Marion Mitchell-Wilson's leadership coalesced into Inlandia, and with her passing, she passed the baton to Cati, who has expanded it in a number of ways, reaching out to underserved communities. I admire Cati for stepping into troubled territory and doing it with grace and with the solid support of her team.

Advice

You've got to have good information. You have to be informed. **You have to speak from accurate information**. If your information isn't accurate, you're wasting your time. I've always been impressed with the women I've worked with, from Joan Donahue, Linda Dunn, to Jane Block, to Linda Wood, that they did their homework. And you don't just shoot off your mouth about something you care about. You speak with a cool head.

You have to have a team. You have to have a group. You have to have dedicated people who can work together and can see the long-term benefit, not the short-term. You don't work as an individual, you work as part of a cooperative.

One of the workshops I did at the YWCA was about taking credit for your work. That too often, when women find success, they say, "Oh, I was lucky." No. You weren't lucky. You worked hard. And you made the right decisions. And things came together, because you cared! And it was due to your diligence, not to luck, that things worked out.

One of my favorite quotes is from Peter Drucker, who said, "Success is not solving problems. Success is seizing opportunities." And that, I think, is the key, particularly for local grassroots organizers. That you seize the opportunity that presents itself and you carry it, kind of like that football, all the way to the end zone if you can. And if you can't, well, go back and start again. But to move toward the opening that presents itself rather than banging your head against the wall that seems to have been erected in the direction you wanted to go.

I understand that leadership doesn't do it all, but it sets a tone, and I think what we've seen in the latest political arena, we see how devastating the tone can be. And also, ideally, how powerfully good that tone can be, and recruiting people, well-intentioned, willing to work together, in spite of differences. I think that taking credit for your work is an important thing that women need to learn how to do.

If we forget who came before, if we forget on whose shoulders we're standing, we are doomed for disaster. We are human beings with a built-in capacity for narrative, and in order to find our place in this world, we have to know who stands with us, who stood before us, in order to go forward.

"Speaking from a well-informed perspective"

Joan Donahue

Roots

I was born in 1953 in Leavenworth, Kansas. I was raised in Kansas City. My dad worked for JCPenney. My husband was in the hotel business for a long time, so we moved around a lot and lived in Chicago, Fort Lauderdale, Orlando, Jacksonville Beach, and then San Diego. We came to Riverside for a job at the Marriott Hotel downtown. We planted ourselves here in Riverside and we've grown here.

Call to activism

I was raised in one of those families where politics was discussed regularly. I was coming up in the 1960s, the Vietnam era, the civil rights era. My mother was always active, and she was active with the League of Women Voters and some anti-war groups. I kind of collected that as I grew up.

I got real active in the League of Women Voters in San Diego. When we moved to Riverside, that experience that I had with the League was what helped me get a job at City Hall as the legislative field representative for a council member Dom Betro. Then I got hands-on experience in government, which was great, and when that job was over, I grew more active with the League here. I think that's when real activism starts, when you're in the leadership position and you tell people what to do, and it's like, "Here's the direction I think we want to go in," that's when I feel like the serious work took off.

Contributions

Working for Dom Betro was fascinating because it was right around the launch of the Riverside Renaissance. There was a lot of money involved, a lot of investment involved, a lot of optimism, and a lot of change. Anytime you have a lot of change, you will also find you will have a lot of resistance. But you look at the rewards now, and it was all worth it, and Riverside is still growing. You look at the development downtown. It was great to be part of that, laying the foundation for moving the city forward, even though, if you recall, there used to not be any parking meters in downtown.

I tried to be an advocate for constituents' concerns, and at the same time try and show them the benefits of what the city was doing and how this would benefit them in the long run. I learned a lot. I found in speaking to people that people are a lot more fearful of things than I realized. People seem to get over-concerned about things. I think most important is to tell people the truth. Listen to them. Try and get them to look at things rationally. At the heart of League of Women Voters is do your homework and be prepared. Argue with the facts! **There is confidence and strength when you know that you're speaking from a well-informed perspective.**

I don't really think of myself so much as a community organizer. I have this great community organization in place, so it's my job to take that out into the community and increase our visibility. League of Women Voters has been doing candidate forums since 1924. We want to broaden our scope, so we reach out to Latino Network, to The Group, to NAACP, and have them co-sponsor with us, and also to the local community groups—if it's a Ward 1 election, you want to work with DANA [the Downtown Area Neighborhood Alliance] or wherever you are. What happened was as we broadened our diversity and widened our reach, the content of the forums became that much better. That really helped to elevate us in the community. I think if you're gonna get anything accomplished, the first place you start is with building a coalition. My attitude has always been there's no point to go it alone. You're not gonna get very far, and you're gonna be that much better if you go ahead and get the other people and get their attitudes and get their ideas. It's a great benefit to yourself, and there's power in numbers. I'm a firm believer in teaming up with people whenever you can.

We also do the pros and cons on the ballot measures. That seems to be really appreciated. I'm really proud of some of the local policy measures that we have advocated for in the past. Some successful, some not. We authored and promoted Measure Q, and we saw it as a voting rights issue, so that in the future, if there's a vacancy on the city council, the council can appoint, but not for longer than one year, because we had this recent experience where we had a vacancy and they appointed a good friend to sit on the council for three years. We saw that as an infringement on voting rights. I looked at all kinds of other cities, looking for best practices, looking at the language in their city charters, how they address vacancies on their city council, and then, with Judith Auth, we put together the changes and went to the charter review commission. We're really proud of that, it passed soundly.

When people think of the League of Women Voters, they think of the voter education work that we do. But really, our advocacy work is the larger part of what we do. And so, on the statewide level, we were instrumental in bringing forth the [California] Citizens Redistricting Commission. Here in California, we're fortunate, we have citizens drawing the lines instead of the legislators. We pick our representatives instead of them picking us. That's the kind of thing we're really proud of, and we're trying our best to get that done nationwide.

Inspiration

When I was in high school, it was Shirley Chisholm. I'm energized again thinking of her now. The woman was fearless! Not just in the fact that she ran for president and broke all these barriers, but she was the first woman to really address gender equality. She spoke to the issues of racism and poverty. She was talking about things that weren't really fashionable for the feminists of the day to talk about. She focused on early childhood education, hot lunch for kids, things that are really important to women, that a lot of women weren't talking about at the time. Shirley Chisholm was very big on diversity, but at the same time unity. She spoke beautifully about being able to do those two things, and she never sugarcoated anything. I just remember thinking, "Wow, this lady is like, she speaks the truth to power." My mom has an expression, "Always a lady, never a doormat." I look at these women I work with—they'll go into a meeting and be concise, direct, always civil, but they will not be walkin' out of that meeting with anybody's footprints on their backs.

Advice

Check out the League of Women Voters. Seriously. Yes, we're a one-hundred-year-old organization, but the League has remained dynamic. It has changed with the times. We have a terrific infrastructure, we have seven hundred leagues across the United States, we have a huge portfolio—if you are interested in any variety of things, we may already be working on it.

Secondly, you can't do much better than take a page from the suffragists. Look at how they did that. You get some other women to stand up with you, and then you start to get the word out there. You grow those coalitions. You get the like-minded groups together for the power in numbers. And then you make a splash. The suffragists held parades. You can still do things like that. Then, depending on what your objective is, a lot of times, the ultimate goal is some kind of legislation. That being the case, you can form the parade, but chances are you're going to need a politician to carry the flag for you. So, then you start with the lobbying, the letter-writing, the personal meetings, and so forth. That is the way that they did it, and we still do it that way today, and it works. The thing that was most fascinating about the suffragists, and the thing that I think holds true today, is that they made it through determination. That holds true, that's what it takes. Ruth Wilson, long-time Riverside activist and one of the founders of the League of Women Voters, told me once, "If I have accomplished anything, it's because the minute I saw an opportunity, I went for it." I think that is such good advice, because we as women tend to be more circumspect. But don't let your self-doubt hold you back. Get out there and go for it.

"Another good trouble"

Nancy Takano

Roots

I was born in Temple City in Los Angeles. I only have sisters, and I have five sisters. By the time I went into camp [Heart Mountain, a World War II incarceration camp for Japanese Americans], I believe I was two or three. We were transported from the assembly center. For some reason, there was some mix-up, so part of the family was at the Santa Anita racetrack, and the other one was at the Pomona center. We stayed there for quite a while, and then we transferred to Wyoming and stayed at Heart Mountain until 1946 when we were told to go ahead and go back.

We went back to El Monte. Then later we moved to Coachella Valley, which is the desert, and we lived half a mile from the Salton Sea. I dearly loved the desert. It is quite remote, but my father and my mother both went ahead and started farming out there with the help of a very good backer. My parents stayed there, and I stayed there until I went to Riverside.

I came here to Riverside in 1958 to go to school. My sister was in one of the first graduating classes for registered nurses at RCC. I rode the bus from Riverside to San Bernardino, and I entered cosmetology school. I agreed to go ahead and do that because of a lack of funds from my parents. From there, I met my husband Willie, and he's a nice man. I don't know why he wanted me! We got married in 1960, and we lived here in Riverside ever since, and we have four boys. Mark [Congressman Mark Takano] is the oldest, and then Douglas, and then number three is Derek—he is teaching at Ramona High School—and then Jerry, my youngest one, retired from the police force in Raleigh, North Carolina.

Call to activism

I felt as though I was always suppressed. From the time I was little, I was reprimanded because I was always out of line. I was one of those kids that used to say, "Tell me why." That was me.

Being Japanese American, you're shaped by what your parents tell you and what you must do—how you are to act. One of the big things is that even if you're wrong, you bow and you back out. The word in Japanese that was used all the time on me is "gaman." "Gaman" means to endure, and it builds you. I was one of those that wanted to fight back. I said, "That's not right! You don't treat people like this!" My older sister used to cry all the time, and I had to stick up for her, and my younger sister did the same thing and I had to stick up for her. And so here I was, always trying to beat up everybody.

When I got to North High School [as the secretary to the vice principal in charge of discipline], I realized how wrong things were there. I had to have been probably about twenty-six, twenty-seven at that time. When I was at North, I began to start speaking out. I began to start saying, "Okay. I am not gonna suspend this person. I will not have my name on there. If you want to go ahead and do that, you do it." They told me that I was promptly fired. I said, "Great, I'll be glad to leave." I think I was fired from that day on almost every other month, because I would not just go ahead, and I said, "This is wrong." I started to stick up. If you can see the position I was in, I was told to suspend a kid, and you know that the kid is telling the truth. Administration is not looking at them as telling the truth, and you suspend them anyway. You start looking at all the things being done, when ninety percent of the people that are being suspended are Black, there's something wrong here. So, I started to speak up. It was racial inequity—it was, but we didn't even use the words. We didn't have time for any of that. Horace Jackson, who was the first Black principal there, had it tough. But I can still remember him hollering out to me, "If you don't do what I tell you, Mrs. Takano,"—hollering to everybody in the whole front office—**"You're fired." I said, "Not today, I'm too busy."** And I just stayed there. I have a lot of scars to prove it, because there was a lot of fighting with the mamas climbing over the counters, and I got hit quite a bit. I don't know why, but I really loved being there at North. North High School shaped who I am.

Contributions

I think I was more of a rabble-rouser than anything else, it seemed like I caused more problems than anything. I have met and talked with John Lewis, and Mark told John Lewis, "I want you to meet another good trouble, it's my mom."

My husband was the organizing chapter chairman for the [Riverside] Japanese American Citizens League, JACL. It's a national organization and there's a chapter out here. We needed to be part of a community. We decided, "Hey, we need to go ahead and show the strength of who we are." They had a play called *Madame Butterfly* at the Riverside Municipal Auditorium. They asked the ladies in the Japanese community if we would wear our kimonos and have what we call a tea, and then hand out the programs and everything else after, which was fine. They told us that we were going to be invited to dinner afterwards. I had nothing to say about it, because the older ones were really running everything. Us younger ones, we were the ones who drove. We got there, and it takes time to get into this Japanese kimono and do all these things. Things went all fine until we went to go to dinner, and we were instructed by the big leaders of Riverside that we had to use the back door. We were told very sharply that we were to serve hors d'oeuvres, which we did. Then one asked, "Well, where are we going to be sitting?" "Oh," he says, "You'll be sitting in the kitchen." So I told the ladies, I gathered them all up, and I said, "All of you are gonna get in the car, and I'm gonna take all of you home, because I am not gonna be dignified with something like this." I can honestly tell you, I said, "This is not *Gone with the Wind*." And I said, "I am not putting up with this." They knew it was wrong. They knew that how we were treated was terrible. But I got chastised because of the way I did it. I got told they've been doing this for twenty, thirty years, and they have got just to the point where we were being recognized and all this and that. So you can imagine how I felt, but I went ahead and told them, "I think we need to have an understanding here." I said, **"I don't want this for my children. I want my children to grow up and go ahead and do just like any other kid that's here. I won't stand for this kind of treatment. I won't let all of you do that."** Slowly but surely, they came around and they did apologize to me, but I did start something. I just told them, "I won't back down." That, to me, was my turning point there, to let them know I'm not going to be treated like this. Now, I can go into a room and survey and say, "I don't see a person of color in here." That's the way it is to me. It's time that people started to speak up.

When the kids got older, I started getting in with the redress [for Japanese Americans incarcerated during World War II]. Then I started to work with more of the Norm Minetas and Doris Matsuis. What I'm really proud of is the younger ones. Mark is very well-spoken, so he doesn't get tongue-tied or start shouting like his mother does. But I noticed that education was everything, and the goals in our family were to get the kids somewhere.

All I do know is I see the students, the Susan Straights, the kids that had gone to North, I see the Black and whites together, and I see the Chicanos. I love seeing how they interact. I can see from the heart how they're talking. I can see where they belong. One of the things that I had always said is there's private schools and there's public schools—my kids, you will teach at a public school, you will never teach at a private school. I said, "You know what you're missing? You're missing the interaction. You're missing the communication going to understanding." I think how important it is to have a public school. You will always get an argument from me if you try to take that away. Private schools are good in many ways. Affordability is not there. But you're just missing out on so much of the interaction that is so important.

I have to tell you the truth, I was a Republican! My father was a Republican all because of Abraham Lincoln. You just fall in line with your parents. When I got married and I went ahead and registered, I did Republican, but I cannot remember if I ever voted for a Republican. John F. Kennedy was running, and I just loved who he was and what his philosophy was, the whole works. My husband used to tease me, "Oh you just always love the way John F. Kennedy looked," and I said, "True, that had a lot to do with it." He was a Nixon man, and so to this day, we still say, "You know what happened to Nixon." We go back and forth. I did finally change, because my whole philosophy was not there. But I love that world, and I don't know why, but I always volunteered, if I was asked if I would help out, I always do. That's who I am.

Inspiration

Woodie Rucker-Hughes, Jane Block, and Connie Ransom. Jane Block, to me, is just overwhelming to the point where I said, "Where did that woman have time for everything?" And Connie's the same way.

Advice

I would love to see the kids today put down that cell phone. I would love for them to interact more. I love to travel—we'll see the tulips, that's one thing—but to find out what exists in the other countries—Taiwan, Nepal, Tibet—I love to do that. For my kids, we would say, "You can paint houses and do whatever it is, and we'll match you, we'll give it to you so you can take off a whole year, or however long it takes to travel." What I give to the kids is to say, "Go on and see the world." I just feel as though that's important. What do you think?

"No enemies, just people who need more information"

Jane Block

Roots

I was born in Montana in 1929, near the beginning of the Great Depression. We later moved to Idaho, where we had relatives. I skied to school in the wintertime and hiked in the beautiful mountains. It was a very lovely part of my young life. My father had gold and silver mining interests in Idaho. He died when I was fourteen. It was a terrible loss.

I came to Riverside in a rather circuitous fashion. I moved from Idaho to Los Angeles in my mid-twenties, and my ambition was to travel and go to Europe. I worked in the credit field, which was very enlightening to me because one of the things that I realized was that we live in a predatory capitalistic society—not that there's any better alternative, but it is predatory. Once I understood that, I was much better equipped to deal with it and to see that I ended up with whatever I needed to make my life comfortable. I succeeded in buying a duplex and working and becoming reasonably prosperous, and enjoyed that, and saved money and was getting ready to go for a year vacation in Europe. But I met Richard Block and he proposed, and I suggested that perhaps we should discuss the terms of a relationship and marriage in Europe. So, he came to Europe. We spent a month in Spain talking about marriage and so on, and ended that month fully committed to each other, so I continued with my year in Europe, and then when I returned, we married. He was at Caltech, and he got an offer from the University of Illinois in Urbana-Champaign, so we married in Pasadena, moved to Urbana-Champaign. I maintained my property here in Los Angeles and we went back and forth on holidays. Finally he decided that maybe it would be a good idea to get another appointment in California, so he got an appointment in Riverside, and we moved here in 1968.

Call to activism

It was sort of an evolutionary thing. My mother was an unusually independent woman. My dad loved her, and so that was the model that I came from, that an independent woman is loved and has a successful relationship with a man, and all that good stuff. So, the concept of being manipulative with men was not an acceptable model to me. Much of our culture is built around women being manipulative with men, and it just seemed demeaning both to the woman and to the man. I became aware of the fact that if I wanted to have autonomy as a human, I needed to develop my own rules, follow them closely so that I wouldn't become an opportunist, and I could be comfortable with who I was.

When we were in Illinois, I would come back to California and was very active and had friends who were very active in the feminist movement. I would take all this material, including material on reproductive rights, back to Illinois with me, and I would have it photocopied at a shop there, and then hand it out to all kinds of people. One time, the guy said, **"You know, I can't run these things off, because they're too revolutionary."**

Contributions

After we moved to Riverside in 1968, I organized a local NOW [National Organization for Women] chapter here and spoke to various groups for NOW and about feminism. It was interesting because somebody in the process mentioned to me that when I was speaking that I was not being very confrontational with people, I wasn't challenging them, I wasn't stirring things up. So the next time I went out, I tried to stir things up a bit, and I found that I didn't enjoy that. That was a big, important lesson that I learned about myself and my involvement politically—that it didn't give me pleasure to be confrontational.

We had consciousness-raising groups here in Riverside. Consciousness-raising was simply allowing women to talk about their feelings and what had occurred to them and what had influenced them, in a supportive and positive environment. This is something that the majority of women had never had the opportunity to do. Maria Cranor and I talked about this, and we decided that the really interesting thing that we could do would be to have consciousness-raising sessions with the women at prison in Chino. So we went to the prison and suggested that to the administrators, and we presented it in a way that they did not find frightening or threatening, so they allowed us to do it. It was a very interesting thing to do. The women who we worked with were often women who had been abused and women who had been forced into prostitution, it was just a tragic kind of thing. They were uniformly women that had not had much chance. I think that that was probably one of the most educational things that I did with the whole NOW movement. I wasn't sophisticated enough at that point to think about educating or trying to influence the NOW organization as a whole to go into prisons and do this, and I regret that I didn't, because that would have made a real difference to a great many people.

In the mid-1970s I got involved with the establishment of the Commission on the Status of Women in Riverside County and an effort to create a shelter for battered women, because there was very little alternative at that point for a woman who was being abused within a marriage. We lobbied and talked to the Board of Supervisors, which was all male at that point, and made our presentation. Interestingly enough, there were a group of women who were opposed to the concept. They felt that it would be destructive to the family. After our presentation, they got up and they told the supervisors that if they voted for this, they would be sinning. The Board of Supervisors then voted to establish the commission. Afterwards, I really didn't know if I should go and thank those women or not. I didn't, but it was an interesting thing—it was so, so clear that these women felt the existing system was working for them, and they wanted it to continue working. It didn't matter to them that it didn't work for women who were abused within the marriage. After the establishment of the Commission on the Status of Women, I met with the chair of the board at that time, and I said, "Thank you so much, but you have neither assigned staff, nor have you allocated any funding for the commission to operate. What would you like us to do?" And he said, "Just be a commission." I went home and I called my friends that I'd worked with to get this accomplished in Palm Springs and in Corona and in various other towns, and said, "Okay, we're going to schedule hearings on shelters for battered women." We did that throughout the county and succeeded in establishing shelters for battered women.

The thing that I have done in organizing repeatedly is I organize things and then I find somebody that's good at administering it, and then I go on to organizing something else. That was true with the battered women issue, and the people that took it over were great. The movement for women to become fuller participants in society was really happening at that time, and I thought, "Well, what could be a real help to women starting to work?" Obviously they needed good childcare and they needed adequate childcare and well-educated childcare. I found a group that had been formed in the Banning area. They organized the community, and they had really great childcare available. I thought, "Gosh, going to each city and doing that would really be quite an effort!" We decided that the thing that we needed was a childcare consortium that would be available to any city that wanted to look at the issue of quality childcare. So, we put the Riverside County Childcare Consortium together, and it has continued to function and has made a real difference for women, because the quality of childcare is very, very important.

It's important to know that women bring a different perspective and a different voice. I became aware of the fact that there were no women heads of departments within the county. We eventually became the second county in California to have a female majority on the Board of Supervisors. That meant that there would be women-appointed heads of departments also. There were a couple of women on the city council, and I became actively involved in supporting them. More women were elected to the city council. There were many women that already had beginnings of movements and a desire for change, and all they needed was a little help in verbalizing where they needed to go to get it.

In the late 1970s, I went to Lou[is] Vandenburg at KUCR, UC Riverside's radio station, and I said, "You know, I really would like to put a program together. I don't have a lot of expertise, I've never done it before. I want the program to be on women's issues, women's space, women's place, what's happening here, and interviewing local women who are doing things." He said yes, which was amazing! I interviewed women who were going to be thinking about running for office. I interviewed women who had controversial issues. It was this really, really positive thing to do, and an unusual thing to do at that point.

I live in a park, a natural wilderness area at the edge of Riverside, and it's because of the efforts my husband and I put together in the Box Springs, along with many, many other people. We were hiking up in the mountains and we encountered a man on a motorcycle. Being from Idaho and always feeling that one addresses people when you're hiking and you encounter them, we said hello, and the man explained that he was going to be building houses and hiding these ugly rocks, so we came home and started organizing. We circulated petitions. I got a *Press-Enterprise* reporter to interview the developer. I talked to the supervisor, Norton Younglove, and found that he had a concept that this would be a good park, so he supported the effort and acted to acquire the land.

After Box Springs, I was involved in other environmental projects to make bicycle paths, to help preserve Victoria Avenue, to preserve Sycamore Canyon, and later to help save the Santa Rosa Plateau near Temecula. When some lands became available for preservation, it was difficult to find an agency willing to take on the holding and the maintenance of the land. We put together the Riverside Lands Conservancy, now the Rivers and Lands Conservancy, and it functioned well. In the early years, it was bouncing around from place to place and didn't really have a home and didn't really have a lot of income at that point. Beverly Wingate was the real estate agent who found property on Mission Inn Avenue that I could purchase with some money that I had from the property I'd had in the Hollywood Hills. I did that and then made the decision that I would donate the space to the Land Conservancy, and I rented the space to the Sierra Club at way under market, and to the Quakers and the desert tortoise people and various other political efforts. It was a very productive use of the land, and the Land Conservancy thrived. It's a wonderful thing, and I should have made the concept more available to people, because it's a wonderful way to invest money. Eventually, when the property is sold, usually, if you sell at the right time, you're going to end up making money, and you can feel good about all that people accomplished because you gave them a secure and appreciated place to be. I feel the investment that I've made in the Land Conservancy is the best investment I've ever made. They've saved thousands and thousands of acres, and they take care of them. The advice that I give to people when they ask me about getting into an environmental project is never, never be intimidated by the amount of money that you have to raise. If it's a really important thing that needs to be saved, just do it. That was true with the Santa Rosa Plateau. When we first looked into it, it was millions of dollars. But hey, we made it happen!

Nobody ever does any of this stuff alone, there's always a group of people doing it, so **I take credit, but I don't take singular credit.** There are people who avoid me at parties, because I'm always recruiting. I was always recruiting. I haven't done anything as a solitary individual. I've done things as part of a group, and I need to share the honor and make that very clear, because **no one ever accomplishes very much on their own.**

Inspiration

The whole National Organization for Women was very inspirational to me.

Advice

I have this philosophy that if I'm involved in a project, **I have no enemies. I only have people who need more information.** If somebody comes up to me and is absolutely insulting, I just smile and give them more information, and I must say, it's infuriating to them, and that's okay. When you're trying to change society and change the way an area functions, you'll be coming back time and time again to the politicians and the clerical staff who take responsible roles. It's very important to recognize that and to not make any enemies and understand that everyone has their own interests, their own peculiarities, and let them be. One very important thing for any activist to realize is that if you're dealing with a city, state, or county employee, never jeopardize their job. You'll find that if they can trust you, that they will help you.

"Sometimes you have to be the one to do it"

Connie Ransom

Roots

I was born in March of 1937 in Providence, Rhode Island. I'm the youngest of five children. My father at that time was an attorney in Providence. His father was from the north woods of Maine, and his mother was born in Philadelphia as a product of a union between a well-to-do and a servant in the household. My mother had gone to Pembroke College at Brown University and was the first in her generation to have a college degree.

My father was very impulsive, but he made some very good decisions even so. One was that in 1941, when I was four, he bought a piece of property outside of East Greenwich, in the country. From the age of four to the age of twelve, I lived in the country in a really fabulous place. My father had turned a shed outside the garage into a darling little Cape Cod cottage for my grandparents, and they lived there, and they were a big influence on me. It was World War II, and my grandfather, who was not working, turned a huge lot on the farm into a Victory Garden. We had that garden and huge chicken houses on the farm. I attribute a lot to my time on that farm, walking in the woods, and there was a brook, there were orchards, there were fruit trees and wildflowers, and my grandfather would take me for walks and tell me to walk so that I wouldn't scare things and that I would see things that I otherwise wouldn't see.

Then my mother and father and sister and I got in the car and headed west. My father had been on a business trip to Arizona and also to San Francisco, and his notion was he wanted to go live in Arizona because he had really bad sinus and it would be healthier. We took off without a clear destination, and he used it as a history lesson. We took five weeks driving and we went to New York and Philadelphia and Washington, D.C. and Mt. Vernon and Williamsburg and North and South Carolina and Georgia and Alabama and Mississippi and Louisiana and Texas, stopping at various hotels or boarding houses along the way. We stayed in New Mexico for a year and a half, and my father got itchy feet again. Then we moved to Portland, and I went through high school in Portland. I commuted to Lewis and Clark College and was majoring in music and theory and sang in the senior choir that year, which was quite an experience because they toured the West Coast, singing at Presbyterian churches and other locations all up and down the coast, including Calvary Presbyterian in Riverside, and at Disneyland, in the first year that it opened. I went to Reed College my sophomore year. Roger [Ransom] was a classmate. We came to Riverside when Roger got a job at UCR.

Call to activism

What I first did was join the Art Center [now the Riverside Art Museum] and the PTA. There were two sort of parallel things happening. I was really intent on pursuing pottery. Betty Parks, another local who had been a potter, and I started a pottery group. We had potters in Riverside who met regularly and had pottery sales. And then, with the kids in school, one of the first things that [my daughter] Charlotte said coming home from first grade at Grant School was, “Mummy, we don’t ever get to do art.” And she was right! There was an easel in one corner of the room, and maybe once a week, you got a chance to go there, and there were three or four colors of tempera paint and you could play around, and that was art. I would speak up at PTA meetings, “Can’t we do more with art, can’t we do more with art?” Our year in Berkeley before coming here was ’67-’68, so those were sort of tumultuous years. While I was there, I was able to work with Peter Voulkos, who was one of the pillars of ceramic art in the country, and so that influenced me as well as the whole art scene in the sixties. I knew there were resources. I wasn’t trained as an artist, but I knew there should be resources available to the schools. We spent another year in Berkeley in ’72-’73, and then when we came back to Riverside in ’73, I got even louder at the school. We opened up a volunteer art room where I trained volunteers, and the students could come for a longer period of time and really get resource materials and learn something. In one of the PTA meetings during that time, when I kept saying, “Can’t we do this, can’t we do that?” a woman whose name was Sheila Bell, who was very active in the community and the Art Alliance [of the Riverside Art Museum] said, **“You know, Connie, sometimes when you have a good idea, you have to be the one to do it.”** My idea was to just throw out all these ideas and let somebody else do it. So that was how I ended up thinking, “Okay, I’ll do this.”

I thought I was very interested in politics; I would listen on the radio from beginning to end to the Republican and Democratic conventions when they happened in the summer. I just found that totally fascinating. But I would never speak an opinion about politics. I didn’t do that through college. I might have an opinion, but I was very quiet. Living through the Red Scare was like a traumatic experience, seeing what happened.

Contributions

After I went to graduate school in the early eighties, I did a lot at the Riverside Art Museum. I volunteered on committees, and I ended up being on the board for a while. The activism part probably showed up after that when I decided to open an art gallery. I had a studio in a produce warehouse on Vine, and I was making big, huge stuff and exhibiting and teaching all over Southern California. My fear was that the landlord was going to sell the building and I wouldn't have any place to do anything with my own work. Roger's father had passed away and he'd gotten some money at that point, so he thought, "Well, maybe we should invest in a piece of property and build a studio." That's how we came to purchase the land on Brockton, which had an old potato chip factory on it. It was going to be my studio, and then I thought, "Well, it's on a commercial street, maybe we should open an art gallery." Nobody else was showing contemporary art; in those days the art museum was very conservative. When we had the art gallery, I ended up being on the Riverside Downtown Association, now the Riverside Downtown Partnership, because I considered my gallery part of downtown. We ended up calling ourselves the Thursday Morning Breakfast Group. One of the goals was to try to figure out a way for these arts organizations to work together as opposed to working on their own little thing, which has been the problem from time immemorial. During that time, the Mission Inn was behind chain-link fence. I said, "Why can't we get rid of the chain link fence on Main Street and put something in the windows so that it doesn't feel dead?" And so, we got them to take down the chain link fence on Main Street, and I worked with the archivist, Kevin Halloran, and he loaned us furniture to put in the windows from the Mission Inn, and then we got art from the Art Museum and put it on the wall. One of my favorite things that nobody else noticed is that we had a Scrabble board and it said, "Mission Inn open soon."

Later, I was involved with the [Sam and Alfreda] Maloof Foundation. That was so important to me. I led the board in the period after Sam died, when we were shaping what the house and gardens and museum would be without him—shaping, in a way, Sam's legacy. It was almost full-time work! But it was so important.

In terms of politics, during the time we had the art gallery, a man named Jonathan Kinsman ran for mayor. He was the owner of a restaurant in Canyon Crest called the Bear Flag. He said, "Can we put a sign in front of your gallery?" And I thought, "I don't know, it's hard enough for me to get any business, I'm not sure if I want to alienate anybody," and he said, "Well, you know, peoples got to know!" So I put a sign out. Then, it must have been around that time that I met Mark Takano at a party at Jane

[Block]'s. He was running for Congress and asked if he could put a sign out, and I said yes, and we had a fundraiser for him. And that's when it started! It was like, "Oh, this is kind of fun!"

We had fundraisers for the RCC board and I supported Bill Hedrick when he ran, and I worked hard on that campaign. When the redistricting happened, Mark called me and said, "Connie, I am thinking of running [for Congress in 2012]," and I thought, "Oh God, Mark, don't do this to me! I cannot lose another election." But I went to work for Mark. I'd never done door-to-door and phoning and stuff like that, but for Mark I agreed, partly because of this young man [Elliot], who was a student at Oberlin, who volunteered for Mark. I don't know whether he got paid anything at all. He was the one who organized the volunteers to go to Mark's campaign headquarters out on Chicago and do phoning. I should have listened to people more, but on Election Day that year, I woke up in the morning and I was so terrified I told Roger, "I'm going to go over to Mark's campaign and I'm going to phone to get people to go vote." He knows that I hate doing that, but I said, "If Mark loses by one vote, I'll just kill myself if I haven't done everything." So I went, I worked, and at four o'clock, Elliot gathers everybody together, "Okay everybody, we're going out to the precincts," and I said, "Well, I'm not going out there." And then I said, "Well, just show me the list. Maybe there's someplace close and I can go." He gave me the Courtyard Marriott on University Avenue. He said, "You go out, you park in the parking lot, you have to be three hundred feet from the voting place, and you hand out these flyers to voters." I called my daughter Charlotte on my way there, and Charlotte came for a little while, and then her son came for a little while, and they both had to leave. I stayed until eight o'clock at night after the polls closed. It was so much fun. Most of my voters were first-time voters who were UCR-connected. Anyway, at the end of that time, my phone was out of battery, I was freezing cold, and I had to pee. I rushed home and changed clothes, and Roger and I went off to Jose Medina's party at Zacatecas. We came up to the back door and I saw Linda, his wife, and she said, "It's wonderful, he's going to win." Raul Ruiz was winning, and Mark was winning, although Mark wouldn't concede that he'd won. It took him a while for it to sink in.

After the election in 2016, when so many tears were shed, Roger and I went to Cellar Door Books. You'd always see somebody you knew when you went in there, like going to Simple Simon's or Jammin' Bread. It's part of the community. I don't remember exactly when it was, but Linda [Sherman, the bookstore owner] posted something about getting together and having a meeting for people to talk. There was no agenda specifically, it was open, anybody could come. There were probably forty people at least. At the very same time, Sue Mitchell and Chani Beeman and Marilyn Odello and other people downtown were getting together. A lot of the discussion was really about what we could do about immigrant justice, but the subject of marches came up at that meeting, and I just said, "Well, I'm too old." Christine Gailey was going to go to Washington. I said, "I'm not going to Washington and I'm not going into L.A., I can't, I'm too old! But I want to do something because I want to be part of that energy." I believe in friction. I think Linda called a second meeting to discuss whether or not to have a march, and that day I stopped in to see her and there were several other people, and Linda said, "I really worry about calling a march and nobody coming." And I said, "Well, I don't care. I'm gonna stand on a street corner someplace." And so, fortunately some really smart people were at that meeting. It was decided that so-and-so would do the PR, Linda and I would get some other people there to work on a program for the event, and we met the next day and she had a couple of people who were young and smart with technology and they made a Facebook page, and it just went! Chani Beeman came and said, "I'm going to be in L.A. for the march there, but if you need any help, let me know!" She's organized march after march and demonstration. Chani gave me the name of the police person to talk to and that sort of thing, and it just happened. We decided we'd start at the Tibbets statue, because I thought, "Well, if there's only twenty of us, we'll just stand someplace then we'll go down to City Hall." But it was so exciting. I've never done anything like that.

I still go to demonstrations and marches, but I can't do it as much anymore, it just hurts too much. My tried and true is writing postcards to voters. And if I can sell a house or two [as a real estate agent] I'll have money to donate to political causes.

Inspiration

Because I didn't think of myself as an organizer, I wasn't looking for that kind of a role model. But I think what Sheila Bell did was wonderful. It was a kick in the pants, you know, you can't just sit around waiting for other people to do anything. Hazel Simon was a sculptor who had a big influence on me. She was deeply committed to the Art Center [now

Riverside Art Museum], and she saw potential in other people. She was somebody who enabled some people to do things. She contacted me and Betty Parks, and said, "There is a ceramic symposium taking place outside of Aspen this summer, and ten of the most renowned ceramic artists will be presenting there. I think you should go!" She said she and her husband Ted, a professor at UCR, had a condominium in Snowmass, and we could stay there, and we'd only have to pay the cleaning fee, and so Betty Parks and I went. I consider Hazel an enabler, and **we need enablers, people to encourage other people to do things.** And then there is Beverly Wingate Maloof. I met Beverly probably in 1973 at the Art Center, because she was a member of the Art Alliance. Our paths would cross off and on through the years, and I'd watch things that she did, including inventorying the historic homes downtown. I thought, "What a huge project. How can somebody think they can possibly do that?" Yet people like Beverly and Sue Johnson worked on that, and it was so critical to the flavor of Riverside that there were these early efforts at preserving the historic landmarks and buildings.

Advice

I think I would pay attention more to what other people were doing who were successful.

"Be that person that shows up"

Sarah Wright Garibay

Roots

I was born in Long Beach, and I grew up in Orange County, mostly in Westminster and Huntington Beach area. I moved to Riverside for the first time in 2008 to go to UC Riverside. After I graduated UC Riverside I was working on Mark Takano's campaign for Congress in 2012, and after the election, after he won, that sort of sparked me to see what would happen if I continued staying in politics. And so after that I moved to Washington, D.C., just to see what would happen. I bought a one-way ticket, didn't have a job or anything, and just said, "Let's see where this goes." I got really lucky that I was able to find a job and a place to live within a month of being out there, hanging out on my friend's couch for a while. I was in Washington, D.C., a little less than a year and a half. Then I moved back to California in 2014 to work on Pete Aguilar's campaign for Congress. Then I came back to Riverside in 2015 and made another transition to work for Mark Takano again, but that time in his district office. And then they pulled me aside, borrowed me for the 2016 re-election campaign. Ever since 2015 I've been in Riverside. It's definitely my home now.

Call to activism

I was going to go to UC Riverside to major in music, and then I had this shift in perspective when I went on this field trip to the South. I went to Georgia, Alabama, Mississippi, Arkansas, Tennessee—to all these different museums and places related to the civil rights movement. I got to meet a lot of different activists from that time period, such as Minnijean Brown and Elizabeth Eckford from the Little Rock Nine, I got to meet Congressman John Lewis, and that was incredible for me. It seemed like, hearing their stories, there wasn't this intention to be recorded in history books—it was just to make a change that was going to result in equal, equitable opportunities, not just for themselves, but for others. So when I first got to UC Riverside, I immediately changed my major to Ethnic Studies. I loved it. I'm so glad that that was my major. I think it gave me so many different things to think about and different perspectives. In our society, there are a lot of things we need to address and a lot of conversations that we need to have that a lot of people are very uncomfortable having, but being in those classes made that uncomfortableness feel comfortable, in a way, like it's okay to challenge different ideas. Then at the end of my time at UC Riverside, I went to Washington, D.C., through the UCDC [University of California Washington Center] Program. The experience itself was great, but my internship I did not like. I was very scared and trying to not make anyone mad, trying to do all this people-pleasing, but I had no idea how to approach this. Then the intern supervisor, she said to me, "I can help you. I know that you're from UC Riverside, and I know that the congressional race out there is really competitive. I know a person who is helping on that campaign, and I can connect you." So I got connected to the Intern Supervisor from Mark Takano's campaign. I went into the interview thinking, "I don't want to do this, I don't want to do politics anymore, I'm not going to like this." My understanding is that he had the same perception, not wanting to trust whoever this person was that's being connected to the campaign. So we both went in very skeptical, and then I thought after the interview, "Well, let me give it a try, see where it goes." I went in very skeptical and not thinking I was going to commit to this, and I committed very fully to it in the end.

Contributions

I don't see myself as the reason for the win on Election Day, I'm just one person out of this large army of volunteers and staff. We were able to get the community on board and have such a large number of interns and volunteers. It was such a team effort in 2012, 2014, all of the campaign cycles that I've done. It was really community-driven in so many ways. I remember our field director said of that 2012 campaign, "This is so weird, there's so many people actually from here on this campaign." And I thought, "There's only like two people from here, there's not a lot of people." She said, "You don't see people from the community on these congressional races." I thought that was so interesting. I'm glad Takano's campaign was not full of outsiders, that we did have a couple community people, because I think that's really important.

I did some volunteering with Planned Parenthood in Riverside. I was just a regular volunteer, but I think after the 2012 campaign, seeing volunteers and other people who had school and work and all these other things still come in and volunteer a couple days out of the week, that told me, there's no excuses. Even if I'm not on a campaign, I need to keep doing this in some way. So I've always tried to stay engaged and involved somehow.

While I was in my master's program at Cal State San Bernardino, I was really involved in the student social work clubs on campus. We did some events about destigmatizing mental health. I was pretty involved with the social work lobby days as a student, going to the state capital each year and volunteering as a team leader to lead the lobbying meetings. Right now I am a micro social worker, but I still am a very macro-oriented person because of my background in politics and organizing.

That day of the Women's March in 2017 was so cool. It all came together so quickly. When you think about community organizing, sometimes it takes a while to get the momentum going and to get that mobility from the community. But something about the Women's March in 2017, it just seemed like this huge snowball. I remember hearing the conversations of some folks trying to get the Riverside one going, and I remember going to a couple of the planning meetings, and I don't think anyone could tell how big it was going to be. And when that day came, it felt like every minute the crowd was multiplying.

Inspiration

My role models were the volunteers from Mark Takano's 2012 Congressional Campaign. Being a field organizer is not the most glamorous job. You're working a lot and sometimes you show up in clothes you wore yesterday. So I remember all the field organizers started all of these growing to-do lists of what to do when we have a day off. But for me, I didn't know exactly where I was going to be heading after that campaign, but seeing all these volunteers show up and commit any little bit of time that they had told me that's going to be me. I'm going to do that. I'm going to be that person that shows up and volunteers no matter what. Those are really my role models and inspirations. I have a lot of pictures from that campaign on my desktop, and sometimes I'll go through those pictures and that's my inspiration.

Advice

Now, being a social worker and being in the mental health field, my biggest thing is self-care. Every campaign season I reflect on that more and more, because I think about specifically the 2012 campaign, because I think that's when my self-care was at its worst. We worked so much! We didn't have time to brush our teeth. If you can't take care of yourself, I don't know how you take care of a community or a cause that you're passionate about. But the other thing is learning to be comfortable with being uncomfortable. Even if that means setting boundaries and speaking up and advocating for yourself—that's huge. When I was a very young organizer, I was people-pleasing, like, "If I do all of this, hopefully it'll get me to the next job or this other opportunity," because that's what organizing jobs look like. They aren't long-term. They can be very short-term, so in the moment you try to push yourself beyond your limits to make sure you can get to the next opportunity, and I wish I didn't think about it in those terms at that time, and I wish I'd thought more about myself—what do I need and how can I advocate for myself? If it's hard to advocate for yourself, it's going to be really hard to advocate for a larger cause.

"Leverage yourself"

Sue Mitchell

Roots

I was born in Dayton, Ohio, and went to college my first three years in Ohio, and finished at the University of Redlands when my husband transferred to March Air Force Base.

I met Zee [Zelma Beard] at an officers' wives luncheon. We had to take a salad with the recipe, and I don't cook! I didn't cook then, I don't cook now. I wrote a letter to my college roommate back in Ohio: "Chris, please help me, I need a salad recipe." So she writes it and sends it back, and I make this Korean salad, and Zee tastes the salad and copies the recipe down. We don't know each other yet, and she thinks, "Boy that Sue Mitchell, she's a really good cook." That was sort of the big joke. We found out that we both liked to play tennis but then I got pregnant and when my son David was old enough, we would put the playpen over at Shamel Park and play tennis.

One day Zee said, "you know, I need a better job. I'm going to be getting a divorce." And I said, "Well, there's someone in my office that wants to open a staffing service, and she tried to talk me into going." I said, "Zee, you should go to work for her!" Zee had a business degree. I said, "You're an office manager, full-charge bookkeeper, paralegal." Then she said, "I wouldn't want to work for her. I would want part of it." That was the key statement. I went to bed that night thinking, "Part of it. Part of it. Part of it." I called her the next morning, and forty-five days later, the three of us were open… Riverside Personnel Services. I was a twenty-six-year-old, and never had a business class. And then I was widowed seventeen days later. Zee divorced that year and we bought the other person out within the year. When we hit Riverside Personnel Service's 10th anniversary, we really celebrated. We shouldn't have made it.

Call to activism

In high school I was the student council president, and I just kind of wanted to run the school. I helped start the first Earth Day in 1970. It was outdoor, we brought speakers in and big loudspeakers and everybody got to dress casual that day and sit out on the lawn. The other thing I really fought for was for girls to be able to wear pants to school. We all had to wear skirts. I never got to take advantage of it, that happened after I left.

I wasn't political at all. My son was just a year old when his dad died. One day he was asking me what his dad's politics were. I realized I didn't know because we never talked about it. I didn't come from a family that was political. I had my "ah-ha" moment when I was forty. I was watching the Republican convention, and Pat Buchanan made that really hateful presentation. From then on, that's when I started paying attention.

Contributions

I started in fundraising for nonprofits. When we first opened the business, we didn't know anybody in Riverside. Any Air Force friends we had were transferred out. We weren't engaged in the community right away, and it was a good thing, because of everything that was happening to us, we just hunkered down. I spent most of my time sitting in my office crying. But finally we got involved. Mary Ann Stalder, Virginia McDonald, and Connie Beasley had a group that met once a month and had dinner, and they were called Women in Administrative Roles, and they were all the nonprofit executive directors. They invited us to join them, and people would say, "Well, you're not a nonprofit," and we were a new business, so we would say, "Oh yes we are!" At this time, there wasn't the leadership class in the chamber, and there wasn't the Pick Group, so this group was the perfect place for us. As young women we were learning about all the issues from all these incredible women who were working so hard, making no money and always needing money, always fundraising. We would go to these dinners, and we'd go around the table. "Well, here's twenty-five dollars, twenty-five, twenty-five," and three hundred dollars later, which was a lot of money for us, I knew it was water in sand, it wasn't doing anything. That's when I started really working on **leveraged giving, leveraged fundraising, and leveraged asking.** Because our community is made up of small- to medium-sized companies, Art Pick taught us, we didn't have the deep pockets, we didn't have the Fortune 500s, we all had to link arms and keep the community up. Well, how do small- to medium-sized businesses survive if they keep being hit all the time for donations? I finally went on this campaign, when all these nonprofits were having five, six, seven, eight fundraisers to only make five or ten thousand dollars, and they all took just as much work. My goal was, "You need to have two fundraisers a year, and maybe a third that's an inexpensive one, so that you can broaden the base, but you need to have fun fundraisers that make a lot of money, because it's our social life, and I am tired of going to boring chicken dinners." That's when I helped start Black Tie Bowling and check signing parties and Shop to Stop Breast Cancer. Let's make it fun, and you need to make fifty to a hundred thousand dollars off your fundraiser. I spent a lot of years focusing on that.

I have kept a chart where I match people up. That's what I've done for a living, so I would do that with volunteers. I had slots, I had my columns, and then I had it broken down by wards and by what their talents were. When I would go to a nominating committee, I would just look at my chart.

This all translates to politics too and Dom Betro was my first campaign. He ran Family Service [Association] for twenty-five years. He grew that organization. He was a mentor to me. He had an Italian restaurant for a short period of time named Calabria, and I went in there one day and he was able to sit down to visit. He was saying that they were downsizing their home, and I said, "Okay, perfect! You need to move into Ward 1 or Ward 3," because I knew that he had had this inkling to run for office. I had these little cards made up that said, "Betro for Council," and stapled dollar bills to them, and gave them to a bunch of people to go into the restaurant and hand them to him, to prove he had support.

He started to run in Ward 3, and they redistricted, and he ended up in Ward 1. The [Riverside] Renaissance wouldn't have happened without him. I was in the Raincross Group, and we kept wanting good things to happen in Riverside, and we couldn't understand why they weren't. One day I made this chart, I went and researched who had been city manager and city council and mayor for the last thirty years, and then I made three columns. The first column was, "Leaps Tall Buildings," meaning gets big things done. The second column was, "Really Nice and Hardworking." And the third column was, "Criminals." Then I went through the list of people and I would put X's where they'd belong in these columns. So the good news is we had no criminals, a few people danced with being a little bit unsavory, but nobody crossed the line into full-fledged criminal. But the problem was we had no one in the first column. We had some people on the line. I presented this and said, "This is why we're not getting anything done." We don't have to have all nine people the first column, but we have to have a couple. Once Dom got elected and then hired Brad Hudson for City Manager, everything broke loose. I would say that's one of the biggest gifts I've given. If I never lifted another finger for this community, I'd have done my part for Riverside in helping to elect Dom Betro. And I didn't get him elected alone, but I did a lot. I get pretty frustrated with people that don't step up to help. We want good leadership. When someone says they're going to run we go, "Yay, thank you," we throw a little money at them, and then we just let them hang out there on their own. It's hard to run for office, and it's hard to be in office, and they need this constant support, and my feeling is, if I'm not willing to serve, I can certainly walk a little bit for them, and I can be uncomfortable a little bit for them.

Looking back, the YWCA and the Junior League trained young women in leadership roles. It was two different kinds of women. I wasn't a Junior Leaguer, but I had the YWCA to go to, and I learned all of my organizational skills, how to run a board meeting, how to be on a committee. Then I started speaking, we helped start a career conference there, and first I started on a speaker panel of four so you don't have to be as nervous, then a panel of two, then you're the lone speaker, then you're the keynote speaker—this is training grounds for women. The YWCA does not exist here anymore, and communities need to realize, when you lose that, what's replacing it? The YWCA trained a lot of women to be great activists for their community, and that may not be happening to the same level. The beauty of the Y was my son was young and they provided childcare for us. You could go home and pick up your child and go from there to the meeting instead of having a babysitter, and then the kids were allowed to come in and interrupt the meeting if they wanted. It was really user friendly for women to volunteer.

In 2008, my belief in the American Dream, hard work brings success, was crushed when a ten trillion derivative Ponzi scheme (legalized crime) caused the Great Recession. Riverside experienced 15% unemployment and it took RPS years to recover. We took little or no income during this time so for therapeutic reasons Zee, at age 62, became a personal trainer and I fulfilled a lifetime dream of becoming an artist.

After a 52 week arts sabbatical, I had a two gallery exhibition at the Riverside Art Museum called "52." I moved my studio into the gallery and was in residence for three months. I learned that I was creative, but that I wasn't an artist deep in my soul. I quickly reverted back to my marketing, fundraising, organizing comfort zone and helped the museum start an adult education program called "The 52 Project." I observed many visitors wanting to do what I had done but couldn't take a year off, so I designed a user-friendly class that meets monthly to help motivate creatives. It's most unique feature is that we teach proposal writing and almost 100 of the over 400 past members have had mini-exhibitions.

[After the 2016 election], Chani Beeman invited a hundred people to her home, fifty showed up, and then Linda Sherman at Cellar Door Bookstore did the same thing, and she had fifty show up, a few of us went over, and we realized we were trying to do the same thing, so we joined up. Again, there's a lot of things I'm not good at, but what I can do is sort of whip people up, and one weekend I just said, there's 250 of us [in the Rise Up Facebook group], and by the end of the weekend, we need to be 2500 of us. And we were. We were having meetings at All Saints [Episcopal Church] and four hundred people would show up in the church, and I finally said to Chani, "We're in trouble. They want a job. They want something to do. We're not a temporary service, we're not set up for this." But then, within three months, Swing Left started, Sister District, and Indivisible. So our job was to push people to these very well-organized organizations, and Rise Up became a place where people could chat and share how to get involved.

Inspiration

I love what Dolores Huerta says: "Every moment is an organizing opportunity, every person is a potential activist, and every minute a chance to change the world." I heard her over in Redlands, and I watched her and thought to myself, "She has said that same thing a dozen times a day every day for sixty years. And she doesn't give up on it." It's being diligent—diligently building your email list, diligently sending those emails at the right times, whatever little things you do, you just stick with it.

Local mentors would be Roger Luebs. He was the first chair of Raincross [The Raincross Group] when I was there, and then I became the second chair. I was very young and I was a nervous wreck, so I just did everything that Roger did, I just followed his example. One of the things he taught was you end each meeting with your action items, and you start the next meeting reviewing your action items, and it doesn't take very long for the group to snap into place, because they're going to be asked, and then they'll have to report that they didn't do it. I learned that lesson very early on. Connie Beasley was remarkable. She found the Children's Center, she taught me the value of thanking people. She wrote thank-you notes for everything. We finally had to beg her, we told her we're never going to give her anything again if she ever wrote us another thank-you note. Jim Erickson, because Jim made you feel good even when you weren't a big donor. Jane Block of course. Jane has the gift of coming up with an idea and finding someone else to run it. Not that she hasn't been behind so many things, but I have watched her and she is just really good at that.

Advice

Figure out how to **leverage yourself.** I can't write BIG checks but I can send out emails to 100, 300, or 500 community members for different causes. So, build those lists, keep them current and don't be afraid to ask for a good cause. Target your asking and don't fret over being rejected by 80-90% on any given request. Focus on how much have leveraged yourself by the positive response of the 10-20%. You will always be surprised by who responds and how generous people can be.

"Go get it done"

Patricia Lock Dawson

Roots

I am a Riverside native. I was born here in 1965 at Parkview Hospital. My mother was a nurse at Parkview. I'm the youngest of five children. We were raised in the Greenbelt, we grew up in the orange groves and packinghouses and running around, so I spent most of my years outdoors. Absent maybe seven years or so for graduate school and my husband's graduate school, I've spent most of my life here in Riverside.

Call to activism

I've never had trouble thinking of myself as an advocate, but I've never thought of myself as an activist. I don't consider myself an activist, and I think it's because I've always just worked. I'm an environmental scientist. I had an undergraduate biology degree from UC Riverside and I went to graduate school at the University of Washington and I got a Master's in Forestry with an emphasis in wildlife ecology. I did wildlife ecology in streamside communities of the Northwest and mostly songbirds. That really started in the Greenbelt, because when I was growing up we used to run or walk on the canal, and I used to always wonder, "What is that bird, what was that song?" We had this stack of World Book encyclopedias that

I used to try to find out what that bird was that I saw. I've always loved wildlife and animals and being outdoors.

After my husband finished graduate school, we ended up back here in Riverside and I worked for the Bureau of Land Management. I started having children, and I did not want to continue working full-time. It was just difficult. I wanted to work part-time, so I started working for the county of Riverside on the multiple species habitat conservation plan. I got involved in the Rivers and Lands Conservancy, and then I started working on the Santa Ana River at Mayor Loveridge's request and Supervisor John Tavaglione's request, and it all kind of led into this career in politics. I like to tell people I was a pretty good wildlife biologist, but I was a much better policy person, so I kept getting dragged into that for whatever reason. While I like being out in the field counting birds, I always get dragged into political discussions and making decisions. I think, as a scientist, you're a problem-solver by nature. I'm a top-down thinker, so one of the first things I do is look at, "Alright, why did that fail? What needs to happen to make it successful? Who needs to be at the table?" You start assembling your pieces. I think a big part of it is asking the right questions and listening.

I recommitted to Riverside when my children were very little, because I was offered a very prestigious position in Washington, D.C., with the National Wildlife Federation. It was a very difficult decision to turn down, but I loved Riverside, I wanted to be with my children, and I wanted to be close to family. Not too long after that, I was offered a position with the agency running the Los Angeles River and Mountains Conservancy to be their executive officer, and I turned that down because I didn't want to be out of my city. I often tell people the measure of a person's success is the opportunities that they let go, because I think these were fabulous opportunities that I had to say no to, but they just galvanized my connection to my hometown and made me double down on being involved here.

Contributions

It's just been my work. I was asked to work on the Santa Ana River project—initially getting the trail built—back in 2003. There had been legislation introduced in the California State Legislature to establish the Santa Ana River Conservancy. There was really very little bringing people along in that effort, and in fact, it imploded. We had people from the Building Industry Association and the Audubon Society that are generally on different sides equally hating it and coming out against it. It blew up and it created a lot of enemies and bad faith. In the middle of that, Ron Loveridge and John Tavaglione approached me and said, "Hey, you want to work on the Santa Ana River thing?" I had "sucker" stamped on my forehead, and I said, "Sure, I can do that!" The problem was that I needed to create an organizational structure for three counties and fifteen cities and multiple jurisdictions to come together and decide, what is it that they want to do on the river? What do they want the river to look like and what can we do? Nobody wanted to form a new agency. So what I did was I wrote and developed a partnership agreement and essentially got them all at the table just to talk, and they all used their existing authority to talk to each other. That led to getting a bond measure passed where we got $45 million for the river. We got additional money, we started building the trail, relationships mended. Then in 2014, I worked with every single jurisdiction and organization up and down the river to get them to either give me their input on building a conservancy or to just not oppose it. Sometimes that's a win in the legislature—if you can just get somebody not to oppose it. That legislation passed unanimously with bipartisan support. That to me is an illustrative tale for a number of reasons. One, it tells you that you lose a lot of time and effort if you don't do things correctly the first run of the game. Secondly, it's amazing what can happen when you do establish goodwill. People are willing to come along and they trust you. We've gotten over $65 million for that trail. We now have a state agency. Everybody's working together, and in the meantime, we had multiple blue ribbon task forces in a bunch of the different cities, we established the Santa Ana River Trust, a nonprofit through Rivers and Lands Conservancy, so all kinds of good stuff happened because of that.

I applied for the [city] Planning Commission when I was pretty young, and I really liked it. I was the only woman for the entire five years I was on the Planning Commission, and I wasn't welcome when I came on. I haven't faced too much overt sexism in my career, but the Planning Commission was a pretty rough-and-tumble group of guys. I would never bite. I would say, "Well, that's an interesting viewpoint," and just focus on the issue instead of personalities. You want to focus on the problem, not the personality. You can't make it personal. I was faced with a lot of not-so-nice behavior, but by the fifth year, I was voted in as chairman.

I was involved in a group called California Women Lead, a statewide organization, and I started a chapter here in the Inland Empire. Their whole thing, regardless of party affiliation, was to get more women in government and serving in elected and appointed positions. I never wanted to run for office. But I got appointed to the Board of Behavioral Sciences, which oversees all the mental health professionals in the state. Governor Schwarzenegger appointed me there. I was up there telling all these women, "You gotta run for office! You gotta run, you gotta raise some money, you wanna do this!" I was like, "You have no idea what you're talking about, Patricia!" So this opportunity came up to run for school board. Lew Vanderzyl, who was a longtime board member, retired and there was an opening. Ron Loveridge encouraged me to run. I never expected to win, ever. But when you start doing something, you get into it and you want to win it. But I really did it so that I could walk the walk of what I was telling women to do. And then I won!

When I ran for school board, there were no other school board members at the time with children in school. None of them. And I thought, you know, "We really need a consumer up there. We need somebody who's consuming the product of the schools." At the time, I had a child in elementary, middle, and high school, so I had all three of them. My kids brought home what was going on every day at the dinner table. I got to know other parents. My kids went to elementary school at Emerson, on the Eastside, a pretty diverse school. It informs your decision-making. I'm pretty proud of some of the stuff we did on the school board. We raised the graduation rates.

I think the biggest thing was another one of those times where you ask a question. I was in a meeting my first year on the board, and they were presenting all of our data on graduation rates among our various subgroups, and among African Americans, they were so bad, they were so low, they weren't graduating. I was like, "That doesn't look right. Could somebody talk to me about that?" That led to this whole program called the Heritage Program and to all this other stuff, and now our Black students are graduating at the same rates as others. The mental health needs of students was really big for me, too. It's not the same experience that high schoolers had even ten years ago because of social media and other things going on, so I brought a broader perspective to that which made some really positive changes. I found out I could be pretty good on the board, and I think that led to some good changes.

The mayor thing came up, again with Ron Loveridge—he and Rusty [Bailey] asked me to run. That was a big decision. I've always wanted to make my city a place where my kids didn't feel they had to leave, because all my brothers and sisters had to leave for opportunities elsewhere. I thought, if I'm going to turn down that job in D.C., if I'm going to turn down that job in Rosemead, and I'm here in Riverside, I'm going to work for a city where my kids don't have to leave. They have opportunities. Our universities are more included in the city. We have more employers, more cultural activities, and so however I could get there, however I could make that happen, I did. And that included running for office.

Inspiration

Jane, Jane, Jane [Block]. Saint Jane. If I could get a little icon of her on my shelf, I would make offerings to her. To me she is the most fascinating person. She gets so much done. Jane never wants credit. I get very emotional when I talk about Jane. She's put me up to a lot, but she's guided me and she's been my advisor on so many things.

I would say the same thing about Ron Loveridge, too. I go to Ron all the time for advice.

Rose Mayes, she keeps her eye on that prize and she doesn't let things get in the way. She's somebody I go to for advice for a lot of things. Woodie Rucker-Hughes was like a saint to me, too. Woodie would give it to me straight. You need people to do that. You need people to tell you when you're screwing up. She would tell you, "This is going on and nobody's doing anything about it. You gotta do something." And I'd be like, "Right away, Miss Woodie!" I've watched Ofelia Valdez-Yeager work effectively. She's always very gracious. I think it's important to be gracious and courteous. My friend Michelle Oullette was instrumental in bringing the Cheech [Marin Center for Chicano Art and Culture] to Riverside. She's just smart, and I like to surround myself with smart people, smarter than I am, that can tell you what to do, help you out, bounce ideas off of. We have so many good people in Riverside. Chani Beeman! Sometimes during my mayoral campaign, I felt bad because I would run to Chani so much. I felt she could speak for me to people. There's not a lot of people that you trust that with. I'd say, "Go talk to Chani, she'll let you know what my ideas are on that," and she could do that.

ADVICE

Policy work is often about bridging divides. It's often about finding solutions to issues and that generally entails bringing different viewpoints to a discussion and figuring things out, problem-solving. When I think of activism, I think it's generally taking a side and advocating for a particular issue, and I'm more about advocating for solving the problem in the middle. I think sometimes when you're working in the policy world, it's better to reserve a little bit of your thinking on something in order to win over people that you may alienate if you come out of the gate with a position. It allows people to hear you and allows people to listen to you a little better.

I don't give a rip who gets a credit, honestly. If it's going to get done, go, go! Go get it done, and then we can all benefit from it.

Don't put something out there that everybody's going to get ticked off at and hate. Do your groundwork. Find out what's important to people. Find out what they would like to see, and then craft whatever you're trying to do that solves your problem, but get some input first.

Sometimes your best advocate does not look like you. I was always looking for another woman, and sometimes the men that could help me would be standing right there and I couldn't see them because I was looking past them. I wouldn't be here today without Ron Loveridge. When we're looking for somebody that looks like us, talks like us, speaks like us, or fits some box that we think they need to be in, we miss a whole universe of helpers. Woodie Rucker-Hughes didn't look like me, but she gave me some of the best advice I ever got. You have to seek out a diversity of opinions.

Focus on the issue at hand instead of getting caught up in emotion or getting your feelings hurt about something. Just keep your eye on the prize; Rose Mayes gave me that. Keep working. It doesn't mean you have to be abused. But you also don't have to be undone by it. Focus on the problem, not the personality. Focus on ideas, not ideologies. Partnerships, not partisanship. Those things have helped me immensely over the years.

I learned that I had to stop apologizing for myself. That doesn't mean that I don't need to apologize for things sometimes, but I have to not apologize for who I am. As young women, we are often apologizing for ourselves, for who we are. You still have to apologize about things sometimes when you screw up, and that's okay! But try to find the place of being comfortable in who you are, and knowing that, "Yeah, that's kind of who I am. I'm a jerk sometimes, I'm nice sometimes, I'm smart sometimes, I'm dumb sometimes." I meditate every day, so I try to live with these competing things in my mind all the time. I think it's okay to be all those different things and just own it.

Connecting people

Ofelia Valdez-Yeager

Roots

I was born in Tayoltita in the state of Durango in Mexico. I was about one and a half when we left there and made our way to Tijuana. My mother's family is from the state of Sinaloa, so there were a lot of relatives there. My father was an American citizen born in Jerome, Arizona, and my mother was born in Mexico in a small town called San Ignacio. My father left Arizona when his father took him and his siblings to Mexico during the Depression. My father subsequently met my mother, started having all these children, and then decided that he needed to come back, that there was not really a future for us in Mexico. So we came to Tijuana while he was in Los Angeles working. He said he would not bring us over until he had raised enough money to purchase a home for us. So he did. Because of the law at the time, my oldest sister was an American citizen, since my father was an American citizen, and then the law changed and all the children in between were not citizens automatically, so when we came to California it was some time before we all became American citizens. That didn't stop my brothers from fighting in Vietnam.

We grew up in Montebello, about 10 miles east of Los Angeles, and I had all my schooling there and then came to UCR in 1965. I consequently met my husband there, and we've been in Riverside since 1965. I arrived at UCR and lived in the Casa Hispanica, that was the Chicano Studies—about as close to it as we had at the time, but it allowed me to feel a little bit at home. There were very, very few Latinos at that time. I was there on scholarship, and it was a great experience. My career at UCR as a student was one of a lot of exposure, meeting a lot of people that I don't think I would have ever met, some great professors. I had a happy experience at UCR, but I also knew that I had received a scholarship to UCR. Dr. Eugene Cota-Robles was instrumental in that. At the time it was fifteen hundred dollars a year, and that paid for room, board, and tuition, which was a lot of money. My father couldn't afford that. **I always knew that I wanted to give back because of that.** That has stayed with me over the years.

Call to activism

I've never described myself as an activist. I see an activist as somebody over there, not me. I guess I did it without a title. I don't know why I had the confidence to do a lot of the things that I did. When you think that I ran for school board, and there were no role models, and so what made me think I could do it? All I can think of is **I had some silent confidence that told me, "Well, why not?"** I just *didn't* think that I *couldn't* do it. I think that comes from just living and being involved. One thing leads to another, and you don't know what is going to trigger doing this and that, but for me, the training that I got as a PTA volunteer and the experience I got working with all those parents with Little League really built on the next steps. In Little League, at the old park, I would clean out those toilets. It's just something you did. All of those are building blocks to get to the point where you're doing something that you feel you're contributing. A job needs to be done, let's go get it done. You get other people to buy in to your passion or your goal. Those are little building blocks that lead you to something a little bit bigger.

There was a person when I was growing up, my father always used to talk about her when I was in elementary school. Her name was Lupe. She'd go to city council, and I wasn't paying attention to city council, but my father was. I always remembered him, thinking, "That lady got stuff done," and it was a person who looked like me.

Then my oldest sister started out at 17 as a clerk at the register recorder's office in Los Angeles. She had to go to work because there were too many of us, and she did not go to college, and she was the smartest one of all. She tells a story that at some point she needed to confirm her U.S. citizenship. Under the law she was a citizen, but you have to go through all this rigmarole. She must have gone to the Community Services Organization in L.A., and she said this little woman just pushed through and said, "Okay, you stand in line here," and was telling her what she needed to do, and it was Dolores Huerta. I think of Dolores Huerta then and Dolores Huerta now, and how she touched my family through my sister, and my sister then ended up becoming the first woman and Latina Registrar-Recorder in Los Angeles County. That's a sense of pride for those of us in my family.

Contributions

Every organization I work with, it's a focus on youth, and usually offering scholarships for students. Maybe that's because I received one and it was my only opportunity. The fact that I went to university was a huge deal. I was the first in the family. I was involved with my children's school and got involved with the PTA. PTA pulls you in, you know. I eventually became the council president, and I learned about many things, and it led me to run for the school board [Riverside Unified School Board]. Because of my position with the council, I really did know all of the schools. I knew the principals, I knew the presidents of the PTA, I knew the different issues that existed among the schools, and I felt I could do it. In the meantime, I began working with the mayor of Riverside, Ron Loveridge. I worked part-time, but that was a real "ah-ha!" because I actually started getting paid for all the things I was doing for free! It helped with the income. I was an assistant to the mayor, and my focus was education and youth. It allowed me to continue my volunteerism on boards like United Way. I think all those volunteer efforts were very worthwhile and allowed me to connect with a tremendous number of people. My key contributions probably have been connecting people.

Around '92-'93, there was an RCC trustee who died, and they were going to fill the appointment, and Andres Soto came forward as someone that wanted to fill the seat. A couple of us asked how we could help, and we started meeting, three of us, to see what inroads we could make and who we could contact. Ultimately they appointed someone else, but we decided that we would continue meeting, because by then there were more people that would come to me, so I said, "Let's just keep meeting, and it will give us an opportunity to come together and share what's going on throughout the community, what issues impacted the Latino community." We would see if we could respond or identify resources. So we kept meeting, and that was like twenty-seven years ago now! That became Latino Network. It was a place you could feel connected. We developed a couple of events that were fundraisers so that we could do our work. We went through, like, five restaurants where we would meet. They would close, and then we'd have to find another place. The last place was the old Centro de Niños. Nati Fuentes was the director there, and when we couldn't use Zacatecas anymore, she said, "Well I can't offer you breakfast, but I can make a cup of coffee," and so that's what we did. It was very important for me that we could look out the window and see children, and that's what our focus was, to make sure we thought of the future, and those were our little kids.

With regard to the Cesar E. Chavez memorial, Ron Loveridge came to us and said he felt that we needed a Latino leader on the downtown mall. We had Ysmael Villegas, and I had worked on that while I was in the mayor's office, so I was familiar. I thought, "Okay, we can do that." He came and challenged us, he had two years left on his term, and he said we needed that. My daughter Marisa was incredible support, because she knew a lot of people that cared about Cesar E. Chavez, and opened doors to her contacts, and we worked very well together and got that done. It was obviously supported by Latino Network as well. It was during that awful recession, and we raised about half a million dollars. I'm very proud of that achievement. Some people think I'm very blunt. **I don't have a lot of time to waste, so if I'm here to ask you for money, I'm going to ask you for money.**

And then the Cheech! I was called, and they said, "Would you consider doing this?" I don't know if I'm just too naïve, but three million dollars needed to be raised in a year, and we said "Okay, well, let's do it," and so we did, and we keep fundraising, and my gosh, we finished the campaign just before COVID. Can you imagine? I can't believe it.

Inspiration

My sister, my mom and my daughters have been role models in that you think about them as you're going through these experiences to give you strength that you can do it.

There are the national figures. Dolores Huerta, thinking of her helping my sister when she was so young, to what she's still doing at 90, is incredible. Hillary [Rodham Clinton] for all that she represented for us. I consider her incredible.

As I was a younger woman involved in the community, the Jane Blocks and the Jane Carneys were very important. I'm grateful to Mary Ann Stalder, who was my neighbor, and was a development person with United Way, who opened doors, who put me on committees to broaden my experience. I'm amazed that Nati Fuentes from Eastside could do all she did, with limitations. And of course Woodie [Rucker-Hughes], who pulled the community together and is very much missed. Ninfa Delgado from Riverside Community Health Foundation and Estella Acuña from Chicano Student Programs [at UCR]. They're strong young women, and they get it. They volunteer for what they're passionate about and try to guide younger women.

Advice

I always say don't fly too close to the sun. You're not here because of your sole effort. You take a little from here, from here, from here, and you can't take credit for everything that's been done. That's probably the most difficult thing, because it takes some maturity to get to the point where you can say "I'm here," and know you stand on the shoulders of those that came before you.

Connecting the resources is really critical, because you will never know when you're going to need someone or someone's going to need you. I say to people now: relationships. It's all about relationships. So be careful how you behave right now. Ten years from now that person is going to remember how they were treated.

Asking for advice is critical. Don't assume that someone doesn't want to give it. It doesn't mean you're going to take everybody's advice, but there may be a nugget there that you need to pay attention to.

Allow yourself to evolve. Be true to yourself today, and maybe next week you're going to change a little bit. That's okay. I don't expect people to be the same way they were ten years ago. I would hope that they would have evolved.

Team player

Marisa V. Yeager

Roots

I was born in the early seventies at Kaiser Fontana Hospital. My parents are Class of 1969 alumni at UC Riverside. I grew up in Riverside, all the way through high school, and then I went to college at UC Santa Barbara. I lived in Washington, D.C., for two years and in Montebello, California for four years. I moved back to Riverside in 2001 and have lived here since then.

I grew up bi-culturally. My mom's family is from Mexico, my father's family we can trace back to the three ships coming over. Growing up in these diverse cultures allowed me to be comfortable in different situations and communities. I love learning about different cultures. That is definitely something that I cherish greatly, because you'll find that there's more commonalities with all of us than differences.

Call to activism

The terms "activism" and "organizing" were never something that I thought about when I was growing up. It's just something that we did. I recall being involved with AYSO soccer, and in soccer you'd learn to be a team player, to work with people to get to a common goal. My parents were very much role models, because they were both involved with their respective communities—my father through the elementary school that he worked at and my mom through the PTA as well as other community organizations like Latino Network, where she's a co-founder. We were always engaged in raising funds for helping schools, school children, book drives to provide books. I remember going to church with the family one Sunday, and my mom wasn't agreeing with the comments that were being made against those who love each other regardless of gender, and as soon as my mom heard that statement, we immediately stood up and walked out of the church. We moved churches because of that. That was impactful. My mom is very much an equitable person. I always learned that. If there is something that is in front of our face that is inequitable, how can we best address it so that we can right that wrong? That was one of the ways I started looking at life. "Why doesn't someone have access to this?" That resonated a lot in what I did in my career.

I was a full-time intern with Congressman George Brown Jr. I started my federal policy work being paid as an aide for Congressman Xavier Becerra, and I worked on natural resource issues, campaign finance reform, and monitoring U.S. Supreme Court decisions. I came back to California from Washington, D.C., because I had a calling to help with my grandmother's care, and so I moved back to help with that. It's a decision I will never regret. I have a new compassion for helping with our elders and the importance of continuing to honor and respect our elder family members and their quality of care end-of-life. I will always take that to my heart. I became a senior manager for government relations for the L.A. County Metro. During my two and a half decades at L.A. County Metro, from 1997 to 2019, I held various government relations positions dealing with 88 cities within the metro region, as well as the sixty state senate, and assembly members, including our eighteen members of Congress as well as our two U.S. senators. It was quite a big delegation, and I loved every moment. I quickly learned that public transportation, similar to education, is a glue. You need public transportation in order to access resources like going to the doctor's office, going to the grocery store, etc., especially in a very urban environment. There's linkages of public transportation through the Metrolink system to link people from the outlying areas, so it's important for workforce access as well. I became the Director of Government Relations for Riverside Community College District. I've always been connected to education too, so this kind of brings it full circle.

Contributions

I'm a connector. My key contributions are relationships, and bringing all of my experiences and who I know from my different roles and bringing people together to see, "Hey, can we do something together to move forward an issue or address a concern?" Relationship building is key to me as part of any community organizing.

When I moved back to Riverside in 2001, I wanted to see how I could give back to the city that gave me so much growing up. So I applied for a position on the Human Relations Commission. That was just a natural fitting for me, and one of my contributions to that commission was to make sure there was a youth voice on the commission. That's something I always ask: "Where do we have the next generation involved in conversation?"

As part of Latino Network, I helped make the Cesar Chavez statue a reality. Cesar Chavez actually did work in our area on behalf of farm workers. He attended the courthouses on behalf of the farm workers in our area. So there was a true tie to our area. It was a lot of money that had to be raised to bring it together, and it happened. Bringing people together for the opening and seeing the eyes of the people when they go by the monument is just amazing and brings me joy. That's what I get out of it.

The Cheech is honestly a family effort. This is a project where we are bringing an amazing center to the city of Riverside. The opportunities that this center will create will be wonderful. It's going to be a testament to Chicano art, which *is* American art. The amount of energy and focus, even from the Smithsonian, about what this collection will be is so exciting. It will continue to be told in stories when we're no longer here, it'll be for future generations. The center space will bring people together, it will bring more people downtown. But it's not just for Riverside. This contribution is for the region, the state, national and international audiences. That's the intent.

In terms of politics, as a high school student I remember being involved with Steve Clute's state assembly race. I remember working and supporting Assemblymember Jose Medina, working and supporting Andy Melendrez in his first race for city council. I was a delegate three times—in 2000 I was a Gore delegate when I lived in Montebello, and then I was a delegate in 2008 and 2016 for Hillary Clinton. In order to be a delegate you have to work your relationships. It's like running a mini-campaign to ensure that you have registered voters within your respective congressional district to come together and vote for you at a caucus for that specific presidential candidate. I did, and I was successful those three times.

In 2011, I ran for city council from Ward 1. I was running against an incumbent. There was another woman in the race, and then there was also the previous incumbent that I supported in his two council races, who came in last minute. I was also working full time in Los Angeles, coming back and forth. I had specific times I could work on the campaign. I don't regret anything. I received 22.1% of the vote running against an incumbent, as well as running against the former incumbent and the other fourth person. I love campaigning, I loved what I learned more about in this ward, in the area of the Northside. I identified where there was inconsistent planning and inequity in how these communities were being addressed. I appreciated everyone who was on my campaign team. I raised over thirty thousand in that race, spent every single penny on that, was not in debt from it, so that was good.

I continue to help elect other Latinas to become elected officials throughout the state of California through Latinas Lead California Political Action Committee. Our mission is to raise funds to elect Latinas into office throughout the state of California. That includes state senator, state assembly, governor, attorney general, state treasurer, all the cabinet positions. On the county level, Board of Supervisors, as well as the cabinet and the various advisors that are elected to judges, to water district boards, to school boards, community college boards, to mayors, city council members. I've been on that board since 2013, and I've been the political director for the last ten years. It was an existing PAC, formerly called HOPE PAC. I was asked to join in my new capacity as I termed off the HOPE C3 board. My contribution was that I modernized the interview application, I modernized the metrics of evaluation and how we determine endorsement to the relationships for campaigns in the Inland Empire and culling of relationships of those elected on those various levels throughout the state. We're able to help with both money and relationships. We supported Riverside Councilwoman Gabriela Plascencia, State Assemblymembers Sabrina Cervantes, Eloise Gómez Reyes and Abigail Medina, Darlene Trujillo-Elliot for Riverside Unified School District, Nancy Melendez for Western Municipal Water District. We continue to expand our support for Latinas running for office and will continue to do so. We offer a network to expand the bench as well as break those ceilings, so we're excited. The next Latinas at the table are important, continuing to have those role models so that people see themselves in people.

Inspiration

Growing up with my mom's influence, and the Mary Lou Moraleses of the world. We have such great women here in the city of Riverside. Ola Faye [Stephens] comes to mind, and others with The Group who truly continue to keep that organization going.

My aunt Beatriz Valdez, the first Latina Registrar of Voters for L.A. County. She was pretty significant to truly understanding the background of elections and the importance of custody of ballots to ensure the safety and also the counting of every vote within L.A. County and every county in the United States.

I always value the historical civil rights and social justice leaders who paved the way. Dolores Huerta and her family members. I've worked with Congresswoman Lucille Roybal-Allard. I've worked with other members of congress like Linda Sánchez and Norma Torres.

I always look to people who, when they bring people together, are bringing different perspectives together so we can provide the best response politically. I feel that we always need to have a balance in discussions on politics, especially on policies, because it never helps any society, nor is it sustainable, if we have one party over the other dominating the policy discussion and implementation of that policy. That has been my experience since my first legislative policy responsibility in Congressman George Brown Jr.'s office.

Advice

Continue to speak your truth. Continue to watch your pennies. We don't need to be making fiscal mistakes that harm messaging and intent of an organization or issue. Keep people that ground you around you in your space. Continue to just chip away. **More importantly, make sure to say thank you**. Make sure to say thank you. That's a forgotten skill that in my life has helped continue my relationships because of the mutual respect that comes from this simple action. And more importantly, have fun.

"Focus on the mission"

Lecia Elzig

Roots

I was born in 1953, so I'm a baby boomer. I grew up in very conservative Orange County, which was difficult because my mother was a Democrat. I think she was the only one in the entire town. I can remember when I was in the second grade, John Kennedy was running for president against Richard Nixon, and we had our little mock election in the classroom, and I was the only vote for John Kennedy. My mother got Nixon stickers, two of them, and she cut them in half so it said "Nix on Nixon." I don't know how many times that thing was ripped off, but she kept replacing it. She would get accosted by people in parking lots, and she was very self-confident, vocal, and had no problem telling people what she thought of their opinions.

I moved to the Inland Empire in the late eighties, and I've lived in the city of Riverside the last eighteen years. I worked for the California Highway Patrol for twenty-eight years. I grew up in a time period where girls were very limited in what they could do with their lives. I wanted to be an astronaut, and my mom says, "Sorry, girls can't be astronauts." "I want to be a fireman!" "Sorry, girls can't be firefighters." "I want to be a policeman." "No, girls can't be police officers." That's how I grew up, but fortunately that mindset was evolving as I became an adult.

I was working [for the Red Cross], and I thought, "This is not what I want to do for the rest of my life." I saw that police departments were now hiring women. I just thought, "You know what? I want to do this. I want to give this a shot. Girls can do this now, you know?" When I was fifteen or sixteen, not a chance, but now, yes! So I applied to a number of different police agencies. I liked the Highway Patrol because it was a large department; I knew it would offer a variety of opportunities, and it would allow me to live anywhere in the state. That's how I ended up there. It was kind of a fulfillment of a childhood dream, "Hey, girls can really do this." I wasn't part of the first class of women that went through the CHP Academy, but we were still a novelty. I'm really, really grateful that I was born into a time where that opportunity was available to me, because the generation before me, it wasn't. I started as a patrol officer. Then I rose through the ranks, and when I retired, I was an assistant chief. As I rose through the ranks, I was a patrol station commander for nine years; the first female captain in Bakersfield and south Orange County. As an assistant chief, I was assinged to CHP headquarters in Sacramento. I oversaw the Office of Equal Employment Opportunity and the Office of Internal Affairs. Everybody used to joke, "You are in charge of the two ugliest parts of the whole agency," but it was really, really interesting. Even though you're part of a situation where misconduct is being investigated, it was inspiring to me to see the degree of intensity that people were held accountable. You do something wrong, you're going to be punished for it. You're going to suffer severe consequences. Also, I got to see how focused the department was on diversity. I'm gay, and I remember when I talked about this to my parents, they were really worried for me at work. I said, "The last place that I'm worried about is work, because the state of California provides extraordinary protections, and I can tell you that the California Highway Patrol enforces those rigidly." I didn't have any fear in my job at all. I know that I'm one hundred percent supported. I'm more worried about the people throwing eggs at my car in the driveway, which has happened here in Riverside.

Call to activism

Right when I turned eighteen, I had a friend who said, you know, "Hey, we're eighteen, we can vote! There's this guy, McGovern, look at what he has to say!" So, my very first involvement in political activism was campaigning for George McGovern. We knocked on doors, we made phone calls, we set up tables at the swap meet, we did all kinds of things like that. When he swept California, I was filled with elation. And then, of course, we all know what happened [McGovern lost the election], and that was very gut-wrenchingly discouraging to me. We know what was happening with Richard Nixon. I can vividly remember just a week before the election, him saying, "The Vietnam peace talks are going so well, it's all gonna be over within a month," and I'm like, "You're a liar." That, among other things, propelled him to re-election, and of course the Vietnam War went on for another couple of years. He lied, and it really, really crushed me, especially with the other things that happened in the Nixon administration. Being a young adult watching Watergate happen, and lie after lie after lie after lie. I always voted, I never stopped voting, but it took me a long time before I was ready to jump back into political activism. Then, of course, life happens. Jobs happen, careers happen, you move around. You support people, you have a yard sign, but you don't really have time to do a lot of things. I was in that position for a long time.

Contributions

I retired in 2010 and spent a year walking the dog and gardening, but I knew I wanted to do more in my retirement. Around mid-May, 2011, I got a phone call from a lady named Michelle Campbell, and she said, "Hey! Are you interested in volunteering for President Obama?" And I'm like, sure, why not? That kind of started everything again. From that point forward, politics has been a big part of my life. I became a neighborhood team leader, which meant that I was in charge of regular phone banks. Things continued to grow where we ended up having this very large team of about a hundred people in Riverside. We needed multiple team leaders, then we needed to establish teams in other cities. Ultimately, I was a regional field organizer, starting smaller teams in Moreno Valley and Perris. We also had several different teams in Riverside. That was really rewarding. We had a really robust team in Riverside. You start developing these teams, and pretty soon leaders develop, and okay, now you have a new team leader in Moreno Valley. Now you're the team leader in Perris. Now you're the team leader in Corona. Watching these people take off in their own local leadership roles and building their teams, that was really exciting. I don't even know how many Saturday morning phone banks we had at my house. We'd have a barbecue in the backyard, and we had raffles. Back in those days, phone banking was done from a paper sheet of names. Every time you turn in a sheet of completed phone calls, you get a raffle ticket. People had a good time.

Although the 2016 defeat was crushing, it didn't kill my soul like the one when I was a teenager. After the election, I just said, "I have to devote every ounce of my life to getting that man [Donald Trump] out of the White House and stopping the horrific things that he wants to do." That got me back in the ballpark in 2016, and I'm right now the president of Indivisible 41. How that happened is kind of funny. I just literally showed up to everything that I could show up to. I got this phone call from Chani Beeman, and she said, "Hey, would you be willing to come to this meeting we're having about organizing?" So, I'm like, "Yeah, sure, okay." So I get there, and another lady, Jane Mitchell, was also there. She'd been organizing pop up demonstrations all over the place. The group looked at us and said, "You ever heard of Indivisible?" We're like, "Yeah, sure, we've heard of Indivisible." "Well, Congressman Takano has been asking why we don't have an Indivisible in Riverside." And we said, "I didn't know that we needed one, I thought it was primarily for districts where there were Republican or conservative members of Congress." At that time, I had a very limited knowledge of what the Indivisible Guide was. They just said, "Well, we think we need an Indivisible in Riverside, and we want you two to organize it." I had met Jane at rallies before, so I only knew her by sight. We just kind of looked at each other and went, "Okay! Here we go!" That's how all the Indivisible stuff started. It's a great organization and a wonderful experience being a part of that. In collaboration with Jane Mitchell, starting and getting a very active Indivisible chapter going was really, really important. I think that it's evolved into something that people look to locally as a guide and as a finger on the pulse of what's happening, not only in our community, but in the state and nationally. One of the things that really drives me to Indivisible, even though I was accidentally drawn to it, is that it's progressive but it's non-partisan. I think it's really important because we can draw in lots of different types of people. One of the things I like about Indivisible is it takes a very strong stance that we are not Democrats, we are progressives. There are things that I don't like about the Democratic Party. I'm a Democrat, but I think it's important that this organization is based on a philosophy that is based on progressive values, not necessarily linked to a party. There are cases across the country where the Democratic Party has kind of tried to influence the Indivisible chapters. The national organization says, "You let your chapter be, your chapter is autonomous." As Indivisible has grown, it started out very, very focused on contacting your member of Congress about this or that. Then it evolved into something that is more about state politics, local politics, down-ballot races. As it grew, they began including these greater and greater objectives. We don't just need the White House, we need the House and the Senate. We need states, counties, cities. We need to have this progressive philosophy from top to bottom in government, from the dog catcher to the president. Things kind of evolved like that, and by the time they began evolving that way, we had the chapter going. We were functioning and we were doing good things.

I think probably one of the things that we're most proud of is March for Our Lives. For us, it started while I was sitting at my kitchen table. My wife and I are watching TV, and she's talking to me about something. I see this national thing that's happening, and I just went, "Excuse me for a minute. We have to do this in Riverside." I immediately got online and started registering everything and putting things together. We got a team of really, really inspiring, smart, dedicated high school kids, and basically said, "You're in charge. This is it, this is your movement. **My generation failed to make it happen. Maybe your generation can make it happen.** You tell us what you want, and we'll do all the work in the background." It was so inspiring to see how that turned out. We had over four thousand people in Riverside. We didn't take any credit for it, very few people even know that Indivisible was involved. It was one of the most inspiring things to see these young activists, see them continue on in their activism. Now they're in college and they're not kids anymore. They're going to grow up being dedicated, hard-working people working for progressive causes, and that's really exciting to see. I think it just was wonderful to see something like that happen in Riverside.

We're all melded together, and that's really an exciting progressive coalition for Riverside. I think it's something that will be solid and active for a very long time. We work together. Nobody's competing with each other, we're all on the same team, we're all working toward that same goal and will continue to do that, and that's really exciting.

Inspiration

John Lewis, and I don't think anybody else even comes close to me. He has such a special place in my heart because he was so humble, but yet so focused and so dedicated. A man that would be nearly beaten to death, but still maintain the commitment to peaceful activism. He was willing, literally, to die for the civil rights movement. That's an easy thing to toss around, "Oh, I'd be willing to die for that." Well you know what, he nearly did, and he still went back out after he was beaten. That just really moves me, also how he went on to have this congressional career, the example he set, and the concept of creating good trouble. I just love that.

Advice

I'd say the first thing is to **be patient.** This is not going to sound very uplifting, but people will fail you. They will fail you. They will tell you they're gonna show up, and they won't show up. They will tell you they're gonna do something, and they won't do it. You can't let that discourage you. You have to realize that people are human, they will fail you. Just be grateful for the people who are willing to work and willing to do what needs to be done. I mean, certainly, be inspirational, be motivational, but the reality is that there will be failures. People will fail you. Don't let it get you down. Focus on the good part of what you're accomplishing.

I would say to future organizers, keep your eyes on the mission. Keep your eyes on what you're trying to accomplish. Find meaning in that mission, in that goal that you have, and let that be your guide. Don't allow disappointment to discourage you if something doesn't turn out as spectacular as you wanted. Take the win that somebody showed up, that somebody answered the phone. Because, in the long run, we may contact thousands of people, but the ten who show up are the ones that get the job done. It's the commitment and it's the dedication. Focus on the mission, focus on what you're trying to accomplish and take every single thing that you do, however big or however small it happens to be, as a victory—because you made a statement about what is right and what is just and what is good. I think that's probably the most significant thing.

Righteous anger, generative action

Donatella Galella

Roots

I was born in 1987 in New York City. I came to Riverside for a job at UCR. It was the week of my birthday, the week of my dissertation defense. I was in the office of the DMV renewing my learner's permit for the second time in my life, because I knew I needed to learn how to drive if I were to get a tenure-track position somewhere outside of New York City, and that's when I got the call with the job offer at UC Riverside. I work on contemporary popular American theatre, particularly Asian American theatre, Black American theatre, and musical theatre.

Call to activism

I grew up quite apathetic about politics and thought that certain kinds of equality had already been achieved and that taxes were too high and people should work hard and then they will naturally succeed, and I made false equivalences between different political parties. It wasn't until graduate school, at the City University of New York, when I started reading more and learning about existing and historical structural inequalities. Then Occupy Wall Street happened, and that was so extraordinary to me to see all these people make these critiques of class oppression and be willing to live in this park for a while and try to create a different way of being together. I was also really inspired by the Black Lives Matter movement as it was manifested in New York City. I was particularly moved by the murder of Eric Garner in Staten Island.

Thinking about capitalism and white supremacy together really rocked my political world because I had grown up so conservative and apathetic. I realized that to be an ethical person, I should be engaging in some way. That's when I started regularly going to protests and learning more and reshaping the direction of my research. When I applied to graduate school, I had pitched myself as someone who was going to study English Renaissance Literature, and then I was taught that actually I could study whatever I wanted, so I turned to these delegitimized forms, particularly the musical, and I began researching why it is so popular, and then realizing that I have these interests in the economies of theatre and this greater interest in African American theatre.

Then at the time of the Orlando massacre at Pulse in Florida, I saw this segment of *Last Week Tonight* by John Oliver where he was talking about how there are only five million NRA members versus a huge percentage of people who support very basic gun control and how we outnumber them, but NRA members and right-wing people are more likely to contact their representatives, so they have an outsized voice. I thought to myself, "Okay, well, why don't I just start calling my representative?" At that point I was living in Corona in 2015 to 2017, and I then learned that Ken Calvert, who represented that district, had the highest total donations from the NRA of any sitting congressperson from California. So I just started doing it. I would call when I was on campus walking from my car to my office or to an event, because what else did I have to do during those few minutes? It made me feel like I was doing something.

Then when the 2016 presidential election happened, I felt so angry and upset, but I guess I felt like it was to be expected, because of how this country is rooted in white supremacy and hetero-cis patriarchy. I made a commitment in January 2017 to call my two senators and my house representative every business day, often at both their D.C. office and a local office. Then I started trying to get other people to do these calls. I was inspired by the Indivisible movement that emerged out of that election, which was organized by former congressional staffers during the Obama era who wanted to make a reverse Tea Party and give tips on how to actually get heard by your representatives. The most effective way is not signing petitions or sending emails, which are easily deleted or passed over, but it's making phone calls, because you have to make a personal connection with someone on the other end. They are forced to listen to you and to take down your comments and to pass them up, and they tally up all the positions at the end of the day and then float to the representative what were the most talked about issues and what the stances were. I realized I'm not necessarily persuading someone because there's no way I'm going to be able to persuade a certain kind of far-right-wing person on anything, but I can make them listen to me and then worry about me. I've definitely seen the consequences of that. Ken Calvert has never had an in-person town hall. As a result of some of us pointing out his absence, he started being much more present on social media and showing the closed-door secret events he had. Now his staff members have to spend time worrying about us and creating these tweets and taking these photos to document this because he's trying to counter our discourse.

I was glad to discover that there was an Indivisible chapter in the district led by Barbara Davis. I volunteered for the Facebook group to put out these daily phone scripts. It's kind of like theatre. You're writing a short play every day, because the idea is that if we all call about the same thing, that's going to make a bigger impact. I was shaken when I learned that so few people contacted their representatives. I remember during the GOP tax scam of 2017, Kamala Harris's office made a tweet about how they received something like four hundred calls that day, and that was a lot for the day and for this big issue. I was like, four hundred calls? For forty million constituents? I made two of those calls that day. That made me want to keep on doing it and realize the power of what happens when a bunch of us can be organized to do this. I also realized they don't have the infrastructure, actually, to deal with more of us to call in, because they don't anticipate that kind of civic engagement on that level.

I became part of the Riverside group when I moved here. We learned Calvert was having a fundraiser at the Mission Inn and more than a hundred of us showed up at the Mission Inn to draw attention to his absence, his lack of town halls, and to his terrible record. Politics aside, he refused to have an in-person town hall and he hadn't even had a telephone town hall between 2009 and 2017. The throughline is I'm always thinking about feelings, and honestly, I am trying to make some people feel bad because maybe that will cause a self-reflection for you to wonder why this is happening? Why am I made to feel bad? Am I doing something wrong? Maybe I can do better.

Contributions

I think it's my persistence with Calvert. I have time. I will keep on doing this. I'm very good at researching and quite a good public speaker, so when I go to his office with people and we'd sometimes offer testimonies, I can very easily rattle off aspects of his record and cite stories personally, as well as various kinds of significant studies to prove how wrong he is and why he should vote otherwise. When they started realizing what we were doing, they stopped putting in the event flyers where they were exactly, so you'd have to call or email and reserve your ticket in order to find out where the event was. I remember one sneaky thing that me and another person did. We knew he had an annual golf fundraiser, and we determined it was the golf course in Victoria and we showed up at like six in the morning, and it was great to spook him a little bit because he wasn't expecting us there. We had things like "missing" signs with his face that we put in the bushes. I had a "Puttin' with Putin" sign. There's also a cleverness and a joy in connecting with one another and seeing certain people over and over again at these events. It's really energizing for us. Again, this was a way to make him uncomfortable to try to drive him into retirement or at the very least also to try to change his votes on things and to try to stop the people who are going to these events and donating to him.

I think I've written thousands of postcards as part of Postcards to Voters and other campaigns modeled on that. There's research suggesting that if you get a personally-written postcard from someone saying, "Hey fellow

Democrat, you should vote for this person, here's the date by which you should do it, here's some more information, thank you so much for being a voter," that kind of messaging is more powerful psychologically than saying, "Vote."

I've contributed to Riverside by helping with Councilmember Erin Edwards' campaign. I organized the postcard writing. I was her social media campaign manager, generating content toward the end of the campaign almost every day and trying to galvanize people and educate people on the issues and on her vision. You know, she won! Working on her campaign and learning more about city politics, I realized how important city councils are. I went to my first city council meetings because of her. I went up to speak and give testimony a few times, I write e-comments regularly now, I've studied the city budget to try to advocate defunding the police and reallocating that funding to help out people who are unhoused.

Another thing I attempted to be skilled at is writing letters to the editor and trying to encourage people to send letters to our local newspaper. Representatives really care how they are portrayed in the media, what the discourse is around them, so you should do whatever you can to try to take up space and shift what that discourse is to paint conservatives as who they are, for the harmful policies that they enact.

The renewal of the Black Lives Matter movement led me to help co-create a group at UCR for our own Cops Off Campus chapter, because of doing more research and seeing how American police kill people and almost always get away with it, and this is not normal globally. I think that reform can in some ways help, but I also see how it re-entrenches the police's presence and their legitimacy. Often, reform ends up giving them more funding, and they just do other kinds of violence and harassment of minoritized people, and so I've come to a position of abolition. That has been something on my mind since the Black Lives Matter movement started, but I really haven't been openly saying abolition until maybe the past year and joining this group of other UCR colleagues. We've organized things like car caravans and Coffee Not Cops conversations where we give people free coffee and snacks and pamphlets and try to engage in conversations. Who makes you feel actually safe and have you had encounters with the cops? Did they help you? They have not for me. And imagine what are the other alternatives we can have that actually would keep us all safe based on our personal experiences, our lived realities, as well as what the research says. That's been a real change in where my directions and my energy has gone in the past year, but it's also hard during a pandemic and also with having a baby, because I can't do as much as I used to before. I called my representatives while I was being induced for labor, and ever since then I still call every day, but I don't call two offices for each representative every day, and it's also been different because ninety percent of the time I'm getting voicemail and not a live person on the other end, because of people not being in offices and how they've set up things. That's really changed the structure of that. And the other big change is with Kamala Harris's office, I was such a reliable caller they trained their interns at one of their offices based on me as a case study. Now we have Alex Padilla, who's also great, arguably more progressive, and I just hope that all those calls I made over the years pushes Kamala Harris further to the left to do things like abolish ICE, for example, because when you say those things persistently to the people with whom she works, maybe that ultimately gets into her ear and she hears that.

Inspiration

Lorraine Hansberry. I just love her. I love *A Raisin in the Sun*. I think it's so much more radical than a lot of people think. She was a communist and she was very open about it. She was queer and wrote stories dealing with this. She was anti-colonial. She did fundraising for groups like SNCC [Student Nonviolent Coordinating Committee]. She understood all of these different kinds of oppression across gender, sexuality, race, and class, and then incorporated that into her artistic work on top of doing direct actions. She understood that there was a place for all of that as well as rigorous intellectual thought.

Advice

It's okay to be angry, and your feelings are valid. So often women of color, especially Black women, are criticized for their anger, or we're told to not feel that way, that those feelings are illegitimate, and there's this false binary between thinking and feeling. But I think anger can be extremely productive. I think about Audre Lorde and uses of anger. So use your anger and use your feelings! Whenever I feel so angry about the latest thing that the former president did, that the Republican Party does, I really simmer in it, but then I try to channel it into doing something, at least making that phone call. Saying I'm outraged about the treatment of the separation of refugee migrant children on Facebook, that doesn't get to a representative who can affect a policy about this, but if I pick up the phone and say that to someone and give them my zip code, they have to record that and take that into account. So think about how anger can actually be really productive. Do not feel ashamed about it. **A righteous anger can actually be really good when you channel it into a generative action.**

"Don't let them erase you"

Rabbi Suzanne Singer

Roots

I was born in New York City. I grew up there, and I went for one year to Smith College and transferred right away to UC Berkeley, so that tells you something about who I am. I lived in California most of my adult life. I came to Riverside as a rabbi [at Temple Beth El].

Call to activism

My mother was a survivor of Auschwitz, so as far back as I can remember, I had this sense of injustice and anger at what happens to innocent people in this world. I always felt some calling to do something about it.

My grandmother was very active in social justice work. She was born around the turn of the twentieth century. Her parents came over from Ukraine. My grandfather ended up making quite a bit of money, and so they lived a very lovely life, but my grandmother devoted her time to trying to help people. She was on all sorts of committees and commissions in New York City. She was on the Board of Correction, which was a watchdog group to try and make sure that the jails in New York were humane. She used to go out to Rikers Island every month to visit people. When they finally built a new facility on Rikers Island for women, they actually named it after my grandmother to honor the work that she did. It's not like she said to me, "Do this," but that's really where I focus most of my energy.

One of my tenth grade teachers tried to get us to wake up to what was going on in society, and he said, "Don't be sheep." That's why, even though I love studying literature and I would have been very happy as a scholar with a PhD in literature, I thought, "I've got to do something that has more impact on society." I chose journalism. I thought that through journalism I would make issues known to people. I was a news and public affairs producer, and I produced a children's series called *The Puzzle Place* that was meant to teach kids to respect diversity and to learn how to get along with each other. I never really felt like I was in the right place though, and I didn't feel that my interests were consonant with television's.

I could give you many reasons for why I became a rabbi, but I think the real reason is something that you can't really explain. I do feel like I was called in a certain sense, so it was beyond all the rational reasons I could give you. Being involved in social justice work was definitely part of it. I do feel like part of my work is activist, as well as educational. I try to connect what I believe we should be doing as Jews to the values that our tradition has taught us. I'm much more interested in systemic change and legislation as opposed to charity work, even though we must also do the charity work, feeding the homeless, being an example—but I'd rather figure out a way not to have people who are homeless than to feed them. Let's find a solution to why people are on the street in a very wealthy country like this one.

Contributions

I got here in 2008, and right after that the housing market started to collapse in Riverside. Reverend Jane Quandt [of First Congregational Church] and I, among others, were trying to get the city to be responsive to the fact that so many places were being foreclosed. We met with the city council and specifically with the finance committee, because they were about to pick a bank that they were going to do banking with, and we wanted them to take into consideration whether the bank was working with the community rather than just foreclosing on houses. We spent quite a long time meeting with various council members and meeting with the finance committee, and finally, when they put out their request for proposals to banks, they did have a tab dealing with community involvement. Unfortunately, in the end, they picked the same bank that they had been banking with, but we did work on that.

Clergy and Laity United for Economic Justice (CLUE) out of L.A. tried to establish a chapter out here, which did exist for a few years, and one of the things they wanted to do was organize warehouse workers in a union. We were involved in that for a couple years. Then we formed the Justice Table, and our focus really was on criminal justice reform. This was with Vonya Quarles, Corey Jackson [of the Riverside NAACP], Luis Nolasco [of the local ACLU office], and Adam Wedeking from ICUC [Inland Congregations United for Change]. We met with supervisors before the jail in Indio was going to be built. It was getting state money and maybe federal money as well, and we said to them, "Don't take the money, don't build it. We don't want more jails." They didn't listen to us, but we did lobby for that. We've held a couple of forums to try to talk about alternatives to incarceration. We did quite a bit of lobbying in that area as well with supervisors over the years, to say, "Look, if nothing else, this is too expensive, and it's not effective." Why are we putting a lot of money into putting people behind bars, and they're coming back within a few years? That's not a successful program, so let's put our money into mental health and drug rehab and job training.

We also visited a jail in San Bernardino County where they have a room for parents to be with their children and to play games, and we're trying to encourage our jails here to do that sort of thing. We have lobbied against the fact that this new jail in Indio has no in-person visiting. It's all video, but visitors still have to go there. If you live far away and you can call somebody remotely, that's one thing. But to have to go all the way to the jail, which is not that accessible, and then have to be on a video call… I've developed relationships with a number of elected officials, and in particular our state legislator Jose Medina and our State Senator Richard Roth. I talked to Assemblymember Medina, and I said, "You've got to introduce legislation that makes it illegal to have no in-person visiting in a jail." And he did! He did introduce legislation, but it would mean putting a lot of money into redesigning jails that were given the permission to build without in-person visiting, and at least so far the bill hasn't gone through, but he did introduce it. I have also taken congregants with me to visit with both Senator Roth and Assemblymember Medina to lobby for legislation.

I've been involved with Adelanto [ICE Detention Center] and worked with Hilda Cruz of the Interfaith Movement for Human Integrity. I've gone a number of times to visit people there and to hold holiday commemorations there. For example, Hanukkah—it's the middle of winter, we light lights and try to shine the light on what's going on in Adelanto and to provide them with hope for the future. I also have a relationship with our Congressman, Mark Takano, and so there was a plan to build some sort of place to hold children as part of the family separation policy that the [Trump] administration had. I went and lobbied my various representatives, and there was enough opposition here from enough people that they decided not to do it here. We were successful in keeping them away. Of course, the question was, is it better to have it built here and we can supervise it, or to have it built somewhere else where there'll be more abuse? Well, the fact is, you can't do any supervision. They don't let you inside. I've gone to visit people at Adelanto, but you go to this very specific place to visit. You don't get to see where they live. It's very hard to monitor what's going on.

I've visited the border with an organization called T'ruah, which is a human rights organization, and also with the Hebrew Immigrant Aid Society. We went down to the border in El Paso and visited a number of shelters and also went over to New Mexico to another privately run prison for immigrants called Otero [County Prison Facility], and we did get a tour. It's not that easy to get a tour, and the warden gave us the tour, very proudly showing us things, like, "Oh look, these people can work in the kitchen, or they can become barbers, or they can clean the toilets, and they get paid a dollar a day. Isn't that fabulous?" You see fifty men on what you can barely call bunk beds, because it looks like they were made out of cheap wood and these thin mattresses, in there with a bathroom that's basically open, with almost nothing to do, and the recreational area is a concrete yard with barbed wire around it.

I'm part of the California Religious Action Center (RAC-CA) and on the Commission on Social Action of the Reform movement of Judaism, which lays out some of the goals of the Religious Action Center. We pass resolutions under which they can decide to promote a particular piece of legislation or lobby for it.

Inspiration

Definitely my grandmother. Ruth Messinger would be one of my important role models. She was the borough president of Manhattan. She actually ran for mayor against Rudy Giuliani. She was the president of the American Jewish World Service. I remember she wrote that, yes, there are a lot of problems in this world, and yes it can be overwhelming, but **we do not have the luxury to be overwhelmed.**

Advice

I didn't listen to myself for a very long time. When I started thinking about becoming a rabbi, it was ten years before I did anything about it. So, one bit of advice is to really listen to what your gut is telling you. My gut was telling me, but I wasn't listening, and I found all kinds of reasons for why it didn't make sense to go.

The other is to have a long-range perspective. Look at Stacey Abrams. She worked for decades. It's not one campaign. That's the way it works with social justice as well. You have some wins, you have a lot of losses. Sometimes you think you've made progress, and then you realize you've taken ten steps back, and you can't take anything for granted, and you have to keep fighting, and you have to really keep your eyes on the prize. What's the long-term goal that you really have, and how are you going to get there? Take the long view of history. Also, know history, because I think we take a lot of things for granted. We certainly learned over the last few years that we took democracy for granted. The advances that women have made, a lot of things that women fought for in generations before mine, are not a given. You have to keep fighting. And don't forget what your mothers and grandmothers and great-grandmothers had to fight for, because nothing is certain anymore.

The beginning of the Book of Exodus has a lot of women, and it's because of the women the Israelites are saved. In the Book of Exodus, Moses was saved by being put in the river by his mother. Pharaoh said, "Stick him in the river," and she did, but she happened to put him in a basket, so she saved him by doing that. There are the midwives who save the babies, because Pharaoh says, "Tell the midwives when the babies are born, make sure they don't get born alive." Well, they save the babies, and they then lie to Pharaoh and say that the Hebrew women are so strong that they weren't able to do anything about the babies. And then the women decide to continue having babies. They make sure that there is a future. All these women are responsible for saving these babies, and they all do it by defying the orders of the dictator. So they're all very brave and important at the beginning of the story. This is all in the first couple chapters. And guess what—they all disappear. Don't let them erase you after the first couple of chapters.

"We co-power"

Vonya Quarles

Roots

I was born in the sixties in L.A. County. My father was from South Carolina and was part of the Geechee Gullah culture off the coast of South Carolina. My mother was Lakota and Irish and was from Iowa. My father had been in the military and then he came home and he met my mom. My mother was in a boarding school—that's what they used to do with delinquent girls—and she met my father, and they were both very young. The only culture that I know about is the Black one. I have Irish and Lakota blood, but I don't know how to be Irish or Lakota. When you look at me, you see a Black woman, and that's been my experience. I was raised in the Harbor area of Los Angeles and South Los Angeles and came out to the Riverside area in 2008. It was a good choice. I came out here because I wanted to purchase a house and the housing market was a lot more appealing.

Call to activism

My parents were relatively young and living the sixties lifestyle, which was full of activism. I went into foster care when I was about five and came out when I was about ten or eleven. My foster parents were very strict, and they weren't part of the sixties or seventies. They were probably more centered in the forties and fifties lifestyle. When I came out of the foster home, it was the women's liberation movement, the civil rights movement—all those different things were happening and the grownups were talking about it. I longed to be a part of that. When we came out of foster care, my mother was in a relationship with a woman, and they were always talking about women's liberation. It was unusual times, and I recognize now that my childhood was rich with experience and opportunities to be resilient.

The activism that I remember most had to do with Mumia Abu-Jamal, who was a prisoner and had been part of the MOVE work in Philadelphia. When he was on Death Row, we did a lot of work around ending the death penalty. It was a long distance between that activism at a young age to what I'm doing today. I took the long road and had some lived experiences. I went to jail and prison. I was paroled. I became sober. My life began to change so that I could really be there for someone in a real way, and that's when my activism began to change and become more meaningful to me and the community that I'm part of.

I don't know a soul that doesn't know struggle in one form or another. I appreciate it's not always the same. It doesn't look the same. But the more I listen to people and their stories, the more I'm convinced that we've all carried some form of pain or trauma. Sometimes it's what propels us and helps to shape us.

Contributions

I came here at a time when the stigma around incarceration was prevalent, and I've seen it change. I can't take credit for that, but I would like to be part of taking actions on behalf of people who have been incarcerated and convicted, and demonstrating that **it's okay to lift your head up and not be tied to who you used to be or to the worst mistake you've ever made.** To say that I'm a system-impacted woman was freeing to me, and it was freeing to a lot of other people who have been able to say that without shame, without pride, but just stating a fact. That's not who we are—that's a status. I feel that I've been swept along and moved with that activism to change the way we identify ourselves and those around us, being part of a movement to change how we even talk about people with the lived experiences of being incarcerated, not as being convicts or felons or any of those other dehumanizing terms that we had once relied on.

When I paroled I went to work in an oil refinery. They weren't doing the formal background checks. They would just ask you if you've been incarcerated before. I didn't wear prison on my face, so when they asked, I said, "No, I haven't been incarcerated." And so I went to work in the refinery, and I was able to go to school while there, and the company paid most of the tuition for the bachelor's degree. The trajectory of my life was changing. I was home. I was free. I was working a legitimate job. I was a mother. I could have gotten an MBA and the company would have paid for it, but the activist in me was seeing the world around us, and I knew by 2005 that getting the MBA and working there forever was probably not going to be for me. I ended up going to a Women Organizing for Justice and Opportunity training that Susan Burton at A New Way of Life was offering in 2011. I had graduated law school in 2009. Because of my past, I had to wait longer for the moral character determination to be made. When I started law school, I didn't know if I was going to be able to practice or not, but something told me to just go, because even if I couldn't be licensed, I would at least know more, and I could do more.

After the Women Organizing for Justice class, I knew that I needed to do something. In 2009, Starting Over started. In 2011, we started the Riverside chapter of All of Us or None. People we were organizing with had either been in jail or prison or our children were in jail or prison. We didn't know what we were doing, we just knew we wanted to do something. Since that time, All of Us or None has been successful in litigation around the rights to vote for people inside the Riverside County jails, for making sure the marijuana records are purged as mandated by the laws, and by helping, and I think this is probably the most important, to change the hearts and minds of people about who we are. We've done different things, from the police to the courts to the collateral consequences that many of us live with and suffer with in silence, trying to live after incarceration. We wanted to help provide housing for people that were unhoused. Once we started doing that, we became aware of how many homeless people had criminal records. We knew we weren't going to be able to put a Band-Aid on it or provide enough beds to make the problem go away, and so the New Way of Life program model was direct services, policy advocacy, and civic engagement. We said, "That's what we need to do." When it came to criminal justice, we were far behind Northern California and Los Angeles in terms of our policies and in terms of the sentiment that public safety resides in the hands of law enforcement. That's the real challenge. How do we help to first understand ourselves and then help others to understand that we are responsible for public safety, and it can't be outsourced to an external entity? We have to recognize that addressing poverty is the way we increase public safety. Addressing mental health with mental health solutions is the way we address public safety.

The programs have expanded and the vision has expanded. We started just doing housing. We didn't have case management. We didn't have peer support. We didn't have an employment or economic development program. Those things have been added. We have peer support, we have case managers, we have an outreach team, we have a participatory defense team, which helps families who are going through the criminal justice system develop social bios for their loved ones so they can present to the courts a more three-dimensional picture of who the person is. So you're not just armed with the police report and belt recorders, but you can see that this person is connected to people who love them, and this is who they are, not just what they did. We have the Family Reunification Equity and Empowerment Project, which addresses the issues with the child protective system as it relates to Black and brown families and poor families in general.

We're a small part of a much larger ecosystem, so we don't have to do it all, but we just need to do something well. I think what we do well is work with system-impacted people.

We don't say empower, **we co-power with people and community.** We work with them, and we're not any better prepared or equipped than they are. Our work is oftentimes showing community members their power and how to tap into it. We want you to know that you already got the power – let's go use it. Let's go to the supervisor's meeting. Let's go to the attorneys. **Let's do what we need to do to help create the beloved community we all deserve.**

Inspiration

Historically, Harriet Tubman, of course, and Sojourner Truth. Of more contemporary people and the people that I can pick up a phone and talk to, it would be Susan Burton, and Hamdiyah Cooks-Abdullah. They are mentors. Michelle Alexander is someone that doesn't mentor me personally, but she has been very important to me as a thought leader about the criminal justice system. Her book *The New Jim Crow* was so on point in terms of how she explained the system in a way that helped me to look past personal shortcomings of individuals and looking at the generational impact of mass incarceration, or more aptly, of racism. When I read her book, it seemed to explain it and break it down in a way that I had never read before.

Advice

Believing in your vision, in your direction, in your power, is important. Being afraid is normal, but the only place to go is forward.

Help create different spaces

Maribel Nuñez

Roots

I'm originally from southeast Los Angeles. My parents were born in Mexico and met here, at the Hollywood Palladium. I've been in the Inland Empire since 1989. This is where it was more affordable to buy a home and there were more opportunities here. I went to Cal State L.A. for my graduate degree in history, but with the exception of going to grad school, I've lived and worked here.

Call to activism

I struggled with knowing where I belonged, because there was a transition when I came from southeast Los Angeles to Chino. Chino Hills was a big difference from where we came from— Compton, Lynwood, Southgate. I didn't even know that I was "the other," until I went to Chino Hills. I think college saved me in some ways and made me really proud of my identity, especially with Chicano Studies. I got my Master's in History and Latin American Studies, and I got to meet a lot of people and I got more exposed to different Latino cultures. My thesis was about the history of EOP, Educational Opportunity Program. At the same time, we were organizing against the war in Iraq, and I got more politicized. I did some work with the anti-war movement, and with some of the discrimination that happened against immigrants.

When President Bush got elected and there was No Child Left Behind, and then even with President Barack Obama with Race to the Top, I didn't like that kind of teaching. I know people could be very creative to go outside the box, but I felt I needed to teach without being told how to teach, so I felt like higher education gave me a broader way of being able to teach and do more co-learning with students and bring those critical thinking conversations. In 2007 I started teaching at Riverside Community College, at the main campus and then the Rubidoux Annex, which I really loved, teaching the high school kids that were in college-bound prep, and so both spaces were great and creative to be able to teach. I was teaching as I was working in organizing. But then the recession hit and the budget cuts were there, and so I found myself with a big student debt, and as the budget got cut, I was underemployed in teaching. Our parents taught us, at least particularly immigrant families coming to this country, that if you work hard, you'll be on that path of economic opportunity. I think that a lot of us face the situation, "I worked hard and I went to school. Why are we in this circumstance?" There's a lot that I respect in my family, but I felt that sometimes, even if you do "the right thing," there could be some barriers.

When the recession hit, I was really motivated working with students at RCC, UCR and Cal State against the budget cuts. I realized in higher education justice, it's so important for there to be resources to fund positions full-time, because you can't do as much good, quality work in the long term when really good organizers move on or are snatched up. We lose youth leaders because they're overworked and it's a ripple effect, when they work multiple jobs and they can't be as civically involved compared to the older generation or seniors that are retired. I did volunteer in community organizing, and then at the same time when President Barack Obama was elected, I got very involved. I was part of the Obama for America organization and started working on the Affordable Care Act. A couple of nonprofits came to me and I was able to have organizing positions in Corona and Riverside—Working Families Win and then California Partnership, now Inland Equity Community Land Trust. Since then I've been organizing and teaching, and I taught all the way through 2016, when the position opened for me to be an executive director.

I came to the realization that **we need to make sure that different spaces are created, that we have different organizing spaces that come from different people, to move the needle**. I also realized more about money in politics. I realized that we have to look at things in a very nonpartisan way. I'm all about looking at values and looking at how we are as a community, and how we meet people where they are, party or no party.

Contributions

I met Ms. Yolanda Esquivel through St. Anthony's, one of the churches here in Riverside in the Canyon Crest area, getting petition signatures for the Affordable Care Act in 2009. We've been organizing ever since. Part of my work was to help to build organizations as a coalition here in the I.E. There were only partisan groups or groups that were led by electeds, so if we're trying to fight against the status quo, then I knew that I had to help create groups so that we could do something collectively. I became a co-founder of LULAC [League of United Latin American Citizens] Riverside with Yolanda and Gilberto Esquivel. They had been organizing in LULAC for a long time. Through that work, there came the opportunity for redistricting. There was a push for a redistricting commission. In 2011, Yolanda and Gilberto said, "We need to organize, because the commissions are going to come and we need to come together to organize and do maps and this and that." I thought, "No, they're not going to listen to us." I was originally a skeptic. But we brought NALEO [National Association of Latino Elected and Appointed Officials], we brought other groups, we did some outreach, we came up with some common ground. I worked with Gilberto to do some maps, and pretty much the maps that we drew were the ones that the commission accepted, and it brought up Takano, Roth, and Medina. We got Ken Calvert to pack his bags and go to Corona or wherever.

Part of my work has been to build capacity for community organizing around the state budget. I got hired to work for the California Partnership, and that organization does state budget advocacy. We moved to do more regional work, from California Partnership to Inland Equity Partnership. We organized state budget rallies. One thing that I learned as an organizer is that it's important that you have one or two things that are your focus. We identify health and housing as the two primary drivers of poverty. We want healthcare and housing to be de-commodified. We got Senator Roth and Assemblymember Medina to co-author the Health for All bill, and getting Senator Roth and Medina, who are from Riverside, to support something like this, is a big deal for this region as we're talking about the long history of where we were to where we are now. We organized county budget response rallies as well. We have continued having the Medically Indigent Services Program, which is a county safety net program, and to expand it to undocumented immigrants. We have shifted to focusing on Riverside, San Bernardino, and to some extent Imperial Valley, to do work here more regionally and be able to do more advocacy with the county and the city electeds to be our leading targets. In 2018 and 2019, using that coalition model, I helped organize with a few other partners—Corey Jackson, Karen Borja from Planned Parenthood—and create a California Partnership Action Fund 501c4 table, Engage Coachella Valley and Engage I.E., so we have convened local tables to do endorsements with the focus of county and local electeds. We were able to help to get Councilmember Erin Edwards in office, Gaby Plascencia, and we did a little bit of support for Ronaldo Fierro. We're happy that they got elected, and we're using those networks to make sure that in Riverside we have a strong eviction moratorium against evictions, an inclusive rental assistance program that includes all our communities, and get the word out. We worked with the leadership of Councilmember Edwards and Councilmember Plascencia to introduce a rental freeze in the midst of COVID-19. We didn't get it passed, but I appreciate that we just pushed it and let's see who voted which way. That helps you when you're looking at the next round of elections. Recently we've been working on the housing element for the city of Riverside. We are partnering with Anti-Racist Riverside and others to look at some data that talks about race, making sure that we continue looking through a racial justice lens, and really mobilizing and trying to make sure that we get through the housing element. Part of the organizing that we need to do is to change measures and change hearts and minds. I think that there's still more work to be done with the people that are middle or upper-middle class to make this reshifting of the city, to make it Riverside for all.

Inspiration

Ella Baker is a major one, because I see her organizing from behind the scenes. I see her leadership development. I've seen a lot of documentaries where some people her same age are saying, "Whoa, how do the youth organizers work with you, how are they able to work with you?" She said, "Well, because I treated them the same. I didn't ask them to call me 'ma'am' or whatever, we're all the same." It reminded me a little bit of my experience organizing with younger students in the higher education budget cuts. We're all the same.

The local one is Ms. Yolanda Esquivel. What I realized about her is she's kind of a float-like-a-butterfly, sting-like-a-bee kind of person. You feel, "Oh, she's a nice lady." But I think she's very diplomatic in her approach. You don't have to yell or anything. She's as progressive as you can get, she's diplomatic, and she's someone that people really respect. The other person that I would say is Elizabeth Ayala, and another friend of mine, Cristina Mendez. Before I thought, "why doesn't she just be more visible or tell people what she really does," but I've learned along the way, that's where some people want to be, and it's not like they're insecure. That's where they want to be—behind the scenes.

Advice

I think that we don't always have to have an opinion. Sometimes it's good just to listen.

I do feel that sometimes there is a double standard in how women are treated. It's very important to see—if a person does something to you, are they like that with everybody or just women?

Read books for sure. If you're an organizer or an activist, I think it's important that you figure out the lessons learned from the past. It doesn't help when there's a lot of effort that has already happened and you're repeating the same mistakes. I think there's ways of learning from the older generation, and adapting it to what makes sense, because we know that in some ways history doesn't always repeat itself, but it could mirror.

Accept criticism from people you take advice from.

Know your place and own your stuff. When you're working with people, it's always good, to be clear on what your intentions are, be honest, wherever you feel safe to do that. That helps to clear up any misunderstandings. I feel that sometimes people always come up with new groups or new coalitions, and it's always easier to do that than try to plug in or make wherever their spaces are there to make better. The nonprofit industrial complex doesn't help sometimes, especially if we're positioned as an organization that just gets grants. It's important that we find different sources of funding so that we stay with our mission, we stay in our lane, because if you are all over the place, you're stepping on toes, and people don't want to work with you and how you're organizing is all over the place or with issues. So it is important to make sure that we stay focused, not only for the community but also just the sustainability of the organization.

Always leave room to carve out youth spaces. They should be there with intention. Either help create the space or don't take it personally if they create separate spaces.

"Think about the lives that are touched"

Yolanda Esquivel

Roots

I was born in Donna, Texas, on April 10, 1951. I grew up there. We moved to California when I was fifteen. When we first came from Texas, we moved to the Coachella Valley because an uncle of mine had moved there, and he told us that the labor in the fields was much better paid in California than Texas. So that was a big motivator for us, because we were farm laborers—that's how we made a living. I was six years old when I started working in the fields, and my brother was younger—he was three years old, a baby, out in the field. I didn't want to move, because I liked school and I was doing well in school, but my uncle said, "You know, Yolanda, in California, pickers earn twenty-five dollars by working from six in the morning to twelve pm." And right away, that did it for me. In Texas, we would work all day long, six in the morning until five or six in the evening, for four dollars and fifty cents. So we decided to move.

The following year, Cesar Chavez came in. I remember him telling us to walk out, and that was really hard. We were just barely trying to make a living, and here comes Cesar Chavez. My mother didn't want to walk out, but at the same time, we understood the message. We knew he was right. And so we did. It was quite an experience, but we were able to survive. My mother said, "There's no way that I can be without a job. I have to go back. As soon as we're allowed to, I'm gonna go back." I said, "Well, I'm gonna go look for another job someplace. I don't want to break the strike. I want to be able to do something else." I went looking for a job. I went to the bus depot and I asked the woman there for a job. She said no at first, then she said, "Give me your number and I will call you." I didn't know that she was one of the most influential ladies in Coachella. Her name was Eleanor Lopez, and she was very involved in the community. I worked with her for a little while, but that wasn't very much, and I was getting a little nervous about how I was going to pay for my clothing to go to school. She finally said, "I've got the job just right for you. You're going to be the secretary for the new youth outpost that's going to be built here." That youth outpost was a program that LULAC of California [League of United Latin American Citizens] started. It brought teachers and activities in, because at that time there weren't any activities for the kids there in Coachella. There was baseball, and boxing, and arts and crafts. There were dances sometimes and we would arrange trips to Disneyland or Universal Studios. I created the schedule. It was wonderful. I worked there my junior and senior year. That position really helped me provide for my clothing and all my expenses. I even bought myself a little car.

I went on to college at Cal State San Bernardino, and I was able to get a teacher's degree there. It was a very good experience. I was the very first one in my family to go to college.

Call to activism

My grandmother was a woman that was very bright, but she hadn't had the opportunity to go to school. She was fluent in both English and Spanish, and she made it a point to always keep up with what was going on in the country. She had a tremendous influence in my life. She would always tell us stories, and she would teach us things that were important, especially how to behave and how to treat each other. She was a very kind woman and very strict also. When I was nine years old, I remember her being very excited and organizing people, telling people that they had to register to vote, and getting money together to buy the poll tax. This was when the election of John F. Kennedy was coming up. It was something very exciting for our community and our families because he would be the first Catholic president. I remember my grandma saying we had to do everything we could to get him in, and her brother coming with one of the large trucks that he had to take people in the back of the truck to vote. They had gotten their money together to go pay the poll and be able to vote. In the evening, we were listening to the radio, and my grandmother said she was very sad, "Mija, we've lost the election." I remember going to bed very sad also. But in the morning, when I got up, she was making tortillas, and she said, "Mija, guess what? A miracle, we have a miracle! The President is now John Kennedy! He won, the first Catholic president!" It was a wonderful, wonderful day for us, and we were thrilled. I think she's where I get it from, and the fact that she would tell me our history gave me a good sense of who I was. In fact, I was born out of wedlock and I didn't grow up with my father, but she would always tell me that my father loved me and that he was a good man. My mother didn't want to marry him, so she didn't! But my grandma made it a point to tell me that he loved me, and that made all the difference in the world.

Contributions

When we got to Riverside, my husband was working at a radio station here, and we would work the fiestas at Our Lady of Guadalupe on the Eastside. I've always believed in registering our people to vote, so I would go out and register people to vote. At that time, nobody else was doing it, especially on the Eastside. I remember one of the men at the fiesta said, "What do you think you're doing here?" And I said, "I'm an American citizen, and I can do whatever I want to do. If you don't want to register to vote, that's fine. I will go to the next person. So thank you very much." We went back to Texas for about four years, and then we came to Riverside, and when we came back, we started doing the same thing, trying to get people to register to vote because it seemed to me that that was the key for our community as Latinos to have a voice. So that's why my husband and I have always worked in that, to try to get our community to register to vote and to vote.

When we retired, some friends of ours were passing out applications for LULAC, and we all decided we would start a LULAC here. LULAC is the League of United Latin American Citizens, and it's a national organization that was organized in Texas in 1929. It's an organization that is completely volunteer, nonprofit, and deals with social injustice, with educational issues, with health equity, housing issues, and bringing political information to our communities. We're very happy that we were able to get it going here, and we have some really wonderful friends that joined us. In order to start it, you need ten people, and we had twelve people, so that was lucky. We decided to address the health disparities that we have, and we created a completely free health clinic, and we would have doctors volunteer also, and we've been able to give dental treatment to hundreds of people absolutely free, and vision exams and eyeglasses. We've partnered with the new University Health System, and they provide all the primary care free, and we've partnered with Walgreens, and they provide all the vaccines. It's only done once a year, but it's open to the most needy people or even people that have health insurance but don't have dental and vision. It's been a very wonderful project. We enjoy it and we've worked with the UCR medical students and we work with RCC. The students from RCC that started with us ten years ago, they're the ones that run the clinic now. We have been able to work with so many different organizations so that we can have this successful clinic that provides health services to the most needy. It's a wonderful project.

When we first got here, we tried to get support for LULAC. We supported Bill Hedrick when he was running for Congress, and he lost by a lot. It made us look into why this happened. We found out of course that our district was completely gerrymandered. We decided that maybe we could do something about it, and it just so happened that California had established a new commission to redraw the lines for redistricting. We got together with our members, we looked into it, and helped redraw the lines. The maps that we created are the maps that were accepted and the maps that we have today. This is why we saw the results right away. Almost as soon as we finished those maps and they were accepted by the commission, they started having elections and we started to see the difference in who our representatives were.

I've been a board member in LULAC, but for many years I didn't want to be. I was the one that provided the snacks when the board met. I've always supported my husband. I never intended to be president of the organization, but at the time, I had to do it. I told everybody there, "I really have never been president of anything in my life. This is not gonna be easy, but I'm gonna try it, and I'm gonna need your support." And they have, we've done it together. I've never been one to get up and speak in front of people. It's very difficult. I had terrible experiences as a child in

Texas with the school system, and it really affected me. We are dealing with inequity in the schools here in Riverside. We work with Casa Blanca to get the school established there. Our friend Mary Figueroa shared the history and all the bussing, and they need a school on the Eastside too. It's a very sad issue, because it hasn't been addressed, and the school board right now, even though I know all of them and even though we discussed this issue with them one by one, they don't seem to understand that this is urgent now. So we're trying to have them prioritize the Eastside Elementary School along with North High School that needs a lot of repairs, because the children from the Eastside are the ones that attend North. Right now we're organizing in the Eastside. We are now five different organizations that are working together to make a difference. We're not gonna put that on the back burner anymore.

Inspiration

My first role model was my grandmother. She had a powerful influence on me. And my great grandmother, and my mother in some ways that no one would expect. My husband has always been able to deal with difficult situations and confront them. I've always admired that in him. He's not one to step away from an important issue, but he's someone that will deal with it and find some kind of resolution.

The question always comes up for me, "Why in the world do I do this?" I remember Kennedy saying, "Ask not what your country can do for you, ask what you can do for your country." I remember the way he talked when he said it. That had an impact on me and it still does. I still feel it.

Advice

When you see something that is wrong, try to address it. Though it's not easy, it's the best thing in the long run. Many times we'll lose a cause. We won't win. But there are other times that we will win, and we have to think about those, and the impact it has and the lives that are touched. **So keep on trying. It might not be a lot, but to help a little bit makes a difference.**

"Train the community to speak for itself"

Elizabeth Ayala

Roots

I'm a daughter of Latino immigrants. My father is from El Salvador, my mother is from Mexico, and they met in English school in Corona, and that's where I was born and raised. I went through the schools in the school district of Corona up until college. I went to Stanford, then to Washington, D.C., and then I moved back to Riverside County, and then the city of Riverside.

Call to activism

I grew up a child of divorced parents, and both of my parents remarried, so I had exposure to various Latino families and a white American family. That created in me a sense of social observation that is the first step to activism, just seeing the difference between all my cousins. In addition to that, I was tracked early on for honors classes, and I started going to classes that slowly became less and less representative of the very multicultural schools I was in in Corona. By the time I was a senior in high school,

I was the only Latina in my AP chemistry class, when the majority of the high school was Black and brown students. Those kinds of experiences taught me to observe: Why is that?

My parents are immigrants. Their opportunity story is intimately tied to legalization in 1986, and that means my opportunity story is tied to that law change as well. I still have a couple extended family members that are undocumented, so whenever I think of what is happening, it's not out in the news, it's that family member.

I had very strong mentors, especially my high school teachers, Linda Linville and Terry Alice. We read Howard Zinn's *A People's History of the United States* and did a very purposeful compare-and-contrast between the textbook, which was called *An American Pageant*, and Howard Zinn. Early on, that intellectual stimulation created the ability for me to see I can have my own viewpoint of history as well, and that everything that my media consumption or family has been giving me isn't always going to be the whole truth. I loved learning history and fed that desire to both learn and understand what was happening around me.

Being the oldest daughter and the nurturing role that's given to the oldest child in an immigrant household to take care of your siblings, to be a trailblazer in figuring out the United States education system, I probably do have an overdeveloped sense of responsibility. When I was an organizer for Inland Congregations United for Change, so many of my siblings and cousins were in school. When we talked about Proposition 30 to fund schools at a higher level, that wasn't just a philosophical value-laden chant for me; it's personal because I have young siblings. I think that also harkens back, again, to my overdeveloped sense of responsibility. I take politics personally. That's partly where my activism began—that love for my family and wanting them to all have the same outcomes. I think there's something to be said about equal opportunity versus equitable outcomes, because I don't think anyone wants to be poor. I don't think anyone desires their children to *not* succeed in life. And so, if that desire is there amongst all of us, then there are structural things that are producing unequal outcomes.

I studied International Relations in college. I had a stint in a couple different nonprofit roles in Washington, D.C., and then after that, my first nonprofit job in the inland region was at Inland Congregations United for

Change. I didn't know exactly what community organizing was when I started at ICUC. I began as an office administrator, but I knew I wanted to learn about community organizing, and I knew this organization was doing good work, so I hoped to be a part of that. Trying out different roles really helped me understand the different ways our intersecting movements can make an impact. It gives me great hope that since I began working in 2006-2007 in the inland region at nonprofits, the sector has grown substantially. There is more funding coming in after some excellent studies from the James Irvine Foundation looking at the disproportionate funding in our region. There are stronger coalitions. There's a learning culture. I'm really happy to see how much our region's advocacy and social justice sector has grown.

Contributions

I have worked on socio-economic issues, such as bank accountability and housing foreclosure prevention. I was involved in the Occupy Riverside movement. I helped start a grassroots organization called 28ers, which is looking at the need to pass a 28th Amendment to change the role of money in politics. I work remotely now for the Solís Policy Institute (SPI) of the Women's Foundation of California. The mission of the Women's Foundation of California is to promote racial, economic, and gender justice—it's very intersectional in its approach to gender justice. In 2015, I was a fellow in the inaugural SPI local program when they did a pilot program specifically in the county of Riverside. It was a wonderful experience because I met so many women—cis and trans women and gender nonconforming individuals. I was a participant in the Solís Policy Institute first, and then I started working for the Foundation as a program manager.

My largest responsibility is curriculum development and the retreat and webinar execution. My role is to recruit the participants and then to look at the essential pieces we think they need to learn how to advance local government policy objectives, as well as bringing in advisors and doing guidance phone calls, because you can't just receive information, we also need to think with partners to process. I've been so excited and fortunate to see teams of fellows do amazing learning and work across the state. One of the most recent achievements was a team of fellows in the county of Los Angeles advancing a board motion at the L.A. County Supervisors level to support finding more funding for doulas to address the infant and maternal mortality gap with Black women, who are two or three times more likely to die in childbirth than their white counterparts, regardless of socioeconomic background. Then they achieved this motion at the Board of Supervisors level, but the skills that they gained from learning policy apply to other local government issues, apply to other government levels. I really appreciated that experience when I was a fellow, and so I'm hopeful that I'm giving that experience to our participants as well. We're also making sure that they're helping us form what a feminist movement looks like. Gender justice doesn't get relegated to just cis women's needs. It includes trans women, it includes non-binary, gender non-conforming individuals.

One of the threads within my work has been teaching or training or facilitating. I'm a board member for a small nonprofit called Child Leader Project where we try to create experiential learning programs that produce that deep reflective thinking that is social justice-oriented for our youth here in Riverside. **As a community organizer, your role is not to speak for the community; it's to train the community to speak for itself.** I have played a large role in trying to educate. In my current role as the program manager for the Solís Policy Institute Local, I facilitate a program where we bring together fellows to learn deep advocacy and leadership development by not just learning what a local budget typically looks like, but going out and advocating for it, by doing. I've also learned a lot from all of the participants that go through our programs. Many of the times they can be the trainer—the teacher in front of the room. We try to facilitate that cross-fellow learning as well.

A common challenge for local community activists or anyone in the trenches as a social justice advocate is you do a lot of work, but you're not necessarily sure when the fruit produces. I was let go from ICUC, partly due to a budget cut and funding not coming in anymore for my particular campaigns. That was a really difficult period right after that, because there was a lot of self-doubt. I knew I had the ability to forge relationships, which is so necessary to create change, but my trajectory has had many shadows of doubt, and that's very common amongst our community members. Sometimes we lose, that could be a campaign, that could be a vote within a city council, that could be loss of funding within an organization that decimates its ability to do some of its work. There are some seasons where I'm like, "What have I done?"

When I was more active in Arlanza Community Garden, that felt good because it was a very physical manifestation where I could say, because of my hundreds of hours of work, that garden revived. I think it's important for those of us who are leaders in the community to talk about those shadow times. There have been other shadow times associated with my mental health. I'm bipolar, and I'm very open about that because it's another social justice issue—there's a lot of shame, there's a lot of stigma, there's a lot of unknowns about mental illness. I have tried to find liberation and leadership and honesty. I struggle with what my story is. Sometimes it seems very disparate, with starts and stops, but I think that's true for a lot of us. I've been working on reclaiming some of that confidence and proud moments where I think, "I can do this work, I am being helpful to the fellows, I am being helpful to the city of Riverside." In my current role, I feel really whole because we're also being there holistically for our fellows. It's not just about the work, it's about their personal tie to the work, it's their personal leadership in the work.

Inspiration

One of my current inspirations is the writer adrienne maree brown. She has written a book called *Emergent Strategy,* looking at [how the] ways that we organize on the small scale impact the large scale, following some of the principles of Octavia Butler, the science fiction writer. Her second book is *Pleasure Activism*. She says the revolution must be pleasurable, or if it's not appealing, why the hell are we doing it anyway? That concept that activism needs to be based in our ability to imagine ourselves fulfilled, to imagine ourselves experiencing joy, has been something interesting for me, because back in 2011, a lot of my organizing was motivated by that righteous, cold anger. But I don't think that's sustainable, and adrienne maree brown says the revolution is for our mutual liberation and pleasure. I'm not angry anymore; I'm trying to add to the concept of well-being in the work, and well-being as the outcome that we want for our communities.

Advice

Reflect on what sustains you in this work. Reflection and just reflection, period. I keep a journal to document gratitude moments but also pride moments. I am very hard on myself, and I know a lot of women organizers are. But if you reflect on both your gratitude and pride moments, I think a lot more organizers would realize, actually, I did do something! I am capable, or I am experienced enough, I am knowledgeable enough. I encourage reflection, especially centered around our moments of courage, our moments where we were the only one in the staff meeting advocating for a different direction in the campaign, where we were the only one at the public comment speaking our truth and the truth about our communities. I'm always inspired and look for those stories of courage amongst my fellow activists, and that's one thing that I hope to keep nurturing amongst myself and those in my circles. How do we sustain and provide inspiration and give sustenance to our courage because I struggle with being courageous in interpersonal conversations with some of my family members that I disagree with? But those moments are necessary. I struggle, and I still get nerves from doing public comment at a local government agency. I still struggle and get nerves when I am being called on to be interviewed by any media outlet. But the courage is what will help us say what needs to be said.

The other advice is to find mentors, and sometimes the most helpful mentors are not the ones with the big titles, are not the ones with the positional power, but the community power, the relational power, the interest in your growth.

I think we need to celebrate more. There's a lot of work to be done in our communities, in our global community. There's a lot that we don't do right, but there are still things that we do correctly, or that we do in earnest and with positive impact, and to celebrate—not just the win or the accomplishment or the thing that was done, but to celebrate yourself. We need moments of joy. That includes celebration, and that includes community care, taking care of yourself, taking care of our communities, being a part of taking care of our communities.

For some of us the fear will never go away. The fear of failure, or the fear that our families face in legitimate physical terms, but we do it anyway. That anger at the injustice, that fear about what could happen to our families if health care remains a privatized business, for example, is not what's going to be fueling us, but it can sit there next to us. What should be fueling us, I believe, is courage and love of ourselves, our community, and our spiritual selves. For me, I think partly due to my growth as a community organizer with Inland Congregations United for Change

(ICUC), there is a spiritual element that we can't ignore when it comes to our movements, when it comes to sacred anger, when it comes to holy joy, that must be fed. And I am hoping, as I grow older, I'm feeding more and more the joy and the love part, and that we're all in a community that has those resources already. We have the resources to be resilient, we have the resources to create joy, to create moments of love, and I don't have to go out and find those, they're within my community, they're within myself. I hope more of the rising activists build that for themselves, acknowledge that for themselves, work on that every day for themselves, because that's what's going to sustain us, and that's the ultimate goal of our work. It's that joy, that love, and that sense of well-being.

I used to think that my singing is a different thing from my activism, but part of that joy that I hope I'm cultivating is in art. Art that inspires is such an important part of our movement. The best marches I've been to have some form of music involved. Sometimes I play music when I'm feeling angry about a situation. Nina Simone has been on my mind a lot recently—that's the music I gravitate to, and it's part of that sustenance that's so necessary.

"We were dismissed as hysterical housewives"

Penny Newman

Roots

I was born on May 30, 1947, in Oakland. We moved to Southern California when I was very young. We first lived out in Coachella. My dad ran the water district there for a while. We moved for a short time into Rubidoux, then settled in Perris.

Call to activism

I think it goes back to my parents really instilling in us that we are part of a community and it's our responsibility to make that community the place we want it to be, that there's fairness and justice and that we need to treat our neighbors equally and to be a part of solving problems.

I got married, and in 1965, we moved to Riverside in the Glen Avon area. As we were being drawn into the Stringfellow battle [over the Stringfellow Acid Pits toxic waste site], we looked at it as a short-term thing: We'll just bring the facts to the decision-makers, since they probably didn't understand that we were having chemicals released into our community, so we would let them know, and then they'd do the right thing. We soon found out that in many cases, they already know the facts. They just don't give a shit about us. That was very life-changing to me. **I had not been around people who didn't care for others. When I confronted that, it really startled me and made me look at the world differently.**

Contributions

When we started with Stringfellow, it was just a matter of some of the local moms getting together and saying, "This isn't right and our children are at risk and we need to do something." As we started organizing, it soon became clear after the first year went by and then the second year went by that this was a long-term battle. It really wasn't just about Stringfellow. This is about the system and the way our system of governance works, and that we need to change *it* if we're going to have changes in our community. So, that made us realize we had to come up with something a little more permanent. We incorporated as Concerned Neighbors in Action so that we were a recognized entity. We had to become incorporated, especially when we filed a lawsuit that ended up going to the Supreme Court.

I don't think in the beginning we thought of it as building anything. **We were just trying to survive and to make sure our families were protected.** We had no organizing training. I didn't even know what organizing was, other than cleaning out your closet or something. But we knew we had to do something, so we got together and just by the seat of our pants tried different things. We found what worked and what didn't. We connected with other communities and saw that they were going through the same thing. We started talking with those communities and finding out what they were trying and what worked and didn't work, and then combining our efforts so that we could have more influence in Sacramento. After a while, we had gotten enough credibility under our belts where we weren't just dismissed as hysterical housewives anymore, but they actually were paying attention, because everything we said happened. Then we started attracting some of the other environmental organizations. They bring their contacts and credibility into the effort as well. The people who have the most credibility are those who are having to live with it day in and day out. They know these issues inside and out. It doesn't take much after meeting with an elected official to find out you know more than they ever will.

We just went through what working-class women do to work in their community, like you do with the PTA. That's the way I became chairman of Concerned Neighbors in Action. I had been a PTA president, and they said, "Well, you know how to run the meeting, so you do it." And then it stuck, because the press likes to have one person to go to. I think that was our biggest mistake in the whole effort, was having me as the spokesperson. I became identified rather than all the other people who were doing such phenomenal work alongside me, but I was the face of what was happening.

We went through that, we went through our lawsuits, we went through our personal injury lawsuits and all that. It got to '91 to'93 when we decided, we're having a lot of people call us wanting to know, "How did you do this?" There's a lot of people who are in a position where they're being harmed, and they don't know how to get through this decision-making process. They don't know who to call, they don't know how the decisions are made. They don't know how to bring their stories forward. We decided after consulting with a lot of people around the area that we didn't want to just create another nonprofit that's going to take a bunch of grant money. We end up competing against each other and we don't accomplish the goals we want to do. We took a long time to think about, do we need another nonprofit, an ongoing one, and what should be the mission of that nonprofit? That's when the Center for Community Action and Environmental Justice (CCAEJ) was born. We turned CNA into the Center so that we could look beyond Stringfellow. We wanted to make some place where people could come and learn the lessons we had learned so that they didn't make the mistakes we made starting out, and could learn a little faster. We thought this would then give a little more balance to the battle if they had somebody to consult with them.

The goal was to change the system. Having one person or one group isn't going to change the system. You need to have the knowledge coming from different communities, and multiply that knowledge and multiply the efforts to change the inequities that are out there. It's that idea of by and for the people, that we need to be involved, we don't just elect somebody and forget about it, that we have to hold them responsible that they are representing us. They're the ones who vote. They have to know that we are either in favor of them voting a certain way or not, and doing what they need to do to represent us.

I think there's been some real significant accomplishments on a lot of different levels, but the fact that CCAEJ is still going strong after forty years, that it has a strong reputation, that we do good, and that's the purpose of the organization. We brought a lot of people through the organization that have learned their own strengths and have learned their own skills and talents and have expanded them that are now out in the community doing other things. I think it's changing the Inland Empire and changing it for the better.

I think we've, number one, brought women's voices forward so that we're not dismissed like we were. We certainly were called at various times these "hysterical housewives." You'd go to the Board of Supervisors and they'd be reading the paper, or getting up. It was extremely disrespectful. I think giving community members credibility to have a voice in local elections and local governance is important, and we've gotten a number of local residents to run for office. We had one woman who was scared to death to talk in front of a school board, but she wanted filters put on the water system. I said, "Well, what is it that you want to say?" She wrote it out and then we practiced it over and over and over again so she would be comfortable. She made me stand next to her when she got to the podium. But she delivered very passionate comments. Afterward, she said, "I never thought I could ever do something like that. You gave me the confidence to do it." I said, "That's all you needed. You had the knowledge, you had the ability to do it, you just needed a little confidence." Those are the successes that I remember. Those are the things that touch my heart the most. I like winning different policies and stuff, but seeing people change and come to their own, find their voice, is such a blessing to me.

When we started CCAEJ and were going through the discussion about what we want the organization to be, we made a decision that we wanted the board to be all female. Because we wanted these women in our community to have the opportunity to serve on a board, to learn how a board operates, to develop their own confidence and their understanding of financials, and developing policies and all of that, how to do fundraising, we wanted another learning space for women to be able to advance through that. It wasn't until just a couple years ago that we had some men join the board, and we've had men on the staff off and on throughout the whole thing. We always hire who we think are the most qualified, but it's qualified in terms of who can work in the community the best. That's not necessarily whether you have a degree or anything, it's how much do you know the area? How much do you know the community? How much can you relate to people? Not everybody can be an organizer. It takes a certain personality.

I think all of the policies that we've developed on toxic chemicals came directly out of our community and the work we were doing. I take great pride in that. I also recognize now that a victory is only a temporary victory.

I was getting ready to retire with very mixed feelings, because I really loved what I was doing, but I really felt it was necessary so new leadership could step forward. When [Riverside County] Supervisor Tavaglione said he wasn't running again, [it] made an opportunity for somebody to step forward. Having an open seat makes a big difference in running for an office. I had a lot of people who came to me and said, "This is the time, Penny. You're retiring, you need to do this. We need you. The board needs a change, and here's an opportunity." I debated it for quite a long time. I even went to South Africa with a girlfriend of mine. We went on a safari and I met some organizers there and really contemplated what I should be doing. I came back and decided, "No, I'm not going to run. There's other people who could do this." But then I went to a meeting and we were talking about who to get to run, and they all said, "Well, Penny's going to," and I said, "Well, no." And they kept saying, "you need to do this." I thought, "There is absolutely no reason for me not to do this." It would be a challenge, it would be something I haven't done. I thought, if nothing else, you'll learn a lot. So I decided to throw my hat in and run. It was a phenomenal experience. I loved meeting new people. There's nothing more challenging than to go to a door that you don't know and knock on it and, you know, talk to them. It brought me back to my organizing days, which I'd gotten out of, because I had been administrating, which is not my favorite. That's why I decided to do it. And I totally believed I could make a significant difference with Riverside County. We held our first fundraiser at my house, because I wanted people to know where I lived, and that I am part of the community, and if you have a problem, you come to me. I'm here to listen to you. For better or worse, that's what we did.

Inspiration

When we started, I never had any role models. I couldn't find anybody who was doing what we were doing. We couldn't get anybody to help us. So my role models are the other women who were involved that nobody will really know—Sally Merha and Christine Smith and Linda Spinney and Elaine Leyva and Lynn Spotswood—they're women who came together week after week, meeting in living rooms, deciding what we were going to do and trying to figure out the next step, and piling into this old red van that one of the gals had to go to a picket someplace those are the ones who taught me how to do things. We came up with it as a group and carried it out as a group and never had anybody saying, "Okay, now is when you do such and such."

There are local people who help guide me. Dina Stallings was a professor at RCC, and she really helped me see where my values were and where I should be going. I was thinking of quitting teaching and doing Stringfellow full time, and it was really hard. She gave us an assignment in this leadership class—she wanted to know what our philosophy of life was. I came up with the idea that everyone is born with special skills and talents, that you have a responsibility to develop them to their fullest, and that you're put here to use those talents and skills at their optimum to help the rest of the people around you. Thinking about that, I said, "How am I doing with teaching versus what I could do with Stringfellow?" Then another very influential woman, Deenaz Coachbuilder, who was my supervisor in special ed. when I was teaching at Jurupa Middle School, said, "Penny, anybody can be trained for speech pathology. We have courses, we have good people to walk them through that. You've been put in a special place. You have unique knowledge. You've experienced this firsthand. You know who you need to be dealing with. You are in a unique space. You need to follow that through. There's a reason you've been put in that position." So that pushed me over the edge, and I quit and walked away and started working on Stringfellow full time.

Shirley Chisholm has been an icon to me. I'm absolutely enthralled with Kamala Harris. She was out here and joined us on a lawsuit. She went to Mira Loma and visited with the residents who were impacted by the trucks, a hundred trucks going by every hour. The way that she treated the residents and listened to them with such respect and gave them so much dignity, especially when one family invited her in to meet their special needs child. We had press galore there, and she told the press, "No, you don't come in. This is private." And I thought, any politician who would pass up a golden photo op and be able to talk with someone, she had me then.

Advice

Know yourself, have confidence in yourself. Don't let people tell you you're not worthy.

I think it's important for people to study what has happened before them, to realize that the reason they can now vote is because there were women who stood up, laying that ground, and that they now have the opportunity to take it to the next step. I've really tried with some of the young people locally to understand the history that they come out of, that this community is the one who has created the policies and laws that have made life a lot better for everyone across the U.S., and that they need to be proud of that. A lot of times the I.E. does not get much respect, and it's important for us to claim that respect and not let others take it from us. I'm thrilled with the new generation. I think that they're much more open to the diversity of our region. I think they're much more open to the differences among people. And I think they've got a heck of a battle ahead of them. We still have a lot of work to do, and we can learn lessons from previous battles.

I think we have to be smart and keep ourselves safe. I think we need to watch out for each other. Trust your instincts. We all have that little voice in us that tells us, "This is not a good situation, I'm not safe here, this isn't where I'm happy, this isn't the job that I should be in." We need to start listening to that instinct. I think a lot of the success we've had is the ability to recognize, "Wait a minute, this isn't where we should be going," and that has led to us being successful in a lot of situations. **We underestimate what our inner voice can tell us, and we need to listen.**

I think I've learned a lot of lessons over the years that have made me a better person, that have made me understand that a lot of people react in ways because they're having a hard time, and I think we sometimes need to recognize that life is hard and people are going through it the best they can, and we all screw up, and we need to cut some slack to each other. Just because somebody doesn't agree with fracking, doesn't mean you write 'em off. It may take them time to get to a point where they would agree with you on that. But we need to be better human beings, just all around. I'm glad I've come to realize that, because then I don't get mad at people who say nasty things about me, you know. I understand that there's a public persona and there's a person, and it's not necessarily the same thing.

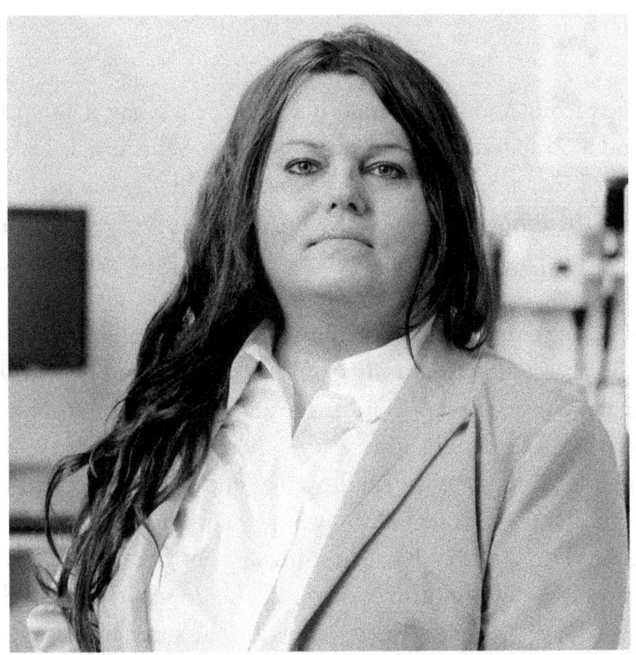

"Everything's a process"

Thomi Clinton

Roots

I was born in 1970 in East Chicago, Indiana, but I was mostly raised in Hammond, Indiana. From there, my family moved to Arkansas, and from there, I moved to California around 2000. California was more embracing and had a lot of civil protections then, and a lot larger, diverse community. So I migrated to Los Angeles, which was stupendous, and then over time I settled in the valley because the cost of living was a lot better. I came to Riverside in 2008. I moved here for opportunity and love.

Call to activism

I was called to activism in 1987 during the AIDS pandemic. I have always been involved, since about 1988 in Arkansas, and at the time I was a gay boy and I was very effeminate. I got detained for putting on the first gay pride picnic, and praise God, if it wasn't for a gay man with a purple tunic and a cockatoo, I probably would have went to jail. I made a decision when I was around twenty-five that I was doing my part. It was horrible back then, horrible, especially in Arkansas. We were told as children that if you kissed a boy, you would have AIDS. So at that age I thought I had AIDS because I didn't know better. We weren't given information to educate ourselves with anything considered to be taboo. I tried to commit suicide because I didn't want my parents to know that I had AIDS because I kissed a boy even though I didn't have it. It was a tough time back then just surviving. I lost about ninety-seven percent of my friends from AIDS complications, and there were quite a few suicides we had to go through in the process. Hate crime legislation was just coming around. It was a tough time to survive. Our gay bar had a metal door because [of] people who drive by and throw Molotov cocktails at the door. When I sit down with people who say, "Oh, my life is so horrible," I share with them, your life has a lot of splendor compared to '87, '88.

Contributions

I was asked to sit on a commission to create the policies for the Prison Rape Elimination Act, which was implemented after the Supreme Court found in *Farmer v. Brennan* that sexual assault in prison is considered cruel and unusual punishment that is not part of being incarcerated. Prior to that, a trans woman could be sexually assaulted, and they had no recourse in the judicial system. They implemented our recommendations, and they created these national correctional standards to ensure prisons and jails are safe for LGBT people. It was a big feather in my cap. This impacts millions of people across the nation. Prisons have to accommodate a trans person, where before, they were just left to fend for themselves. Now there are precautions so maybe their ability to rehabilitate is higher, instead of more PTSD and rape trauma syndrome which make it more difficult to rebuild. I've also created police contact policies for the city of Riverside and the Sheriff's Department and other cities.

I was the co-founder of the Inland Empire Health Plan Gender Health Policies and Program, which serve transgender, gender non-conforming, and intersex people in the Inland Empire. I was recently appointed to the county Mental Health Initiative to make sure that trans people are included in the Mental Health Initiative, and I'm part of the committee for the Riverside University Public Health System and their suicide prevention programs. Riverside County has one of the highest rates of suicide in the nation. We started the first Transgender Health and Wellness Center with the Transgender Community Coalition, and now we have four locations. I struggled for some time. But I have twenty employees, where it was just me in the beginning. We actually employ the most trans people of a non-profit in Southern California at this time. I've been told someone was trying to compete with me, but good luck! Sometimes competitive is good, because it helps you improve things all together.

I, myself, do not believe that you get a vacation if you go into activism to help others, because people are depending on you. You have to be there for those people, no matter who it is and when they need you. It's important that people who decide to get into it establish themselves as someone there if someone's in crisis. If you get into this, you're going to get messages through Facebook, you're going to get text messages, you're going to have to do all this stuff, and you have to prepare for that. It can be challenging, especially dealing with a highly marginalized community like the transgender community, which is still fighting for the rights to use bathrooms.

I know that my people are harvesting the fruits of the hard labor. They're able to access health care, housing, the rescue missions are becoming more inclusive as best they can and police officers are being trained. There's all these things that are going on now that weren't going on. It can be a very bumpy ride, but it's rewarding to be able to see people access equity.

Inspiration

Laverne Cox, Marsha P. Johnson, and Sylvia Rivera. They all came from struggle, and they all were strong willed. They were like, "I'm changing this, and there's nothing you can do about it." And I really liked that. I really appreciate that type of mentality.

Advice

Follow your heart and realize that those that try to put you down, that it's not about you but about them. Through my years of activism in Riverside County, I've had to be very strong willed, and I've had to push. You have to understand that the system is not designed for us, so navigation to accomplish your goal is never going to be a straight line. The challenge that the trans community faces is some trans people do align themselves with cis-gender people and some cis-gender people are uncomfortable sharing privilege. Unfortunately, male privilege is a big issue, and we within the LGBT community have had to evolve and work with each other, too. **It's a process and that's okay, because everything's a process.**

"The gay people to talk to"

Connie Confer

Roots

I was born in Milton, Pennsylvania in 1942. It's a small, blue-collar town. I went to Penn State. All my family were Republicans. I registered as a Republican when I first got old enough to register, and actually was a Republican until I was moved by Ronald Reagan's first term as governor to register as a Democrat.

My aunt and cousin lived in Riverside and I stayed with them for a little while, thinking about staying permanently. Then I moved around a bit more and ended up in Riverside in 1969. I worked as a social worker for a number of years in Sonoma County and in Riverside County. I eventually realized that I was as far as I could go in social work with a bachelor's degree. I went to law school at night while working and passed the bar the first time. I became a lawyer and went from working at the county welfare department as a child welfare worker to being a Deputy City Attorney and eventually Assistant City Attorney with the city of Riverside.

I was aware at a fairly young age that I was a lesbian. When I was in third or fourth grade and we started studying homonyms and word relationships, I thought that since homo meant the same as, and hetero meant different than, I assumed that I was a heterosexual, because I knew then I was different than other people. I didn't really understand the terminology or what was really involved, but I knew that I was different than other kids from a very early age. In the forties and fifties, there weren't people to talk to about that, and so my early years were not spent politically, they were spent trying to figure out how I would live in the world as a person who was in the closet. How will I ever find anyone to love? It's a very lonely place to be. I didn't quite know how that was going to work out. Although my family was very loving, I never felt comfortable until I was in my thirties discussing the fact that I was a lesbian with them. So there were lonely parts to my childhood, but in general I was a very supported, loved child, and I had grandparents around and some aunts and uncles, and I felt very loved and cared for. I had a nice stable early life except for that one issue, which made things a little weird.

I did suffer some of the kind of disrespectful, unhappy things that happen to people who are gay. I was refused a hotel room when I tried to register with another woman. I was told, "We don't rent to your kind." When I first went to work for the county in 1969, one of the questions on the medical questionnaire for new employees asked if I had ever had sex with someone of the same gender. I lied. I think I wouldn't have been hired if I hadn't. That makes your whole employment feel very tenuous because they could always say, "Well, you lied on your application, so we can fire you for lying." I had those kinds of experiences, but meanwhile I fell in love with a woman and was making a life with her, though we were very, very closeted and not political. But in 1969, I was aware of Stonewall. I was tuned in somewhat to national news, especially about gay people. I knew that Illinois was the one place where it wasn't illegal to be gay. I knew that in California, it was illegal. I knew that *Life* magazine did the big spread in the sixties about gay people who were starting to express their desire to have equal rights with other people. Believe me, at that time we were not even talking about marriage.

Call to activism

I certainly became aware in this pre-activist period of not being treated equally, of a feeling that there was an unfairness to the way things were. But there was an organization in town that had a very closeted name, and it was for professionals who were gay to get together. Once a month we would have dinner at a local restaurant and we would have speakers come. Then we had a men's rap group and a women's rap group, and we separated for that, but at the main we were men and women together, and there were a lot of women who participated in it. It was wonderful. We had people come who were sort of famous in the moment and come and speak to us. In 1978, there was a proposition in California, Proposition 6, directed at school teachers who were gay or other school personnel who would speak in support of gay people. It was an outgrowth of the Anita Bryant campaign in Florida, and it was very vicious. There was a local group that was doing local organizing with respect to that proposition, and I went to a few meetings. I wasn't very involved in it, but I was very interested in it. And I would say that my activism really began when I told friends that I regularly went out to dinner with, "I'm going to put a 'No on 6' bumper sticker on my car, and you may not want to ride with me anymore." This was a huge step for me. I did, and they continued to ride with me. From then on, I was step by step by step taking a greater step out into activism. **I can say basically that it all started with a bumper sticker.**

My partner from 1979 on and my friend for the ten years before that was Kay Smith, and Kay and I did this together. She was a little older than I and she was very involved when she lived up in the Bay Area against 1964's Proposition 14, which repealed the Rumford Act, which was the act which made redlining illegal in California. That proposition passed, however, then the California Supreme Court found it unconstitutional. Kay went door to door, dragging, as I understand, her two children along with her. We were really close friends and then we became lovers, and I was inspired by her and we did our main body of our political work together.

Contributions

Kay and I were among the founding members of PACE [Political Action Coalition for Elections], which was the political action committee active from 1985 to 1998. Our call was local elections. We interviewed candidates and we raised money by having fundraisers to give to candidates. We would schedule interviews with candidates, and we learned a lot! Initially, the first go-round, people would say, "Well, but I don't want you to give me any more than ninety-nine dollars," because that was the level where then their contribution would be public record. Some reporter would go and find out that this person had taken money from an LGBT group! So the first time, we allowed people to do that. We hadn't thought it through completely. But after that, always part of our interview was now of course, "If we do endorse your candidacy, we will be providing you with more than ninety-nine dollars of financial support." That was an interesting stress point for some people to whether or not they would even ask for our endorsement. Some of them didn't want us to come to their home because we were gay, which apparently meant we were sexually uncontrollable and we might do something embarrassing, so there were people who wanted to meet at Denny's, or at the library, or who wanted to only meet us in a public forum.

I had been on the board of the spouse abuse coalition, and I had other board-type experience, so I was recruited to come on the board of the Inland AIDS Project when it started its work in Riverside. Kay was on the Human Relations Commission at the city. She was an openly lesbian person on the board. She encouraged the board to recommend to the city that they include HIV and AIDS anti-discrimination in the contracts that the city had with people, and that actually was done, and the city of Riverside has a clause relating to that nondiscrimination on the basis of sexual orientation and HIV status, as well as the other list of things that you don't want to discriminate on before it became part of state law. It caused at that time the development of a petition on the part of community members who thought that was a terrible idea to have that stricken, and that was when People for Responsible Behavior had people coming out from Orange County to support their position. It was a very dramatic time, and Kay was vilified at board meetings, at city council meetings. It was disgusting, the things that people said about her and about gay people in general.

There would be public hearings with people lined up along the side of the council chambers, hot, sweaty bodies very distressed and late into the night. It was a very dramatic time. Eventually, the city hired outside council to give an opinion. They said that they really had to follow the law, the constitution, and that they should not put their proposition to take out those provisions on the ballot. The city won at the superior court level, and then it went to the court of appeal, and I was able to work with ACLU and Lambda Legal defense and education lawyers on the city's response. It was so exciting because I was working with these nationally known lawyers who were living in my conference room in City Hall, working with me on these briefs and on the documents to be filed, and then I was able to be one of the attorneys that argued at the court of appeal. That was a high point of my legal career.

Kay and I got to be known as "the gay people to talk to." We were on everybody's rolodex. We also went to the LGBT March on Washington. We were very involved with the [AIDS Memorial] quilt. We marched in Sacramento, we marched every place there was a place to go march. We marched in gay pride in Los Angeles. I was working with the AIDS Project, I and two other lawyers set up a legal clinic so we could work with people who were having legal problems as far as their illness. And, you know, everybody died at the beginning. I mean, there weren't any people who didn't die, so everybody needed to have help—setting up who would be the guardian of a woman's child after she died, sitting on a bed of somebody who was obviously going to die soon, taking his words down so that I could do a quickly drawn will for him to sign, writing letters to creditors saying, you know, the guy is going to die. He has no money. You can sue him if you want to, but our advice to you would be to just forget it, because there's no hope for you, you're never going to get your money and just stop harassing this guy.

Kay and I were more of the suits. There are streets and there are suits in political work. We were more the suits than the streets, although we went to a lot of demonstrations. But we weren't the down-and-dirty folks. We were more board members. But in some respects we did get down in the weeds with people that were needing real help. Kay worked on the hotline at the gay and lesbian community center for a long time as a volunteer. We were part of their training, we did a unit for them on LGBT issues and how to handle a call if someone called in. We were just sort of everywhere about gay stuff, and if anybody needed someone to talk at their meeting or something, we often got called. I overheard Ron Loveridge telling someone else one time that he thought Kay was the most effective public political activist, citizen activist, of anyone that he knew.

We registered as domestic partners the first weekend that we could. We were, I think, couple 124 in the state, because we mailed it in, and so we couldn't be down there at the Secretary of State's office at eight o'clock in the morning, but we did it as quickly as we could. And then we were married just a few months before Kay died.

Inspiration

Kay was a big influence and inspiration. We both were very inspired by Dolores Huerta and her story of activism early on and her raising all these kids in labor camps and fighting with such incredible intensity. She was down in Riverside the week that the Cesar Chavez memorial was dedicated, and I got there early and had a chance to talk with her and tell her how her having included LGBT issues at some point despite the distress of the men in the union, the farm workers union at the time, that she did, and that her insistence that, no, she had to work for everyone's rights, was so inspiring to us. We really loved that she did that, but also just admired her whole posture of resistance.

Advice

You have to be passionate about what it is you're being an activist about, because being an activist is exhausting. And it is sometimes crushing. And if you don't have that fire in your belly about the issue, if it doesn't mean something very important to you, then you won't be able to sustain it.

In my early life I was dealing with being a lesbian and not having support or dealing with negative things that happened to me, and feeling that anger and seeing the lack of fairness, the lack of knowledge that people had. We know the most important political act of a gay person is to come out.

Love and Riverside

Erin Edwards

Roots

I was born in Peru, Illinois in December of 1983. We moved here when my partner Liz got a job at the University of California, Riverside. So, love brought me to Riverside. When we moved here, I said, "Well it's so wonderful for you, Liz, that you have a job. What am I going to do?" I feel very lucky to have found meaningful work here. We really do love this city.

Call to activism

I can't remember a moment where I was called to activism. I've always been a reader. I'm an only child so I spent a lot of time with my imagination, and with books and characters. The books that I read when I was young had very strong female characters who would ask questions and test boundaries and would stand up for what they believed was right. I used to actually stand in the driveway of my house in rural Illinois, in a subdivision, and read these books out loud to myself almost as if I were in a play. They were really a part of me in a lot of ways. The characters felt very real to me so I wonder if some of that was what inspired me to ask questions and to stand up for what I believed was right.

It wasn't until much later than I wish to admit that I thought about privilege and equity in the ways that I have come to understand them now. I grew up in the same town and I was there until I left for undergrad. I went to a liberal arts college on the border of Illinois and Iowa that at the time was the perfect fit for me. I did a lot of growing there in many good ways. It wasn't until after I graduated from undergrad and went to work for AmeriCorps that I really understood the idea of equity. I remember people I admired in my AmeriCorps cohort telling me about books they were reading. I was reading bell hooks in the gym because someone had recommended it to me. I very clearly remember a moment where I stopped moving on the treadmill and almost fell off. I had, for the first time, the understanding that I was white and what that meant, and the privilege that came from it. I'm embarrassed that it took so long for me to really understand and start to have those critical conversations. As I'm trying to live values of equity, part of that value system is to always be asking questions.

I worked for an organization which is now called College Possible, at the time it was called Admission Possible. Now it's a national model, but at the time it was only in Minnesota. Their work is to help low-income high school students get into college. I had so many extraordinary opportunities in college. I really grew there, and I wanted everyone to have that experience. While I was doing AmeriCorps, it was all-consuming and it was a foundational experience for me in understanding the systems that held people back and the privileges I had, and didn't have, but mostly had.

I made the decision to apply for a master's program at the University of Wisconsin, Madison, and did the international development track there.

In doing my own research and building on research I had done in undergrad, I was very interested in the Caribbean, particularly in Haiti, and I wanted to do my internship there. The master's program has someone who tries to pair students with internships and they didn't have anything to send anyone to Haiti and I said, "But I'm going there." I ended up spending three months living in Haiti and working for a nonprofit. That experience set me off on a different trajectory because I had always loved to write. I had developed a pretty good skill set in writing and people would say, "You know, you'd be a great grant writer." I said, "I don't want to be a grant writer. I don't want to think about money all day. I don't want to write for money, I have no interest in that." Then my first day working for this nonprofit in Haiti, the secretary said, "Thank goodness you're here because we need you to write a grant for us this summer. It's June and we haven't been paid since April." I did spend the summer writing a grant and it was quite a crash course in how money is perhaps one of the most important things that we can be paying attention to if we have an interest in shifting power, because often money is seen as power. **If we want to shift power, we have to understand where the money is, who has it, how it's distributed and what systems exist to distribute that.** That moment really changed my thinking and pushed me on a longer trajectory within the nonprofit and philanthropy sector. **It got me thinking about what my role could be and should be and where I could be the most useful. It's a question I've never stopped asking.**

I thought I would do work in international development. I thought that's where my niche would be, and then I realized the laws were different, and if I wanted to work for the UN, my same-sex partner wouldn't be able to come with me or could come but at my expense and wouldn't be recognized. I thought, "Maybe this isn't what I'm meant to do."

I went from this very local U.S. context to an international context and then to the very local again. I ended up directing a network of soup kitchens, food pantries, and homeless shelters on the North Side of Chicago. It gave me another lens and another hat to wear in a nonprofit organization. I went on to be a grant writer for an organization in Chicago, and I really got to dive into the role of how you write for money and what it takes to fundraise. From there, I was looking for a role where I could flip sides and come from the philanthropy grantmaking side and distribute the grants and understand how that was done. I had a role at United Way in Canada while Liz was doing her Fulbright where I had a portfolio of health investments and got to be in the role of the grantmaker.

When we were living in Winnipeg, I started volunteering for this organization called the MATCH International Women's Fund [now The Equality Fund]. I met their executive director at a dinner and learned more about her and the organization and left that night thinking, "I'm going to work for this woman." I stayed in contact with her, and she wrote me an email one day out of the blue and said, "We have some short-term needs. I want to talk to you about a job." It was really the dream scenario. I had a phone conversation with her where she offered me a job to move from Winnipeg to Ottawa to start working for this extraordinary organization to think about their marketing and branding campaign around International Women's Day. Liz, my partner, was at a choir rehearsal that night and I remember she came home and I was bursting to tell her that I had just been offered my dream job in Ottawa. She came in the door and she said, "I have amazing news for you!" and I said, "I have amazing news for you!" She said, "I just got a job!" and I said, "I just got a job!" Her job was here in Riverside and my job was in Ottawa so we did what you do, which is try to make it work. Luckily, my new boss was willing to be flexible, and she said, "Well, come for six months before you move to California. Work on this project with us and then you can be on your way." We did that, we moved to Ottawa for six months, we lived in five different apartments, slept on couches and on people's floors. We then moved to Riverside. But the job for me was so wonderful, and I was growing and learning. I felt like I had a lot to give there, and I think they felt the same because they said, "Why don't you just stay on?" I was able to do many roles there with communications, fundraising, and strategic planning.

I never would have thought that I would run for office. When someone brought it up as even a possibility, I remember thinking it was so absurd. I was working on a story for my job at the MATCH International Women's Fund where I interviewed a woman from Kenya who was running for the second time to become Kenya's first elected female senator. In interviewing her for an article that I was writing, I learned that she was a single mom with a toddler, she was called names, people threatened to burn down their home just because she had the audacity to think that women should be represented in government. At the same time, there was an issue that I heard was coming before Riverside City Council and I had been encouraged to go and speak or listen in at a meeting. I thought "I've never done that, I'll go." I remember I pulled up the website and the headshots popped up of all of the council members and I thought "Wow, they're all men!" Here I am writing about this woman who has the grit and the guts to do the hard work because she believes so deeply in representation, and, in my own backyard, we have a very similar situation, and I didn't know about it, and I'm not saying anything to fix it. I did some research and learned about Emerge. There was a woman who had been on the city council in Perris that I really admired and when I heard her speak, she talked about how she had done the Emerge program. I thought, "If she did it, I'm going to try." At the same time that the application was due, my partner gave birth to our daughter. So, I snuck away a couple blocks for a few hours just to write my application at the Starbucks and then make sure that I went back home so that I could be supporting Liz and our newborn. I really didn't think I had a chance of getting in, but I did, and look what happened!

I was so lucky that Denise Davis, who lives in Redlands, was in the same cohort as I was. Because the Emerge meetings were all around Southern California it made more sense to carpool than to try to go alone, so Denise and I carpooled to nearly every event and training. I learned a lot in Emerge, but it was those car rides that were really the most motivating to me. I'll never forget Denise wanted to run for Redlands City Council, and she was further along in the process than I was. She had already announced her campaign and was already starting to raise money. The more I learned in Emerge, the more I thought on one hand it could be possible that I could run for office and on the other hand that it was the most preposterous thing. I remember crying on the way to one of these trainings because I just didn't think that I could run for office. I'd been through the training and thought "This isn't the right time, I'm not going to do it. I just can't." Then I came home and I said to Liz, "I'm not running for office." She said, "Okay, you don't need to run for office." Then I was going to community meetings and becoming more and more engaged in what was happening on the city council agenda. I didn't stop doing any of that. Then finally, Liz said to me, "You know, for someone who's not running for office, you sure seem a lot like you're running for office." I think I just realized that it was the idea that wouldn't let me go even when I tried to let it go and that I really needed to keep following it and so I graduated from Emerge in April and opened my campaign committee in May. We had our primary election the following June and then the runoff election the November after that.

Contributions

When I won the seat, it was certainly a lot of hard work that I put in, but it was really a movement of people who put in a lot of time and energy and money to get us here. When I won the election, I had a dais to sit on, an office in City Hall, and within the first three weeks, after I figured out how to log onto the computer and what extensions to press on the phone, I sat down with my assistant Paloma, who had also helped with the campaign. We outlined what our three goals were for the office, then within those goals what the policy goals would be. The three goals that we outlined were transparency, everybody heard, and moving mountains for the greatest good. Certainly, much of my role is policy, as it should be, and thinking about how to move mountains for the greatest good. The first year was an unprecedented one, with a global pandemic. Much of the role and contributions that I hope we've made in the first year is really around the "transparency" and "everyone heard" pieces. Looking at the communication that comes out of City Hall offices in our case, ours and how we're communicating with people, how we're growing that audience, the language that we're using. Are we speaking in English? Are we speaking in Spanish? Are we using both? Are we taking issues that are written in a very government way and making them accessible to people who have twenty seconds as they're scrolling on their phone, to understand what this is and why it's important? I think we've made some great strides. We've had to, for literal life-and-death reasons in a global pandemic, make sure that people understand what's happening, what we know, what we don't know, how people can engage, where people need to act, what those actions are, why and who controls it. I'm very proud of some of the policies that have come out of my office in the first year.

Inspiration

Deborah Wong has been a role model since the second we moved to Riverside. I have learned so much from her and from other women in this city who have been organizing and advocating for years. I was really quickly put in touch with Chani Beeman in Riverside through the Downtown Area Neighborhood Alliance, and I sat down with her for coffee at Molino's. I very hesitantly brought up this idea that I might run for office, and I really thought she would laugh me out of the room. She listened to me, she talked to me about what I hoped to see and accomplish in the city, she shared some of the extraordinary work that she has done in the community and helped me think about the tools I would need locally if this was really something I wanted to accomplish. Meetings with Maggie Hawkins and Juliann Anderson and hearing about ways that they've been fighting for women and for the LGBT community. Connie Confer and her partner and getting to know the shoulders I stand on. The Human Rights Campaign does a municipal equality index every year, and Riverside was at a 61 out of 100. Then, in 2020, we announced that we reached a score of 100 on our municipal equality index showing equality in our city systems for LGBT people. I sent the press release to a group of phenomenal people who've been working in this community for years. I showed up at the very end that got two points for being an openly LGBT elected official and then asked some questions and we got to one hundred, but these are the women who've been doing the work for decades. I have just wild respect and so much more to learn from you [Deborah Wong], from all of them.

Advice

Take care of yourself. There's always more that we can do and we need to take care of ourselves and of each other to get there.

Where I've found any of my success, it's been in building a network of people who are all working toward a goal together. This campaign would never have left the ground without the early adopters who breathed life into it and offered different perspectives. Then the movements of people who knocked on doors and who made phone calls and sent text messages, that's the real story. It's how to work as a movement, so my advice would be don't try to go at it alone.

The first

Gaby Plascencia

Roots

I was born in Los Angeles in 1979. I lived in South Central. My dad was a welder for a company in Azusa and he had a friend that lived in Riverside, so in the eighties when there was a housing boom in Riverside, we bought a home in Riverside. We were renting in South Central, and I have four siblings, so it was nice to be a homeowner and have a bigger house. I'm a product of Alvord Unified, and I currently work as a school counselor at the middle school I attended. That's very rewarding to go back to the school district that gave me so much.

Call to activism

When I started high school, I wanted to go against the grain. I didn't want to be that statistic. So I got involved with clubs on campus. My math teacher, who later became my colleague at Loma Vista, was the MEChA advisor, and I really got connected to MEChA. I became president of MEChA. I got really involved with educating myself. I wasn't the straight A student by any means, but I did well in school. But I had a high school counselor that just didn't believe I was college material. Thankfully, my MEChA advisor and math teacher, Mr. Andrade, pushed me towards a "don't take no for an answer" kind of mentality. I think that really pushed me to say, "Why not? Why am I not college material?" So I just kept pushing. I was in high school in the '90s when Pete Wilson was pushing Prop 187 and there was very anti-immigrant rhetoric, and so I organized the school walkout at the time. Students have been such a big part of activism and movements throughout our history. I think being a part of MEChA was the catalyst to educating myself and breaking that cycle of poverty. There was a program through City Hall where if you opened up events to the community, you could get funds through the city, so I would go meet with Mayor Loveridge to talk about the events we would have. Loveridge was my first endorser when I decided to run for city council, so it came full circle.

After high school, I moved to Los Angeles, I earned an Associate's in Liberal Arts, a Bachelor's in Psychology with a minor in Spanish, and a Master's in Marriage, Family and Child counseling and a credential from Cal State L.A. I worked full time in college. I started my career at Ramona High School in Riverside Unified, then a friend of mine at Norte Vista told me there was an opening for a counselor, and I should apply. So I did and I got the position. It was great to tell the students I sat in those seats, and they could go to college, do more, give back, and then come back and give back to the community.

When I started my career at Ramona High School, I was the only Latina counselor. Ofelia Valdez-Yeager was part of Latino Network and they were sponsoring Latina students to attend a conference in Los Angeles through HOPE, Hispanas Organized for Political Equality. I was a chaperone and took high school students to this huge conference with hundreds and hundreds of Latina professionals. I fell in love with the organization. I reached out to Ofelia and told her I wanted to get involved in the community. She suggested the Latina Women's Health Forum, so I got involved with that nonprofit, then I got involved with Latino Network. I also stayed connected with Hispanas Organized for Political Equality, and in 2013, I participated in their statewide leadership program for young professional women. My friends from the group were running for office in

Long Beach and Fresno, so I started helping them with their campaigns. I helped Marisa Yeager when she ran for city council.

I started getting involved, but I wanted to have a family. I didn't have kids yet. I knew I was going to run for office one day, but it was about timing. So I stayed on nonprofit boards and helped others with their campaigns. I always thought my trajectory was going to be school board, being an educator, but I made the decision to run for city council when my daughter was old enough and I felt the timing was right. I was going to run regardless of whether Chris MacArthur was going to run again, but he decided to retire, and the rest is history.

Contributions

I am the first Latina to serve on the City Council and the first woman to represent Ward 5. I knew exactly what I was getting into. I think when you're the first at anything, there are hardships. I was a first-generation college student, and it was very challenging, there were a lot of hardships and lots of stumbles, and running for office was the same way. I knew it was going to be challenging to go against the status quo, not being a white male, not being someone that comes from money—I knew it was not going to be easy. A year into my tenure, I fought a recall, but I'm still here. I still love it and think things happen for a reason, and I was meant to be in this position because I'm good at fighting back and holding my ground, and I know who I am and where my values lie. I think it's important for people to know who I am and what I stand for. They don't always agree, and I'm okay with that, but I have to look at myself in the mirror.

I like to be out in the community. I'm constantly hosting community coffees. I don't spend a lot of time at City Hall, especially since I'm in Ward 5, and it's very far. So I try to stay in the community and come to my constituents whenever they invite me. I have my office hours at Hunt Park. I have office hours monthly just for students as well.

Being a woman, and a woman of color, and talking about racism and discrimination and looking at our policies that don't work for everybody has been unpopular to some but necessary to move the city forward, so that when we look at City Hall inside and out, it reflects the community. We need to continue to have those conversations and push policies that work for everybody. You never heard Spanish being spoken at City Hall, you never heard translators. We don't even have a translator department at City Hall. So, it took until 2019 to elect the first Latina, and the first Latino was elected in the 1960s. So what are we doing wrong? And what do we need to do differently? I want people of color and people that speak different languages to feel welcome and feel that they have access, that you don't have to have money or power to get a call back from your council member. That's our job, regardless of if we align politically or not. I talk to people all the time that are surprised when I call them back. I tell them, "I'm here to do my job. My job is to serve you and improve your quality of life, period."

It's hard. I have a family. I have a full-time job. The decisions that we make are not easy ones. The system wasn't made for us to govern well. So one step at a time, we're trying to change the system so that it works better for us so that we can really move the city forward. It takes time. But elections matter, and I hope that it gets easier for those that come after us.

Inspiration

Ofelia was one of my first mentors here. Assemblymember Jose Medina was a mentor as an educator as well. Nationally, I think of Sonia Sotomayor. These national and local figures keep us fighting; when you have those losses, you just think, "Well, all I can do is pick myself up and keep fighting." Students also continue to motivate me.

Advice

When one door closes, you just keep knocking on the door 'til you knock it down. Women of color and people of color are used to being told no and used to being left out. So I think it's about persistence. I tell people all the time, "I have a lot of energy, and I will outwork you, I'll wear you down." Whatever I'm trying to push, it's going to get done because I have a lot of energy and I'm persistent. But what I've learned between MEChA and education and now governing is that there's this sweet spot between being an activist, a policy maker, and advocate. **I'm always down for a good protest, but how do you turn that activism into policy?** I will continue as a policymaker to be out on the frontlines with folks, but at the same time, nothing will change if we're not in the system, changing it, changing the policies that don't work for us. So we need to turn that activism into advocacy by getting into that policy seat.

Planting seeds

Clarissa Cervantes

Roots

I was born and raised in Riverside County. I was born in Indio and was raised in the Coachella Valley in the city of Coachella. I went to Cal State Northridge to get my bachelor's degree, and then afterwards I came to Riverside. I've been in Riverside for twelve years, and this is where I choose to call home.

Call to activism

I was called to activism at a very early age. My mother has been teaching at Cesar Chavez Elementary School in Coachella for over thirty-five years. She would guide me to the history section of our local library to books about Rosa Parks, Martin Luther King, Jr., Cesar Chavez, Dolores Huerta. **I was called to activism by reading about their stories,** by learning about who they were and their struggles, how they used their voices to inspire other people to take action. I was so inspired by who they were and that they look like me. I was born into a space of believing that I could make a change. My older sister, Sabrina Cervantes, is an assembly member who represents Riverside and various portions of Riverside County. My sister and I would sit out in the backyard and think about what we were going to do, and it was always about people. It was always about helping people. I feel we get that from our parents and our grandparents. My father was a mayor and council member in Coachella. We grew up with him championing and advocating for our community. My grandmother on my father's side was a fighter. She owned land when it wasn't common for women. Whenever farm-working migrants who were coming to work in Coachella were passing through, she provided them with free housing on the ranch, little casitas, and she didn't charge anybody rent. My relatives and her older children would say, "You need to make them pay!" She said, "No, they're not paying. They need to save up money for their family, for their kids." So at a very young age, I witnessed my grandmother taking in families and making sure they had affordable housing, somewhere to live, that they were able to keep their dignity and didn't have to sleep in cars with their kids. I grew up watching her protect people in the community. My other grandmother was a migrant worker. My mother came from Mexico and became a citizen when I was eight, so I'm first generation on my mother's side. They were always advocates of citizenship, talking about how we came over here for a better life, for opportunity and wanting to make sure that we were safe. I feel that they inspired me just by telling me what they went through so that we could be here today. I never took any of those stories lightly.

Contributions

I'm so proud of the voter registration work we've done here. That's how I came to Riverside. We focused on the areas that were intended to elect

Senator Richard Roth and Assemblymember Jose Medina. And then we continued to do the work. I will never say I did it alone, because each time I had a team, but I was able to lead, to train, to champion, to talk—I've had thousands of conversations with people from Perris to Moreno Valley to Riverside, Jurupa Valley, to Corona, Eastvale, and out in Coachella Valley as well. We didn't just go out to register Democrats. We went out to teach voter education. We went out to teach about voting on the whole ballot and to tell about the importance. You can register someone to vote, but if you don't teach them how to vote, if you don't show them how to vote, and if you don't leave that door where they actually feel inspired to vote, you going through that process won't make a difference. I know we've been able to move people to turn out in this region by having conversations, coming to their door, and by doing the hard work. Every time I heard, "I'll never vote," I had to walk away and believe I was going to convince the next person that their vote mattered. The one person who would say, "This is my first time ever going to vote, just because you came I'm going to finally do it," that person would outweigh the ten people who weren't willing. **We planted a lot of seeds that we're so excited to see now today.**

I was a field representative for Andy Melendrez. When you work for an elected, usually you're convinced you never want to be an elected. But it was always something in my head. When I was in kindergarten, I wrote I wanted to grow up to be the president! I ran from that when I started being an organizer, because when you go lobby electeds and see behind the scenes, you see what electeds have to go through and how much pressure they get. But I feel that when you care how we care and if you have your heart in the right place, it is something that you have to do. It is a responsibility. When Councilman Melendrez decided he was not going to seek another election, the only thing I could think about was the communities that I loved and that I represented with him for many years. All those people that I knew that lived in those neighborhoods. When people asked, "Why are you running?" I would say, "I'm running because of the people that I care about and my neighbors, and I didn't have a choice." It was a choice, but it didn't really feel like a choice.

Inspiration

Audre Lorde is definitely one of my role models. Maya Angelou always stood out to me. When I was little, the story of the Underground Railroad and Harriet Tubman made my heart race with energy. I would feel like I was supposed to be there helping her. African American women are so, so inspiring to me, because they've had no choice sometimes but to be resilient and to show that there are better ways and lives that we all deserve to live.

Advice

It's easy to lose yourself with what people want you to be. We have to be able to first love and accept ourselves. Then from there, we are able to welcome and receive the people in our lives that really align with who we are, what we're doing and trying to accomplish.

I identify as bisexual and queer, and when I finally came into the space that I knew this was my truth, it was hard to not be accepted and embraced by all the people I want to be embraced by, but to see a whole new community that was ready with open arms to love and accept me has helped me to further understand that I have to be who I am. And that the right people who are going to love me are going to see me. And in return, I see the people who are being authentic. And I think that authenticity heals our communities. Whatever it is that pulls you and calls you, it is meant for you. And honor what pulls you in.

A ripple effect

Riverside Resistance Revival Chorus: Kris Lovekin, Jerri Mendivel, Dawn Pia

Roots

JERRI MENDIVEL: I was born in Miami Beach, Florida, but I ended up in California at the age of five. I grew up in Orange County, and when I was a young mom, my husband and I decided we wanted me to be able to be a stay-at-home mom and we needed to buy a house, and we moved to Riverside in 1985. I ended up working in the medical field and along the way I've been a music director at one church or another.

KRIS LOVEKIN: I was born in Heidelberg, Germany, because my father had dreams of being an opera singer, and my parents decided to go to Germany and try for that. They spent five years in Germany and they came back to Perris, California, and then when I was six, we moved to Riverside. I grew up going to Riverside schools and graduated from UCR.

My dad taught music in the Riverside schools and my mom taught math. I was with *The Press-Enterprise* as a reporter, covering mostly education, then I moved over to UC Riverside and did media relations.

DAWN PIA: I was born in 1955 at Community Hospital and went to elementary, junior high, high school, and college in Riverside. Most of my career was working for the city of Riverside in Parks and Recreation.

Call to activism

KRIS LOVEKIN: I did not consider myself an activist before Trump was elected. I've always been a voter, I've always been an engaged citizen, I've always been a community-minded person, but I never considered myself an activist. I didn't take Trump seriously as a candidate because I didn't think that the United States would be backward enough to elect such a man. I really thought he was a joke, and so the shock of election night sort of woke me up. Then as the inauguration approached and as there were protests being organized, calling it a Women's March, I thought, "I have to go there." It was a very singular moment of thinking, "I don't care what anybody else is doing, but I'm going." I was so proud of my community, because there were thousands of people in downtown Riverside, a place that is considered by some people to be sort of a sleepy town. It was an emotional moment and I experienced it alone, even among four thousand people, because the chorus was not together yet, so I was by myself and in the midst of the crowd and feeling proud.

Before I went, I had to ask myself, "What should my sign say? What am I here for?" And I decided it is for the climate and that we deserve human rights, including a planet that is livable and that will continue on for our children and our grandchildren. I feel like I maybe missed the boat in some ways and I could have been more active before, but I kept a lot of neutrality because of that professional responsibility as a reporter and then in PR. But when I retired I was free. I work with 350 Riverside, which is an organization that is named for the parts per million of carbon that is safe in the environment, and we are well above 350 now, so we're in deep trouble. We are betraying our grandchildren, and there are so many important things we need to keep fighting for, but none of it's going to happen if we're in desperate climate struggle. I try to use my skillset to help people promote good causes. I try to use my singing and my writing in the support of community building.

JERRI MENDIVEL: I was raised in a conservative family, in which things were black-and-white and right or wrong, and you don't question authority. I credit my two daughters for getting me involved in activism, because they are both bisexual, and that caused me to question everything as I knew it. I got pretty involved in LGBTQI activism back before it had that many letters in the acronym, because that was part of their journey from high school through college. And as a mother, when it comes to your kids, that mama bear personality comes out. I started getting a little more active and committed when I started realizing a few months before the election in 2016 that Trump actually had a chance of being elected, and I was starting to become terrified. So that's when I started getting a little more active, a little more vocal, and maybe more public in my activism. I reacted with terrible grief and despair at the outcome of the 2016 election, and that's when I felt like I needed to really stand up. I did go to the Women's March in Riverside with a number of friends from church. That was a phenomenal event, a very unifying experience. My next participation was the March for Science because I offered Trinity Lutheran Church as a meeting place.

DAWN PIA: In my childhood there was civil unrest and there was the Vietnam War and things like the farm workers union. I was exposed to looking at these things from a different point of view from a very young age. The desegregation in Riverside allowed us to form relationships with people that weren't in our neighborhood. I know there's downsides where people were taken out of their immediate neighborhoods. A principal named Horace Jackson addressed the situation by gathering a crew of about sixty students and sat us all down in libraries and had some very candid discussions. That was my first moment of being involved. After college I kind of had to cool the jets, working for the city government. Then the election of 2016 was shocking, and I went to the first couple of meetings for Rise Up and became involved in that organization and with Indivisible 41.

Contributions

JERRI MENDIVEL: I think around August of 2017, I saw a video of the New York Resistance Revival Chorus, and I thought, "We have to do this." I just posted that we'd meet at Trinity Lutheran. I got clearance from the pastor and the council. And we had an amazing turnout! I think we had like thirty people, and I had no idea if we were going to have three people. And then I realized I don't know if any of these people can actually sing. So we just got in a circle, and I taught them a very, very simple Melanie DeMore song. Melanie's a vocal activist who's a friend of mine. And the circle sounded absolutely beautiful. I think we all got goosebumps from that. What was so appealing to me is that music is the universal language. A lot of times you're sitting with somebody in the same room, and everything about you is polar opposites, but a song will bring you together. I thought that music would be sort of a healing, joyful way of protesting and might speak to people who wouldn't necessarily give us the time of day otherwise. I talked to my friend Melanie about it because she's been a vocal activist for decades, and she felt like there was a real need for music, because there's always been music throughout civil rights movements and other eras of political unrest, but there wasn't a whole lot of music coming out of this era of protest. And so she just sort of felt like the environment would be really ripe for that. I knew I could teach the music, provide the accompaniment, organize the concerts, but I didn't have the skills or the connections or the knowledge for public relations, for organizing and getting everything running. I was an AYSO volunteer for a million years, but that's not quite the same. So Dawn took me aside and kind of said, "I can't really sing, but I'm really good at organizing and doing these other things." Turns out Dawn actually can sing, and I consider her to be an invaluable member of the chorus. We chose a few members to be on the chorus committee, and that's when things really took off, because different people had different skills. I felt very supported. We had women with the knowledge and organizational skills and enthusiasm to really make the chorus into a viable organization. Somehow it came up that we would be able to perform at the Women's March in 2018. That was a huge, huge deal to us. Our first actual, official performance was in front of a few thousand people, and it was really wonderful. Melanie DeMore came to teach us some activist songs. One of my big concerns was us misappropriating Black culture in some of our singing. Melanie really helped us with that.

DAWN PIA: I think at the peak we were probably at about forty people. Some faded away, other people joined in. Typically we get a request. The committee reviews our ability to have a core group of singers in attendance at an event. When we first gathered together as a committee, we talked about having some mission as well as some goals that we were trying to reach. So as long as the events that we were being asked to sing at touched on that mission statement or our goals, then typically we were more than willing to be a participant of it, and then if we had the numbers, to support it. I think the only time we kind of shy away from things is if it's a political event for, let's say, city council people, because maybe some of our members might support one council member over another. We made a decision on that early on—that we wouldn't typically go to those types of things. I have a strong background in policy governance, which is not the fun razzle dazzle stuff, but I found with my history of working in Parks and Recreation that when you have good, solid policies in place, then it helps in the decision-making, and you kind of keep from decision-making in an emotional sense rather than a fact-based sense.

JERRI MENDIVEL: We were interviewed by *The Press-Enterprise* fairly early on, and we did get some pretty nasty responses and a couple of threatening phone calls. So that was unsettling, a little bit intimidating. We said we're going to have to walk each other out of our cars to and from rehearsal. We need to lock the doors after a certain time, and if somebody's late to rehearsal, they need to text us and let us know that they're out there, because we don't want some nutcase with a gun coming into the church and shooting it up.

DAWN PIA: My daughter would tell me, "Be careful out there." And there was always a general awareness that there was a risk that we were out there. I worked with a few other people to put some posters up or banners up around town or do light brigades, and I was always ripe for a good lecture from my daughter for that one.

JERRI MENDIVEL: My kids had an intervention for me after we'd been together about eighteen months, when Trump just kept exacerbating, ramping up the volatility, and they were really worried about that.

KRIS LOVEKIN: The Resistance Chorus decided we were going to march in the Martin Luther King Walk-a-Thon to support our racial justice mission.

JERRI MENDIVEL: The chorus has tried to be very diverse in the events that it's agreed to participate in. We've sung at Temple Beth El, we've gone out to Adelanto detention center. We did a concert called Music Without Borders to support Casa del Migrante in Tijuana. We did the Bayard Rustin concert at the Fox Theater. We did the Concert Across

America to end gun violence.

KRIS LOVEKIN: That was exciting. There were young people who were singing with us from their own performing groups. That was exciting, but then we all sang together on "Shine," and that's what we were trying to accomplish, is that kind of community.

JERRI MENDIVEL: In the pandemic, a lot of us have become involved in Anti-Racist Riverside and other Black organizations since this has come up, and I think we'd like to really expand on that and fight the good fight in terms of anti-racism. During the pandemic, a small contingency of us went to the Stop Asian Hate gathering. We wore white, we knew we couldn't sing, but we just wanted to demonstrate, "We're here, we support you." It's just been such an honor to serve in this way, because we know that we're on the right side of history, and that it is a calling, and what a privilege and a blessing to be able to respond to that calling.

Inspiration

JERRI MENDIVEL: For sheer courage, literal grace under fire, Malala Yousafzai. Dolores Huerta is a phenomenal voice for those who don't have a voice, but also what I really admire about her was that she spent a lot of time developing future leaders. She wanted to see her work continue, and so she built a contingency of that. Being from a performing arts background, I always really appreciate artists and musicians and poets and authors that are more worried about social justice than selling records, Joan Baez and Holly Near and Nina Simone, people who've used their creativity as a form of advocacy.

KRIS LOVEKIN: Pete Seeger is my role model, and also there's a group of women in Riverside called the Why Nots, and they created a group of singing women. The Why Nots came to sing at my elementary school, Washington Elementary School, and I saw women with their guitars, probably about the age of my own mother, and they had kids at my school, I knew their kids. So these were women who chose to make music together and form a circle, in a time when women were not encouraged to do that. They were encouraged to raise their kids and self-sacrifice. These women did raise their children well, they could do that and also appreciate each other as friends and musicians and performers and go on retreats together to Mexico. So the Why Nots are a particularly Riverside model for activism, that you not only do your normal things, but you also get involved in civic life. Some of them helped create Victoria Avenue Forever. The first yoga classes in Riverside were led by a Why Not. They're a group of folk singers in Riverside who I admire, and some of them are still with us and still singing. They have a song called "While We're Here, We Should Sing," and that is also a philosophy of life, while we're here, we should sing.

DAWN PIA: Sue Mitchell's been a great cheerleader in our community, and she's a person that can move masses. For her sheer smarts and willingness to put in the hard work, Chani Beeman is someone that I'm always just amazed by.

Advice

JERRI MENDIVEL: Get to know the other grassroots organizers in your community and network with those women and connect, because you're going to get encouragement and support from those people. Those people will be there for you when it seems the cause that you're working for is overwhelming. We have a song that the chorus does called "Lineage," where we talk about how strong our grandmothers were. We have several centuries worth of phenomenal women that have really paved the way for us. Tap into that community as well, that energy. Local activism is not that glamorous. Half the time nobody knows we even did anything, and we may never see the actual results of our actions. But **even though you feel like you're a drop in the bucket, that little drop ripples.** You are making an impact. You may never get to see what it was.

KRIS LOVEKIN: Don't be intimidated to contact public officials. Sometimes they don't get as much input from the people who elected them, and so a phone call or postcard or conversation could be important. And do the thing that scares you. If you feel a tinge of, "Wow, that's probably too hard for me," it might be that's what you're called to do, so go for it.

DAWN PIA: I'm all about having a structure in place, a framework, and some of the stuff isn't the glamorous part but it really does pay dividends if you pay close attention to your communications, if you have a good mechanism for communicating, and if the leadership team is listening. Understanding that you're working with other human beings and being respectful of them and not overriding them.

Building community

Sherry Mackay

Roots

I was born in Nova Scotia, Canada. When I was born, we lived with my mom, my dad, my older brother, my grandmother and my five uncles, so I was born into this large family, but when I was young, we moved to a mining community in northern Ontario, and my grandmother and my uncles did not join us. That's where I was raised through high school.

I went to Toronto and a few other places along the way and ended up in Riverside in 1999. We came to Riverside because my husband got a position at UC Riverside, and I joined him. I left my job that I loved, I left my family, my friends, and I moved to the U.S. Within a month, I got a job at UCR Extension. I was hired by the International Education Program as an ESL instructor, and then I eventually became special programs coordinator, so when groups of students would come, they would come to study English, but then there'd be another component to it—perhaps they were law students or business students, and I would connect them with businesses or would go to the courthouse. That was a way that I started to know more about Riverside and appreciate the Sister Cities that we had and really connected with those Sister Cities through their students and faculty coming.

Call to activism

I was a young person who didn't have a clear vision. I worked, and eventually I got a BA. I wound up working for the Dean of Agriculture and interviewing grad students and professors about agricultural research. I'm not a scientist, I don't think I'm a great writer, but I was interviewing all these people, and one of the things I kept on hearing from so many of them was that their wives were with them and their wives were isolated and struggling, they were away from their country, often experiencing winter for the first time. Many of them didn't speak English, and they were just really lonely. So I just thought, "Well, let's get them together!" We would meet every week, and one of the weeks, I would do some kind of an impromptu English lesson, even though I wasn't really trained. We had access to a kitchen, so some weeks they would teach something—how to prepare some Thai dish, or they would teach us some words from their language. This is what I became really passionate about, so I thought, "How do I make this into a job?"

I saw the power of language and how you need to have the language to succeed in a country. I went and got a BEd in TESOL, Teaching English as a Second Language. I moved to Toronto and was teaching in a program called Language Instruction for Newcomers. It's a great program throughout Canada where any newcomer is entitled to English classes. I taught the same students five hours a day, five days a week and had students from around the world in my class. My neighborhood was very diverse, so in my class I had students from Guatemala, Italy, Japan, Pakistan, Afghanistan, everywhere. I love that program and teaching these amazing newcomers, and that was my introduction to the immigrant and refugee population.

I moved to Riverside after working with refugees in Canada, and then in 2012, we moved to Albuquerque. In Albuquerque I got involved with an amazing program called the Refugee Well-being Project. Jessica Goodkind from University of New Mexico is the person who started this concept and had this study going on in Albuquerque where she interviewed newcomers, and then she taught a class and undergraduate students would learn about the countries where these refugees were coming from. Then they learned about the resettlement process, and that's when I learned about the process in the U.S. and how refugees were just getting three months of support from the government. So these students learn about the refugee process and what it takes, and then eventually they're partnered up with the college students supporting the refugee, but of course learning so much in turn. It was really empowering for them to have that kind of impact on these families' lives. Each year, the refugees who graduated from the program would come back as the interpreters. Eventually they came back as liaisons, facilitators, and were really active in the program as well. It was really eye-opening for me, and I was just so impressed with these families and this program.

Contributions

Selin Yildiz Nielsen, a friend of mine from my days back at UCR Extension, had moved away to Iowa, and then to Eastern Turkey, very close to the Syrian border. She was working with refugees both in Des Moines and in Turkey. She moved back to Riverside in 2015, the same time we moved back. So we had both been working with these populations and started asking, "Are there refugees here?" And then exactly at that time, that photo came out of the drowned Syrian boy. We wanted to do something. We put a message on Facebook for our friends, "Who wants to come together?" We realized that the United Nations International Day for Peace was coming up, so we decided to have a peace walk. We met at UCR Extension and we walked to Cesar Chavez and we had our peace signs, and that's how it started. Then we started asking around, "Are there refugees?" We connected with Catholic Charities out of San Bernardino, and they were resettling refugees here. The director of Catholic Charities Refugee Resettlement Program connected me with this family that had just arrived from Afghanistan. The husband came with what's called a special immigrant visa because of his work with the U.S. military. The husband worked with the U.S. military and had strong English skills, and the wife had never gone to school, and had never held a pencil, and she grew up in a village with all of her brothers and sisters, surrounded by a lot of people all the time, and they moved here, to this apartment. When I moved as an English speaker from Canada to the U.S., I remember it was difficult, so I can't even imagine what it was for her. I started tutoring her, and then word got out, and another Afghan would want his wife to come too.

Then I was introduced to Professor Amy Stumpf from Cal Baptist University. She had pulled together this impromptu English class at Palm Baptist Church. I said, "That's my background, I'd love to do something like that." She's like, "Do it!" So the next week, I pulled the women that she worked with the summer before from Corona and these other three Afghan women. We needed volunteers because transportation's really difficult here. So I just put it out there to friends, and we brought these four women together and we started this English class. I started from the lens of the teacher, "Okay, let's get right down to English." Then halfway through, the women would say, "It's time for our tea break" and they would be chatting in their language. I learned that they wanted to socialize, and they were sharing information, and over time they started opening up. One woman said she cried every day until she came to English class. Coming to English class to them was a time to meet their friends, to connect. Of course they wanted to learn English, but the community part was really important.

The mission of Glocally Connected is to promote community building in order to support refugees, and that community building component is everything. I think there are three major keys to building community: The first is trust, the second is collaboration, and then it's uplifting those you're with. In our case, the trust started in the classroom. Some of these women were really scared. They saw that people here did not like Muslims or people that were covered, and that they would not be welcomed. They came very cautiously to my class. They did not open up right away. First, I built that trust. Every time I brought a volunteer in, I was very, very cautious because these women trusted me. With that trust, we were able to open doors for them to connect to the larger community, because they trusted.

What we started in the class reverberated out. There was a ripple effect. The women started getting more involved with the community. **We just built so many beautiful collaborations within Riverside**. I reached out to a lot of people for different reasons. Sometimes we needed volunteers to drive them into class. I always loved to share the story of Beth Miller, who's very active in our community, [who] said, "I knew I was going to drive, but I never knew I would love." The volunteers opened up their hearts and they gained so much from meeting these incredible women.

We saw that the women had a lot of talent, and they were always bringing amazing food. We started with the Alternative Gift Fair at [First United] Methodist Church. For some of the women, it was the first time they ever made their own money, let alone money in the U.S., so it was so exciting for them and it was really empowering. We had collaborations with the Art Alliance [of the Riverside Art Museum] and a beautiful one with Inlandia Institute. We worked with the women in getting their recipes together and we published our first book, *A Taste of Afghanistan.* We had a special program for the kids where they came together to write poetry and do art, and again, it just introduced these families to their larger community and the larger community to them.

I know the volunteers felt uplifted by their friendships, and then of course we wanted to uplift the families and support them, understanding their personal goals and dreams. It's a matter of hearing that and then connecting them to the right person. It just became interwoven in the larger community. With businesses, we partnered with Max Medina and his hair salon, and Le Chat Noir, the French restaurant, and we had a fashion show. It was beautiful, because we had Toni Moore from downtown, and then a young woman who's originally from Nigeria who designed some beautiful, African-inspired clothes, and then three of the Afghan women from the class had their first fashion lines, and we had this fashion show, and it was so beautiful. This was one of my favorite days in Riverside. We had the models over in White Park, and they walked across Market Street, right by the sister city signs. We also had collaborations with students from every college in the area. We weaved in really strong collaborations that continue today.

One thing that has been really eye-opening and really heartwarming to me is seeing different faiths coming together in Riverside. There were pockets of different organizations, different groups doing different things, and we tried to collaborate as much as possible. What we're doing is for the families, but there's a larger vision for humanity.

There's a power in contribution. The women love to share their food, and two years in a row during the holy month of Ramadan they shared that part of what it means to them is helping those in need. The church where we held classes served a hot meal every Thursday, and so the women took a turn and prepared a hot meal for the homeless coming to the church. They were so happy to share their gift. **When somebody can contribute to their community, they feel more like they're part of the community.**

Inspiration

There are incredible leaders we have all witnessed like Martin Luther King and Gandhi and Mother Teresa, and I still love to turn to their quotes or their readings for inspiration. But my first true inspiration was a young man named Terry Fox, a Canadian, who in 1980 was a college student and got cancer and had one of his legs amputated. He was this really soft-spoken, very sweet young man. He decided he wanted to raise money for cancer. Every day he would get up early and he would run like twenty-some miles, and his best friend would follow him in his van slowly. Nobody really paid much attention to him in the beginning. But then he just kept running and running, and there was a song, "Run Terry Run." He went through the maritime provinces, and you see everyday people running with him, and he just picked up a lot of coverage, and he was a very quiet person, but he would speak out. He raised a lot of money for cancer. Sadly, when he got to Ontario he got sick and the cancer came back and he died. But the morale of Canada was lifted by watching him run. And every year in Canada, and actually different parts of the world where there are Canadians, there's a Terry Fox run, and we raise money for cancer research. He wasn't that loud person, he was this very gentle being, but with a vision, and he was very powerful. Definitely, he was probably the first person who really inspired me in my youth.

I started Glocally Connected without experience running a nonprofit, so it was really by working together with so many people in this community that it all worked. Selin is very passionate. Cati Porter is a poet but also has those business skills to get the grants written, get the people in place, get the book published; she gets it done. Kris Lovekin is always lending a hand, always thinking of ways to support the refugee population. Suzanne Singer stands out in my mind as a strong voice in this community, bringing different religions together and supporting refugees and immigrants. Really in Riverside I can look to many, many people for inspiration.

Advice

You need to really know yourself and be true to yourself. Know your strengths and ask where you need to bring people in. It's all these little steps. You have a vision and just follow along. The clearer your vision, the more it's going to come to be.

I advise people not to get caught up in the little ugly details. You can be in the know; you don't need to know everything. I think if I can do something about it, then I'm going to investigate further, but if I can't do anything, maybe I stay in my lane.

"Everywhere can be home"

Selin Yildiz Nielsen

Roots

I was born in Ankara, Turkey, in 1969. I came to the United States with my family in 1987. My parents worked for the State Department in Turkey at the embassy. My mom's closest friend lived in Riverside, so we came here because of her. I had just finished high school, and I didn't know much about the educational system in the United States. They told me that there's a system where you can just sign up and go to community college. In Turkey, you have to enter an exam that's just once a year, and some students are placed in colleges, but the rest cannot go to college, so it's a huge privilege. When I came here, I found out that anyone could go to college. That was mind-boggling for me. So I signed up at a community college. I went to College of the Desert for a few years, and I transferred to UC Berkeley. I finished college and went back to Southern California.

My parents were involved with UCR Extension. They were the overseas representatives, bringing students from Turkey. I decided to be involved with international education. I went to Cal State University [San Bernardino] to get my master's in the Department of Education with the TESOL emphasis, teaching English to speakers of other languages. I got my master's and then I started teaching at UCR Extension in the English as a Second Language program. Then I got married, I had children, we moved to Turkey, we moved back.

After September 11, 2001, they asked me if I was Muslim, and I was a little bit surprised. They knew me already. I said, "I don't know, I grew up as one," because my family was never very religious, but like 99.9 % of Turkey is Muslim, so that's how I grew up. And then I lost my job two weeks later. It didn't occur to me at first. A lot of people were being laid off, a lot of students canceled their trips to the United States, and so I thought that it was a part of that. But I found out that they hired someone instead of me. I was hurt because I thought I was a good teacher, and the timing was very suspicious. I was the only non-native speaker teaching ESL classes, and I thought maybe people didn't trust me, because I'm not quite American. It took me a long time to realize that it wasn't fair. That's when I decided to get a doctorate. I wanted to get more education so that I could be more qualified. My goal was to work in international education and work with immigrants.

Call to activism

I was really interested in immigrant education. We moved to Iowa, and I was involved with this nonprofit organization working with refugees in Iowa. Iowa is a refugee resettlement state. There were a lot of Bosnian refugees, Sudanese, Cambodian, people from all around the world in that small state. There were integration programs, there were education programs, nonprofits, educational organizations, governments—there was a lot of support there. Then I taught at Drake University about cross-cultural communication. It started becoming a passion of mine. I really was interested in the cultures people came from and how we can communicate from different cultures. Then I went to Turkey as a visiting professor in 2012. I was teaching there in the department of education, and I was teaching comparative education classes, and I was teaching immigrant education classes and global migration classes.

The Syrian crisis had started, and where I was in Turkey was on the

Syrian border. There were refugees coming into Turkey, not knowing what was going to happen, not knowing if they were going to go back home in a few weeks or months. There were a lot of unknowns. I got really involved with the situation there, because I knew that education was being interrupted, especially for children. Even though it was projected that it would have been a few months, it's usually never like that. I wanted to establish some programs so that the kids would get some education. My university did not want to be involved. I was kind of on my own. I had to find my own ways of getting into the camps and trying to find out what was going on. I found out some horrific things. There was continuous trauma, and the kids were completely traumatized. I met children whose parents were killed in front of them, women who picked up pieces of their children in a plastic bag, it was just unbelievable trauma, and nobody knew what to do or how long it was going to last. We set up trauma management workshops for the refugees and for the volunteer teachers. The workshops were really amazing. It was a revelation for many of them. That really got me involved with this—working with refugees, researching and teaching about forced migration—that was kind of interwoven with my career and my interest in refugees.

Contributions

I had come back from Turkey, and I lived in Washington, D.C., for a year, then I decided to come back to California. My best friend from teaching ESL at UCR Extension had moved away then moved back to Riverside within a couple weeks of us. I worked with refugees in Iowa, I worked with refugees in Turkey, and she had worked with refugees in Albuquerque, New Mexico, so we were both involved with similar work in completely different places, and we started talking about it. That was when this picture of the dead toddler went viral around the world and brought attention to the refugee crisis. Up until that time, not very many people were interested or finding out about what was really going on. There were people trying to get to Europe in boats, and this was one of the boats capsizing, and then this child washing ashore, and the whole world responded to this picture.

Even before then, Sherry and I were talking and thinking, "We should do something, we have done all this work, we should find out if there are refugees in the area." We didn't know what to do. We didn't know if there were refugees living in Riverside or what their needs would be. We didn't know what we could do, so we had to find out first. But before, we organized a peace walk. September 21st was the International Day of Peace and Ceasefire, and we decided to gather our friends and make a walk downtown. We just wanted to bring awareness. We were talking about maybe joining an organization that was helping refugees, so we looked around. We couldn't find one in this area. So I said, "Why don't we have our own organization?" We can just find out what's needed and maybe we can contribute, **if there isn't one, we will make one!** And that's when we decided to have an organization, without even knowing what we were going to do.

We did a lot of research. It was like detective work at first: "Who are the refugees, where do they live?" It's not really a straightforward thing. There are many organizations that resettle refugees, and some of those organizations are really far away, and they can resettle within one hundred miles, but they don't take care of them. We found out that refugees don't really get much support. From the moment they arrive, they have like three months' support, and in those three months, they have to learn English, they have to find jobs, they have to sign their kids up for school, they have to get health screenings. I couldn't do that if I moved from Riverside to Corona. There's so much involved, and without speaking the language, without knowing anything about the culture. We just decided, okay, "What is the first thing I needed when I came into this country?" Or, "What is the first thing the Syrian people needed when I was in Turkey?" And the number one thing is communication. You need to know the language. If you can't communicate, you can't be a productive member of the community, you can't define your needs, so that's number one.

We were both ESL teachers. We decided to teach English, and then we met Amy Stumpf from CBU [California Baptist University]. She was tutoring two or three Afghan refugee women, and she introduced us to them. We started teaching them English at Palm Baptist Church on Palm Avenue. We started with two or three students, and then we were getting success because as we started our classes, the refugees were very interested. They were excited to learn. When you have small children or if you don't have transportation, it's very difficult to get anywhere, so we would ask around for volunteers to drive these women to class. And most of them had small children, and we would have volunteers take care of the small children. We developed this little thing which was very, very useful, and it worked! It just took off from there. That was the inception. As we got to know the people, it just became much more than that. We realized that's how we could bring the community together, members of the community that would not otherwise get to know each other or have a chance to meet were becoming friends. That is very powerful. **I felt my calling was the integration—refugees feeling at home and people feeling that the refugees in their communities belong here.**

When people think of an "other," like a Syrian or whoever it is, they think of differences, not, "Oh, this person is just like me." But that is the truth. They have the same fears. They want the best for their children. They think about what to have for breakfast or how to solve problems. There isn't really that much difference. I wanted American students to get to know that. There was this girl, Rawdanur, who I met in a Syrian camp. Because of my parents' work, they had this scholarship with the UCR Extension, so I got her the scholarship to come to school to learn English—a Syrian refugee coming to Riverside. We were so afraid because the day she was coming, people were stuck in airports, being turned away because there was this Muslim ban with some countries that people couldn't come from, and it was a really bad situation. But she got to come! It's really about person to person. You blame institutions and things like that, but her experience was this Syrian coming from Turkey just when the Muslim ban was going on, and this passport officer asks, "Why are you here?" She said, "I'm going to learn English," and then they look at her forms and paperwork, and this officer says, "Welcome to California! Don't forget to go to the beaches." She was so amazed. When all of these adverse things are happening, this person is welcoming her. **No matter what happens, we should never lose our faith in people.** She gave a lot of speeches in many places and at many universities, and the students were so interested because all they hear is from the news or social media, but here's this person in front of them, live! When she says, "My dog died. They bombed my village. I walked through the border," they're just amazed—"This person is standing in front of me, she's just like me, she's wearing these jeans." It brought it close to people and made it real. It's really powerful when you bring people together. Rawdanur became an activist, this little girl that I met in a refugee camp. She attended the Women and Girls in Science day at the United Nations. We both spoke advocating on behalf of the refugee girls in science, and we have also established through Glocally Connected two scholarships from a local business to help girls studying science.

I like giving presentations and giving the information about refugees, sharing my personal experiences, bringing it home, especially to people who are not familiar with the situation. It was very exciting and I felt proud to be invited to the United Nations and conferences and summits, but it was almost like preaching to the choir. I love teaching at the university or giving presentations to a high school. When people don't know and they learn, it's the most delightful thing for me. That is advocacy, that is how we get the word out.

Every time I went back to Turkey, I would visit those camps, and there were some makeshift camps too. There were so many needs. There were children without shoes, handicapped kids without wheelchairs, and sick people without medicine, and it was overwhelming. I know there are many organizations that provide these kinds of help, but I took it upon myself. We went to the school, and we saw that the kids didn't have shoes. **So, I called Riverside, and I called Glocally Connected, my friends, and said, "What can we do? Can you just get me like a thousand dollars tomorrow so I can buy shoes for these kids?" And that's what happened.** We raised it in one day, and I went and I got the shoes, we went there, we measured them, we put them on their feet, and the next day I came home. I know that you can call the Red Cross, and you can try to figure it out, but I just experienced that you can do things. If you want to do something, you can just do it. These kids didn't have shoes, so I said, "Okay, I'm just gonna get them shoes." And people are amazing! They contributed! They said, "Okay, here! Here's the money, do it!"

There's so much more involved in growing an organization—it's a little bit of a dilemma for me—the desire to be on the ground doing something and doing the things that are necessary that are not so exciting. Without doing that, without raising money, without finding grants, the organization is not sustainable. That's the reality of it, and that bugs me. I see smaller NGOs trying to get grants and money from larger NGOs, larger NGOs trying to get money and grants from governments, it just turns into begging for money all around, and it shouldn't be that way. It shouldn't be on the shoulders of these organizations trying to pick and get the money. I think it should be on the shoulders of the big organizations that have the money to find us and do something good for the community. I think there should be enough conscience or community service developed in people, maybe taught in school, that every company should have people go out and find these kinds of organizations in the community and say, "What can we do for you?" so that we can do what we do best—building community.

Inspiration

I grew up with a mother who was proactive in doing things for others. I remember when I was little and she worked for the American Embassy, there was a kid who needed a rabies vaccine or something like that right away after being bitten by a dog, and they couldn't find this vaccine. Time was of the essence, and my mom just took it upon herself. She called the embassy, and then the diplomats, and she said, "Do this! Find it!" In the middle of the night, she woke up ambassador assistants, and then they found it in Greece, and they had it shipped overnight so that it could be given to this kid. She just decided to do something about it, and she did it. She didn't know if she could or not. She didn't know if she would have the opportunity, but she didn't want to *not* do it. Whenever I take on something, it's very personal, and I see my mother was one of the models for me of the, "If not you, then who?" kind of thinking.

Advice

I do think that it's the people that make a place worthwhile. I believe that everywhere can be home, as long as we feel connected and welcome and included. I'm an immigrant too, I'm away from my home country, and I've been to many places, but here with you, with the people for Glocally Connected, I just found home here. You could go to Hawai'i or the most beautiful place, and you could feel lonely, and that would not be a beautiful place. It's important to connect with people.

"The education of women"

Friba Dawar

Roots

I was born in 1972 in Kabul, Afghanistan. We lived peacefully in a beautiful village –surrounded by greenery and the scent of pure earth and water– that was approximately 20 miles away from the capital city. I was six years old when the war started; at the beginning of the war, their tactic was to destroy anything that had to do with women's education, and enemies of education burnt down the only girls' school in the village. The incident led my father to send me and my older sister with my mother to the capital so we could continue to attend school.

When I graduated from high school in Afghanistan, I was filled with dreams of a bright future. I eagerly began my studies in law, majoring in international law and diplomacy, with hopes of making a significant impact. However, my aspirations were shattered when war engulfed Kabul. The city, once vibrant and full of promise, became a battleground. The departure of the Russian forces did little to quell the violence that swept through the city, forcing my family and me to flee our home.

We sought refuge in Pakistan, where the harsh reality of being a refugee quickly set in. My father, who had once thrived in accounting and finance, faced a grim new reality. Despite his expertise, finding work was nearly impossible. He returned to Afghanistan to earn money for us, but the exchange rates and economic conditions diminished his support. Each day was a struggle, yet we clung to hope.

In Pakistan, I desperately sought ways to continue my education, but opportunities for refugees were limited and often prohibitively expensive. Determined not to give up, I discovered the International Rescue Committee (IRC), which offered diploma courses for young girls to become teachers. I passed their entrance exam and joined the program, eventually being hired as a teacher at a refugee school. My hard work and dedication led to promotions, and I began to lead academic programs, helping others while continuing to learn and grow.

Then came September 11, a pivotal moment that changed everything. The U.S. military's intervention in Afghanistan marked the beginning of a new era. As the Taliban receded, a new government allied with the U.S. started to restore some sense of normalcy. Schools and universities reopened, and with renewed hope, we decided to return to Afghanistan.

Returning home was bittersweet. I had married and started a family, now with two young children and a third on the way. Despite the challenges of a growing family, I vowed not to abandon my dreams. I re-enrolled in university, determined to complete my education despite the obstacles.

Graduating was a triumph, but it was just the beginning. Armed with my degree and a heart full of resolve, I set out to make a lasting impact. I founded my own school, driven by the desire to provide others with the opportunities that had once seemed so elusive. My journey, marked by hardship and perseverance, led me to a place where I could make a meaningful difference for future generations.

Call to activism

From a young age, I dreamed of establishing a school for girls, especially in the villages. This dream was born from my childhood experiences and further fueled by my work in education. As a refugee in Pakistan, I saw firsthand the struggles faced by families, particularly girls and women, who endured violence and societal challenges. I realized that education could transform lives, offering solutions to these problems. I believe deeply in the saying, " If you educate a man, you educate a person. If you educate a woman, you educate a family, a society."

In 2008, I seized the opportunity presented by the post-Taliban era to found a girls' school. The new government was encouraging the establishment of private schools, and I was driven by a deep desire to make a meaningful difference. Despite having limited resources, I started with a small, humble beginning. My vision was clear: to create a place where girls could receive an education and forge a brighter future.

My school quickly became a beacon of hope for many young girls. Although I charged a modest fee, I was acutely aware of many families' financial challenges. In Afghanistan, it is common for families to prioritize boys' education, often believing that girls will eventually leave to join their husbands. Determined to change this mindset, I worked tirelessly to encourage families to send their daughters to school. I kept fees as low as possible and introduced scholarships for those who couldn't afford the modest costs.

Understanding the broader impact of education, I also offered after-school classes for women over 18. These classes allowed them to gain knowledge and skills that could transform their lives. I needed to extend educational benefits to all eager to learn, regardless of their age or economic status.

My passion for education extended beyond my own school. I became involved with the Afghan Institute of Learning, which aimed to promote education for women, especially in rural areas. We trained educators and health professionals to provide in-home education on topics like contraception, family planning, and basic literacy. We also empowered high school girls to become community leaders, challenging the belief that leadership was only for men.

However, my work was fraught with danger. The enemies of education and peace knew that spreading knowledge would foster resistance. Reluctantly, I decided to relocate temporarily. Leaving my home and school was heart-wrenching. I could hardly sleep, overwhelmed by the thought of my daughters having the same fate as me.

In search of safety, We decided to pursue our move to the U.S., where I had some family support. Despite the longing to return to our old life—my children missed their friends and school—we were granted a one-year visa. I packed our belongings into a suitcase and left everything behind: my school, our home, and the life we had built.

Initially, my husband stayed behind due to his job. I struggled with the burden of relocating with four young children. I urged him to join us, threatening to return if he couldn't come soon. He insisted that staying in the U.S. was the best choice for our family's safety and future. Despite the difficulties, he reassured me that this sacrifice was necessary for our daughters' education and safety.

Contributions

When I first arrived in Riverside, I was overwhelmed with sadness and longing for my past life. The transition was tough, and I missed my work. One day, as I was at the mosque for prayers, I had a conversation with some Afghan women. They spoke of a place called Glocally Connected with such enthusiasm, sharing how it had helped them learn English and integrate into the community. One woman gave me Sherry Mackay's number, suggesting I reach out.

I discussed it with my sister, who kindly called Sherry. Soon, I found myself at Glocally Connected, which was like a lifeline. Day by day, I felt my spirits lift. I made new friends and quickly became involved. Families in the community turned to me for help with translation and navigating various challenges. I stepped into roles as a translator, facilitator, and anything else needed. I was driven by a desire to help families build strong relationships, believing this would positively impact their children's futures.

My journey with Glocally Connected also led me to the Inlandia Institute, where I participated in publishing projects like *A Taste of Afghanistan* and *The Stranger Is My Friend.* Inspired by the positive feedback on my cooking, I ventured into catering with "Taste of Afghanistan." Although cooking wasn't my passion, I enjoyed sharing my food with others, and the catering business took off.

Enrolling at RCC was another milestone. It was a unique experience to attend classes alongside my two daughters. Being the oldest student in my class didn't bother me; I felt proud and exhilarated to pursue further education. It was a reminder that learning has no age limit.

Living in Riverside has been a transformative experience. I've built a network of friends who have become like family. They introduced me to influential people and opportunities, including Congressman Mark Takano, and connections with local institutions like UCR and Cal State University. Since moving here in 2016, Riverside has welcomed me with open arms, and I've embraced every moment. The community has become a cherished part of my life, and while I hold my past close, I am grateful for the new chapter Riverside has brought.

Inspiration

I grew up in a family where education was more than just a value; it was a way of life. My father, an orphan who made his way through school alone, was the youngest child in his family but had an immense love for learning. He often said, "I want all people in Afghanistan to be educated." Education was his sole focus when talking to us—not wealth, not material things, but the power of learning. He treated both boys and girls equally, believing in opportunities for all of us, and his unwavering support paved the way for my education.

As a parent myself, I've come to understand the struggles my parents faced, even though they never showed it. My parents were always ready to help others. My mother took special care of women, while my father assisted men, often stepping in to provide for those in need. I remember how he would quietly leave food at people's doors if he noticed they were struggling. In season, my mother would invite anyone who needed it to take apples and peaches from our garden, especially families who didn't have farms.

Growing up with such values instilled in us a deep sense of responsibility. Each of us wanted to give back, to offer guidance and support, and especially to help others receive the education that had been so crucial in our lives. The lessons we learned from our parents shaped who we are today and continue to inspire us to make a difference in the lives of others.

Advice

I have four daughters, and my greatest wish is for them to become exceptional leaders, regardless of their paths. I encourage them to pursue their passions and follow their dreams because true fulfillment comes from doing what they love.

To me, a great leader treats everyone equally and with respect. It's not just about speaking; it's about listening, too. Sometimes, the best ideas come from unexpected places. I always remind my daughters to treat people with kindness and to recognize that, in the eyes of Allah (God), we are all the same—just human beings.

Having traveled from Afghanistan to India, Saudi Arabia, Dubai, and finally, the United States, I've seen firsthand that, despite our different backgrounds, we share the same humanity.

"Behind the scenes, below the surface"

Paulette Brown-Hinds

Roots

I was born in 1967 in San Bernardino. My parents, Hardy and Cheryl Brown, still live about two blocks away from where I was born and where I grew up. Actually, they didn't leave the west side of San Bernardino, so every home we lived in was near that area of San Bernardino. I came to Riverside when I started graduate school in 1990. I started graduate school at UC Riverside after spending four and a half years in undergrad at Cal State San Bernardino. We had always had a connection to Riverside. The *Black Voice News*, the newspaper that my family has been the stewards of for almost forty years now, was founded at UCR. Students founded it in 1972 at UCR, and then its circulation was still in Riverside, so we always had kind of a connection to Riverside.

Call to activism

Growing up, my parents were very involved in community activities, and they were the PTA-engaged parents who would go down and advocate for their kids, and all kids, at the school board, before my dad was elected to the school board. They were doing activism around their kids, around education. My parents were both very involved in scouting. My mother was a Girl Scout leader, my dad was a Boy Scout leader. My dad did the first big Boy Scout camp on the west side for Black and Latino kids. No one had done that before in that area of the region.

It was just a part of growing up in our home. **Around our table early on, it was conversations about what you did at school, but then also what needs to change at school.** It was about the neighborhood and how we can make things better. That was just the way we talked, and I think it comes from the way my parents were also raised. My grandfather was a sharecropper from North Carolina. My grandparents used to pack up the kids and at certain times, harvest time, they would move the whole family to this one farm and they would all farm, so my dad was also a sharecropper. My grandparents were really involved in NAACP. My grandfather helped register people to vote in this rural part of North Carolina under the threat of the Klan. My grandmother on my mother's side was good friends with Maxine Waters. When Maxine Waters got her start as an activist as a Head Start parent, my grandmother was one of the Head Start teachers. They were always involved in voting, we always talked about voting, we were registering people to vote. So that's the background for activism.

The reason we had the newspaper is I think two reasons. One is, my parents were both looking for community service. My mother was kind of volunteering, I think taking photos, and my dad was writing a column, and he had his day job at this point. His first big job was as a meter reader. He was the first Black meter reader for Southern California Edison. Back then it was called Cal Electric, and he started working at Kaiser. But he always had these other interests. He was writing columns for this newspaper. So, part of it was community service. The other part of it was my dad was always concerned about losing his job and not being able to support his family. And the reason he worried about losing his job wasn't because he wasn't doing a good job, but because he was outspoken and because he had this kind of advocacy, he was concerned that he may one day be asked to leave and he always wanted to make sure he had something that could support his family.

And so we have the newspaper, and then that became our vehicle for a lot of the advocacy work because it was started in the spirit of the Black press even though we didn't start it. Providing a voice for the voiceless and making sure we're telling our own story. Then the advocacy became around key issues. When South Africa was still under apartheid, there was a community of South African expatriates here and they found my parents and wanted to get messages out, and I remember conversations about divestment. When I was in college in undergrad, where I'm working with teachers or professors in my university, we were doing these big forums on divesting and having meetings at my house. I was on my own at this point, so it was with my roommates, but we would have events at our house. Miriam Makeba came and spoke at our house even though at that point I didn't even know who she was, really. It moved easily from kitchen table conversation to taking all of that conversation that we had as a family at the kitchen table to, okay, now it's the newspaper, and we have a larger voice.

Contributions

Honestly I don't like being in the forefront of things. Most of the time I'd rather be kind of behind the scenes. I'm not necessarily comfortable with being the face of things. It's always a challenge to me, I kind of have to force myself sometimes to even say yes to those kind of opportunities. I have the newspaper and we have the nonprofit, but I also have the strategic communications work I do, right now the Black media and communications lead for the 2020 census. So I have a whole team of really good experts working with me. I have a lot of Sacramento contacts. Some were from my mom, but some are from my communications work, one is Governor Newsom. Even when I'm talking to the governor, it's like "You need to pay attention to those neglected parts of the state," and luckily he came into that position and he hired some key people who grew up in the Central Valley or they're from the Inland Empire, so we have some key people who are trying to make sure that that stays an important part of his commitment to the people, that he is making sure that resources are allocated more equitably and that places like ours that have been neglected may get more resources. It's a constant push but he at least has that mindset. I try to even use the political connections for that, not just philanthropy.

I find that I'm able to use all of the experience and all of the relationships that I've developed either through the relationships in my family or that I've developed on my own to use those to benefit communities. And I care a lot about the Black community, I really do, but I also care about our region, so I try to be a voice for our region when I'm in these statewide conversations. When I'm in Sacramento, when I'm in the board room at the [James] Irvine Foundation, I'm thinking not just of our region but inland regions, those regions that have that have been somewhat under-resourced for so long, I'm always saying how can we do more? I'm always thinking like that. I was fortunate with my family to have a solid and great foundation. The work I'm doing, I consider it built on that foundation, and I've been able to extend and do more.

I care about the Black community, I care about our region, but I also care tremendously about the news media and its important role it plays in our society, so that's why I was really involved with the California News Publishers Association as a board member and then finally making it to president, being the first African American, actually the first person of color to lead that organization after 130 years.

My interest in GIS came when I met Jack and Laura Dangermond, the founders of Esri, back in 2016. One of my team members, his wife worked for Esri, so they mapped our Underground Railroad tour. And I thought this was kind of cool, so I started looking into it and we did another map that I still really like. It's about the history of segregated beaches in California called "Segregation by the Sea." Our team really enjoyed the kind of multimedia aspect of it. They enjoyed being able to visualize data in different ways. Everyone got excited about it. Part of the challenge we found is so much data that you would think is easily accessible may not be desegregated by race. It may be hard to find. So sometimes even when I want to create maps based on Esri's ArcGIS platform, my team is like, "Paulette, we don't have the data!" I have one of our team members who's writing a grant for this concept we have for this data hub that will be accessible to Black media—journalists who are writing about the African American community and supporting the African American community will have access. And we got a big Facebook grant when the pandemic started for some of our work with GIS and telling the coronavirus story. One of my graphic artists decided to go get a certificate in GIS. They're making it easier and easier for people to use who are not technical, so they have a platform like StoryMaps which are great for media. It's kind of immersive-type storytelling and so it's wonderful. That's how we started, but because I met Jack and because we started creating the maps, I sent them to him, and we just started a friendship. I went to their partner conference they have in

Palm Springs, and as I was looking at the technology, I got so excited. I'm not a technical person, but I was seeing the value and it was just so clear and especially—you know, we talk about some of our foundational work, as I mentioned, as a family, of empowering people, and in that kind of advocacy **I saw this as a tool of empowerment for the Black community.**

Jack [Dangermond] had me come to Esri for an annual event they have with students from Boyle Heights. It's a STEM academy, it's a STEM public school, but the kids are in English and History and Social Sciences and Humanities, but they're learning to solve problems in their communities using GIS. They identify, as a group, a problem and then they either get the data to show the problem or they use GIS to find a solution. When I saw it, Jack looks at me and goes, "You know I want you to see this," and I'm like, "Yes! Black kids need to be engaged. Black kids need to be educated and informed on this technology. They need to know it's right here." So I ended up taking my mapping interest and expanding it, learning about community mapping projects and saying, "Okay, we're doing the one piece with our media where we're trying to tell the story, but can we work with organizations that are educational NGOs, so community-based organizations, and just basically present this as an opportunity?" So I ended up with two different organizations. One was a coding camp. They were doing more teaching kids to code and we brought Esri in, and so they incorporated GIS into their coding curriculum. The other is Shirley Coates, who's here in Riverside, who has a leadership academy for girls, middle school girls, called the Society for Extraordinary Women, and she has a signature program called Ignite Leadership Academy. She saw data about especially Black girls and how far they were behind in middle school, so she's like, "Let me focus on girls in that age bracket and create a leadership program for them." And so it's a Saturday academy, she works with them for ten weeks. We connected her with what we call Geo Mentors, somebody who does GIS, and she's had over a hundred girls now who have been exposed; they've learned StoryMaps, they've learned surveying, so they're able to look in their community, as part of one of their activities, and identify places that need, like if there's a pothole, or just things that need to be fixed in their community, and they undergo this survey tool, so they learn how to take a geotagged image and upload it. So they're working with these geo mentors on how to solve the problems that they see right around them. They learn how to tell their story using GIS also; talk about where they were born, where they live, where they traveled. That's the more exciting part for me. I am not a GIS expert. I consider it part of my advocacy work. I just see the value of it.

Inspiration

My parents, definitely. People like Sylvia Martin James, who we loved. She's one of those folks that there was this kind of passion about community and making sure we have the best, most inclusive, equitable community, and knowing that it's going to be the fight of your life, like it's never going to be easy or perfect, but never backing down and always staying committed. Just having ideas, like the idea for the Grier Pavilion, this idea that can become this kind of beacon for that ideal of diversity, and then saying, "Okay let's do it!" I marvel, especially, at the women of color, and especially in our community—Rose Mayes, Jennifer Vaughn-Blakely, Woodie Rucker-Hughes.

Advice

There's a strategy to community work to actually achieve certain goals. It's not always about marching in the street, and it's not about, "I'm the leader, follow me!" But it's seeing, we know what we want the goal to be, and then how do we get there, and then backing the steps up. **A lot of it is below the surface, so people don't see all of that strategy that goes into making something happen.** It's all the things that are behind it and underneath it that are really making things move, and I think that's what I've seen, especially in the women I really admire, is that kind of movement, that kind of strategy. Most of the women that really make things happen aren't necessarily the ones that are out front fully. Even like the big Women's March—knowing that a small group of women at the bookstore are meeting and starting to plan this thing, and you end up with thousands of people there. I think those spaces are where the strategies can really be developed. Those are the women I admire and that I try to emulate in the work I do.

The power of place

M. Rosalind Sagara

Roots

I was born in 1976 in Monterey Park, California, which is not far from downtown Los Angeles. I grew up in Alhambra, California, in the San Gabriel Valley. My family moved to the Inland Empire in the late eighties, and I have been living in Riverside since 2018. I consider myself to be a native of this region.

Call to activism

Following my undergraduate studies at UC Riverside, I went to grad school in the Midwest at the University of Iowa to pursue film studies. I had a keen interest in studying film and in documentary films in particular. I was there for a little over two years and ended my academic career at that point with a master's degree, and came back and worked with some independent documentary filmmakers. I worked in different aspects of filmmaking, including production and film distribution, in a number of jobs. I was really interested in that work, but I was looking for something different, and by the mid-2000s I applied and was able to get a job with the Hotel Employees and Restaurant Employees Union, which later merged with UNITE. UNITE HERE was working hard to organize Indian gaming casino workers, and we have a number of Indian casinos in the region. I worked out of the Palm Springs office, and I was mostly working in communications and helping to tell the story of Indian casino workers and their struggle to organize their workplaces and improve their working conditions. Through that work, I got a lot of exposure and training to community organizing. I really learned and honed skills in campaigning, from getting out the vote to learning how to develop leaders and build a campaign.

My introduction into activism probably began as a student in college in learning more about Asian American history, the history of communities of color, Ethnic Studies classes, and becoming a member of different student organizations and really seeing the power of people coming together. Especially as an undergrad student, I began to feel or to gain more of a social consciousness in terms of my political identity as an Asian American, but also as a daughter of an immigrant. At the time I was a student at UCR, I think there were a number of issues in bringing to the forefront the importance of diversity and inclusion, which we continue to see today. Those were my first introductions into what that work might look like.

That continued as a grad student when I was in Iowa, as that was the first time that I had been out of Southern California and into an environment that was very homogeneous that was not as welcoming to, from my own perspective, students of color. At the time, there was a student effort to preserve two older houses that were being used by students of color at the time. There was one house that was being used by Black students on campus and the other was used by Latino and Native American students. They had been used as places where these students could come together and feel connected to other students of color, where there were cultural activities, places to study, a place to have cultural programming. The university felt that these houses were dilapidated or deteriorating, and they weren't interested in maintaining them. The plan was to move these student groups into a new student union. We wanted the university to maintain these cultural houses because they were needed. They were needed as safe spaces. They were needed for students of color who felt like they wanted a place where they felt like they belonged. And so there was an effort to preserve these places. I didn't think of it at the time as historic preservation. I didn't even know that there was such a thing as historic preservation. I was looking at it in terms of creating a sense of belonging, creating a sense of place, and creating a sense of students providing input into the campus life. Students organized to save those two houses. It didn't happen while I was there as a student. It took some time later, but those houses were preserved. It's a testament to the power of students coming together and letting administration know the importance and the value of those places.

In 2008, I became aware of the issue in Riverside with our Chinatown archeological site. At that time, I had been doing some family genealogy research to learn more about my family ancestry on my maternal side. My mother was born and raised in Mexico. She is of Chinese and Mexican ancestry and she's third-generation Chinese Mexican. Being a fourth generation Chinese Mexican myself, I had longed to be more closely connected to my Chinese heritage. I had been really delving into my family history and finding that a lot of the places that family members or friends of family members remembered that were associated with the Chinese community in Mazatlán, which is where my family is from, were gone. They had been developed. They were in disrepair. They were slowly disappearing. When I learned about this issue close to home, about a site that had been recognized for its historic significance and was potentially going to be destroyed by a development project, I really felt strongly that I could really try to get involved in this issue. It was bringing together a lot of my interests at the time. It was an opportunity to connect with other Chinese and Asian Americans here locally to talk about how we were going to put together a campaign to stop, at the time, this project.

My father was born in Gardena. He's Japanese American, nisei, second generation. I understood what being Japanese American meant to me growing up in a way that was different than my Chinese American heritage. We would go to Little Tokyo to buy fish or buy sushi or go to Nisei Week Festival. I felt like I was part of the broader Japanese American community. My father and his family were incarcerated, first in Poston and then they were moved to Tule Lake. In college, I spent time reflecting on these places and the importance of preserving them and understanding their place in history. I wasn't really thinking in terms of myself preserving them or how I would get involved in that until much later, but certainly it has been an interest of mine to bring attention to the long-term preservation of these places of Japanese American and Asian American heritage.

Contributions

I learned about the threat that the Riverside Chinatown site was facing in 2008 from a friend who had attended a meeting or gotten an email or something alerting her to this development project. I started by attending a community meeting, and I learned that there was a project being proposed. Shortly after that meeting, several community members who had attended that meeting got together separately to discuss what could be done. Our group at the time formed an organization called Riverside Chinese Cultural Preservation Committee. This group included members of some of our local Chinese schools and other members of the community, some of whom were affiliated with formal organizations, but also just folks who were interested in this issue, people who lived in Riverside or this area and also people who were of Chinese ancestry, but a lot of people who were not of Chinese ancestry coming together to think about what we might do. There was a public process which allows the community to participate and provide comment at meetings, in person or in writing, and so a lot of effort was made to attend meetings.

For several months, we followed the process and attended a lot of public meetings, but also additional meetings with city staff to try to see if there could be a compromise. This was all leading up to a city council meeting. We packed the city council chambers with people who spoke up about their objection to this project. What was proposed was a medical office building, and the way that it was proposed would have really destroyed the site. There would be no way to preserve what remained. We were not opposed to the development of a medical office building in the neighborhood, but we were opposed to the placement of the building atop the archaeological remains, which would destroy the site. Unfortunately, we were not able to convince the city council to reject this project and it was approved. At that time we looked at our options and decided that we were going to legally challenge the decision. We formed a new group called the Save Our Chinatown Committee that was really focused on that first step of taking legal action to try to overturn the decision. At that time, the Save Our Chinatown Committee was an informal organization, as was our previous group, but in time, we incorporated into a nonprofit organization, in part to be able to raise funds for our legal campaign, but also because we wanted to be able to continue to educate the community about the history of Chinese Americans in Riverside and the region, so we felt that becoming a nonprofit would help up facilitate that.

We set up an executive committee to provide some leadership in the RCCPC days, and I had volunteered to be on that committee. When we created the Save Our Chinatown Committee, most of the founding members became board members when we incorporated as a nonprofit organization, and I was a member of the board. At the time, our chair was Deborah Wong, who is a professor at UCR. When she stepped away from the organization, because she's so busy and she's involved in so many things, she remained supportive of our work, and I stepped into the role as chair when she left. We launched our legal challenge following the city council decision. Our lawsuit was against the owner of the property, which was Riverside County Office of Education. It was also against the city of Riverside. That fight took several years to come to a conclusion. Shortly after we had filed our intent to start a case, we were surprised to find the owner of the property had allowed the developer to bring some heavy earth-moving equipment to the property and do some grading of the property, which really should not have happened. I think that really upped the ante in terms of our need to remain vigilant of the property. We had to file a temporary restraining order and later a permanent injunction, to cease activity at the site until our court case came to a resolution because we couldn't count on the owner and the potential developer to do the right thing. But that also provided more of an opportunity for us to tell the story through the media, and because there was more attention, we were doing some rallies around the property.

At the time we were also working a lot with students at UCR who were organizing other students to support our efforts, and they were trying to put pressure on Riverside County Office of Education to really come to the table to see if there was a way to preserve the site. That was really helpful. We were organizing students and other residents to continue to voice concerns over this issue. We were meeting weekly. It's incredible that people really felt so strongly about this issue that they would give their time to really help support the cause. We finally got a ruling, and the ruling basically would overturn the city approval of the project, and so the project was stopped. It was a huge win for our committee and we were able to breathe a sigh of relief for a moment. This developer was really intent on building a medical office building, and so following that court ruling, we actually did work with the developer and some of his new partners to find an alternative location for a medical office building in the neighborhood, and that building has been built and is in operation. We had never been opposed to the project; we were opposed to the siting of the project. The legal effort was costly, but we were lucky to find a local environmental attorney who worked with us at a highly reduced rate. He did so much work for us. He did not charge us what he would have normally billed somebody, and so we were really lucky to find him and to have his help. But there was a lot of work to fundraise over the years.

We believe that the Chinatown site should be made a public park, where there would be limited development, but an opportunity to learn the history of the community that was there and that contributed to the city in so many ways. We do walking tours in partnership with some other community organizations, the Japanese American Citizens League and the Young Oak Kim Center for Korean American Studies at UCR. In terms of bringing forth those stories of Chinese Americans in Riverside, we've been conducting a lot of historical research and working with the National Archives at the Riverside facility to digitize their records of the Chinese Exclusion case files. We're really excited to get those materials accessible to the public.

My involvement really set me on the path to pursue a career in historic preservation. I started attending some of the National Trust for Historic Preservation conferences and learning more about the profession and talking to people who were working in the field. I decided that for me it would be helpful to go back to school. There was a program at USC in the School of Architecture that focused on heritage conservation and it seemed like a good fit, and so in 2012, I became a student there. I was there for two years. Following that, I worked as an independent consultant for a bit, and now I'm at the Los Angeles Conservancy, working as Neighborhood Outreach Manager.

Historic places have served many purposes in our communities. People have various reasons why they care about a particular place and various reasons why they get involved in preserving such a place. Given recent attention to anti-Asian hate crimes and violence, I ask us to think about how historic places associated with Asian American Pacific Islander heritage can serve as places of healing for community, not only for the AAPI community but for all people. People often go to the places that are most familiar, and sometimes those happen to be very old places.

Inspiration

My experience organizing with UNITE HERE alongside other organizers in the Indian gaming industry in the Inland Empire was so inspiring. The majority of people will never know their names, but they take on such risks in their workplaces to try to improve them. They've really been great role models for me in terms of learning to find inspiration in yourself and in your current conditions and how to struggle towards a more equitable future.

When I think back about members of my family who have struggled through so many things in life—I think about my grandparents on my father's side as immigrants and having to go through incarceration during World War II and really just enduring and surviving that time and rebuilding their lives—it gives me great comfort and inspiration knowing that I come from a lineage of people who have gone through some really difficult things but have survived.

Advice

Believe in yourself, believe that you can make a difference. You can't do this work alone, but you can definitely contribute.

Practice self-care. This is something that I have to remind myself too, and I haven't always been that great at it. Sometimes this work gets really heavy and overwhelm sets in. **A lot of these projects or issues are not going to be resolved immediately, so you need to really pace yourself and really take time to take care of yourself,** because this work can be long and hard. I advise other activists to really practice self-care and to incorporate that as a regular practice.

"Be tenacious"

Carol Park

Roots

I was born in 1980 in Paramount. I grew up in Cerritos and moved to Riverside in 1998.

My parents were immigrants. They came in the 1970s. They met here, they got married here, and they had me and my brothers. I have two older brothers, and we're all a year apart. Growing up, my mom only ever really spoke to me in Korean. She raised me to be a Korean traditional daughter—save face; don't shame me; when you get married, cook well, clean well, be beautiful. I took all those lessons and was like, "Okay, I get that, but I'm not living in 1970s Korea, mom!" So I grew up thinking, "I'm Korean, but I'm also American." As Colonel [Young Oak] Kim would say, "I'm one hundred percent both," and I embrace both of my heritages.

I grew up working for my mom at her gas station in Compton. I started working with mom in late 1990 because my dad had died earlier in the year, and so mom had to take over the family business. Everything was a struggle. I went with her to work because the gas station was open seven days a week, twenty-four hours a day. This was typical of Korean kids at that time. You went to the shop with mom or dad, and you worked. We were behind bulletproof glass windows at a gas station in Compton, California during the eighties and nineties, at the height of the crack war, turf wars, you name it. Being Korean American also meant that I was growing up in this very specific time which shaped the Korean American community as it is today, because the birth or the rebirth of the Korean American identity happened after the 1992 Los Angeles Riots. That's where my Korean American identity is.

Call to activism

When you think about this notion of activism, there is a sort of paradigm attached to it that I think we need to be bold about and say, "It's not just signatures, it's not just protesting, it's everything in between." It is doing that coalition-building work. It is going into the community on the ground level, or going up to your neighbors, and saying, "Hello! I'm your new neighbor!" **I think we have to go beyond this paradigm of what we usually think of activism as. It's more than that.** When you're being bold, you're breaking through stereotypes, breaking through these binaries that keep us in these very specific categories.

I started to think about community and community activism in different ways. **What I was doing began with my love affair with karate.** I started doing karate when I came to UC Riverside. I started in 1999, and I didn't quite get into activism when I began my training. But years later, when I switched styles and dojos, I started to teach kids, and I would do it free of charge. I started teaching at Bryant Elementary after school programs. That began my love affair for giving back in that way.

I also started doing activism when I began working for the Young Oak Kim Center for Korean American Studies at UC Riverside under the leadership of Professor Edward T. Chang. I went there as a grad student and started working there in 2010 as a graduate student researcher when I was getting my master's degree. While I was there, the scope of my work just broadened in a way that I would have never imagined. I was doing karate, I was doing my thing, and then when I got into the Center, I realized just how much more you could do in terms of education. So I started participating in seminars. People would say, "Hey, you know about some Korean stuff, you have these experiences, could you come and talk about that? Could you give back in that way?" And I said, "Sure, why not?" And then I thought to myself, "Well, why don't we start an intern program here at the

Center?" Professor Chang said yes, so under his leadership, we began an internship program where we mentor and guide undergraduate students and graduate students to learn more about race, ethnicity, and identity. You don't have to be Korean. We've had I think forty interns pass through in the last ten years. They go on to do some wonderful things. Some have become graduate students, some of them are in doctoral programs now, some of them have gone on to become producers at movie studios, some have become community activists, teachers, it's just wonderful to see them grow and become these things that you just hope and wish that they would become, and then they do.

Contributions

I wrote a memoir [*Memoirs of a Cashier*] to give voice to the Korean American community during the L.A. Riots of 1992. I did hours upon hours upon hours upon hours of research and interviews with my mom and my brothers. I worked on it when I was getting my master's degree in creative writing. The author Deanne Stillman would tell me, "Carol, you tell these stories about your mom's gas station, these stories just come out of your pores. You should be writing this." So I started writing drafts. Then one day, Deanne forwarded me a press release from Bettye Miller, who used to be a staff PR writer for UCR and who also was an old friend of mine from *The Press-Enterprise*, because I used to work there. She had put out this press release about a new Korean American study center being founded at UC Riverside by Dr. Edward T. Chang. I ended up reaching out to him. He hired me as a graduate student researcher, and then I realized this was the dude that I was reading about in all of my research! I was like, "Wait a minute, this is the Edward T. Chang that published that thing on the L.A. riots! Whoa!" It just came together from there, and then the book was published in 2017 through the Center, and it just took off. It's a lot of work, but I enjoy it. This is what my calling is. This is the work that we need to do to raise that Korean American voice and identity and also the voice of Asian Americans. This country is multicultural, and we have to be able to understand each other in order to, to quote Rodney King, in order to get along. That's part of our activism work, is to connect each other, to understand each other's identities, our cultures, our backgrounds, our histories, who we are and why we are where we are, what are all these structural conditions that we're talking about, and how that fits into our communities. When we start to understand those connections, then we understand each other, and then hopefully in that way we can make the world a better place.

Each piece has its place. I'm teaching English at California Indian Nations College, and I teach Ethnic Studies at UCR. The academic informs my community research, because then I know what the heck I'm talking about! The teaching helps me to put into practice what I'm researching. I do activism stuff because I know that we have to understand each other, and racism is systemic, so in order to deconstruct and disrupt or frustrate those kinds of systemic narratives of racism, you have to go into the community. The writing aspect of it is what also puts it out there so that people who are not part of academia can learn. Academia is lovely and I love it, I'm part of it, I can't knock it. But when we publish these twenty-five page papers on the structural conditions that created the riots of 1992 and use all that language—it's good, you need that—but homie down the street, whom I knew when I was working in Compton, he's gonna look at me and go, "Whatcha talkin' about Carol, I'm not gonna read that, are you nuts?" So, my thing is, if we're going to do activism, we also need to do it on a level that reaches as many people as possible, and that means Facebook Live-ing, that means doing the projects, that means taking these papers and rewriting them into shorter papers, doing these different things that speak to the population in a different way because not everybody's going to read that twenty-five page article, not everyone's going to go to that seminar or to that colloquium or to that conference.

Some years ago, Dr. Chang discovered that Pachappa Camp was actually the first organized Korean American settlement in the United States. People thought that it was in Hawai'i, people thought that it might have been in San Francisco, but through a great deal of research, both in the Korean language newspapers, English newspapers, Sanborn maps, you name it, he confirmed it. In Riverside, Dosan Ahn Chang-Ho, a Korean American patriot, came and saw that there were a lot of Koreans, and they needed help in getting jobs, and so he created the Korean Labor Bureau. Sometime in early 1905, Dosan established Pachappa Camp as an organized Korean American settlement operated by, run by and rented by Korean Americans. They borrowed money from Cornelius E. Rumsey, a member of Calvary Presbyterian Church. He was impressed by Dosan and lent them fifteen hundred bucks, so they rented these bungalows that once housed Chinese railroad workers. Calvary Presbyterian Church established a Korean mission there. There are records of this in their minutes, which I was very blessed to be able to look at. I was looking at this cursive handwriting from 1904, 1905, and even earlier, and they mentioned the Korean mission and they mentioned Dosan Ahn Chang-Ho. Dr. Chang said, "This is a huge discovery." We decided to ask the city of Riverside to designate it as some sort of a landmark, and they said no, because there's nothing existing there anymore. However, I thought to myself, just because there's no landmark, "Can't we just somehow still designate it something? Can we put a sign, a placard," and then the city said, "well, we could, but you'd have to get permission from SoCal Gas Company, there's all these hoops that you need to go through. You need to get the permissions." I was disappointed, but I still thought there's got to be something we can do. So Professor Chang and I thought about it, and then I said, "Well, how about we make it a point of cultural interest," because I was doing the research, and I realized you could do that, Riverside just hadn't done it before. We asked their preservation officer, Erin Gettis, and she said we could but there was no civic code for it. Long story short, we got in touch with SoCal Gas Company, and they said, "Yes, we would love to work with you on this." The Cultural Heritage Board of Riverside said "Yes, we'll create a provision for a point of cultural interest," and the city now will designate a site as a point of cultural interest even though it has no building. So now when you go to 3096 Cottage Street, you'll see the Pachappa Camp sign that we put through, the first point of cultural interest in the city of Riverside. From now on, people who have these kinds of sites can apply to the city to make points of cultural interest! I never thought that I would do something like that. To me, it was just this neat little project that we were working on, and then here we are years later. It's our work to be able to bring these stories to light and educate others so that we can keep growing together and hopefully understand each other and not have these stupid racial stereotypes of each other and conflicts. There's no reason for that.

Inspiration

Dr. Chang—he's my mentor, and I kind of follow in his footsteps. He's part of the Council of Korean Americans, he goes overseas to Korea to talk about Korean American identity and how we should all understand that the diasporic communities are still Korean, that we should not discount each other, we should help each other.

My mom was a role model to me—her strength and her ability to carry on despite all the hardships. I look up to her very much in that way, and thought, "I gotta be strong like her," and if I'm gonna pursue this route, I'd better be just as strong, because it's gonna be hard. I am trying to emulate her strength.

Advice

My advice is to be tenacious. Be strong. And don't be afraid. We face so many challenges as people of color, as women, as women of color, and to not have the tenacity to fight back and to stand up would be the greatest pitfall. If I wasn't tenacious back in the day, I wouldn't have become a reporter. When I became a journalist, I was, I believe, the only Asian woman in that entire bureau, and the news staff at the time was predominantly white. The tenacity was what got my foot in the door in the first place. I worked as a clerk at *The Press-Enterprise* for a number of months before Nels Jensen, who was the editor at the time, gave me a call and said, "Go ahead and apply for that reporter's position." I was in the San Bernardino bureau. There was no other Asian person. But had I not been tenacious, our Asian American voice wouldn't have been heard there, so the tenacity is important.

And be you, find your own voice, find what you're passionate about. If you don't know what motivates you or drives you or gets you up in the morning to do what you want to do, you gotta find that. Every morning, I get up, I know exactly what I want to do. I'm going to work for this, I'm going to do this project because it fits into this larger purpose. Be passionate about what you want to do, so that when you wake up in the morning, although it may be hard at times, you're still going to be happy that you did it.

"Be the archivist of your own life"

Precious Pipeloluwa Fasakin

Roots

I was born in Pomona, California, in 1999. My parents immigrated from Nigeria in 1995 and then lived in Los Angeles and then in Pomona and quickly I was born. I'm the last of four. I'm an I.E. native, but I was brought to Riverside in 2016 when I began attending UC Riverside. My family moved to Riverside as well, so I'm really a Riverside girl.

Call to activism

When I was fifteen, I began working with a nonprofit organization called Global Girl Media. They're a fantastic group, all about giving the voice, the tools, the microphone to young women everywhere. The organization exists in Los Angeles, in New York, in Chicago, South Africa, Guatemala, so many places around the world. I was affiliated with the Los Angeles group, so I would take the train every day and I would go down there for about two months during the summer. I was interested in journalism and storytelling, and I started telling stories about immigration, telling stories about mass incarceration, sharing stories about depression in communities of color, specifically my household. We were looking at many different stories that girls have to tell. I began interviewing people, I began interviewing my family, people within my community, I learned video editing and filming. That's where really I began to peek my eye into activism. Then I realized that not only I but all of these communities that I recognize have these stories to tell, and Global Girl Media really gave me the lens through which I still look at the world. I really started to become human, to develop that conscious empathy. I think that storytelling in a strange way, although it's fictional, is really about trying to imagine a world that you actually want.

I came to UCR and I lived in the dorms right next to KUCR, Pentland Hills, and I remember my dad was driving me in his old 1995 Toyota truck, and he's just clinking down the road, and I remember I looked at KUCR because we were driving so slow, and I said, "Daddy, I'm gonna work there." And he's like, "Okay, get good grades first, focus on school!" So I moved into the dorm and I began bothering KUCR constantly. I would walk down from my dorm, probably every week, twice a week, saying, "Oh, are you hiring? Are you looking for a new journalist? Are you looking for reporters? I can do that, how do I apply?" They got tired of me very quickly. I was lucky enough to apply and become part of KUCR. I wanted to interview people, and I wanted to be sharing stories on the radio. I found out that first, I would have to be a music DJ, and that was a really interesting experience for me, and even now I still have my music show. That's actually the focus of a lot of things that I do at KUCR, because I realized that there's so many avenues of storytelling. It's not just asking people questions, doing interviews. Music is a powerful and continual avenue of storytelling and activism, and I wanted to explore that through the lens of Blackness everywhere, and that's pretty much what my show does, through music from the African continent and the African diaspora.

I'm a double major in economics and anthropology. When I got into college, I didn't want to look at economics as a dirty word. I think that a lot of people who go without money, we view the role of money as taboo. I wanted to look at that a little bit differently, and include anthropology, because I never wanted that consideration to be dehumanized. It's all about storytelling.

Contributions

I view KUCR as the intersection of all of it. At first, I did not view it as a form of activism. I came to KUCR through journalism, and then I started to realize its very tangible impact on its listeners, especially those within our airwaves. In doing my show, I realized how critical not just radio is, but community-based radio stations are. **There's something so impactful about giving communities the tools to speak for themselves.** KUCR is a radio station for and by people from Riverside and its surrounding areas, and I think that is so powerful, and that notion of for us, by us has become so central to the work that I do at KUCR, at Underground Scholars, with Global Girl Media, and with the course I teach. It's this idea that we can speak for ourselves, although we've been silenced for so long. Now is the time for our voices to be brought to the forefront by us. I think KUCR does that so beautifully, allowing its DJs so much creative space to grow, to share their opinions, their music with their listeners, and it really is a special place.

Underground Scholars really idealizes what it means to use the academic space as a place of empowerment for people who've been historically outside of the ivory tower. Underground Scholars looks at the experiences and the presence of formerly incarcerated, system-impacted, and even some currently incarcerated individuals within whatever city it serves. At Underground Scholars UC Riverside, we're looking at Riverside and serving the Inland Empire as a whole. A lot of the work we do is contacting people who are in Riverside jails and Inland Empire prisons so they can see that there is an opportunity for support once they are no longer incarcerated, and a pathway to schools. We're trying to create a prison-to-school pipeline. In serving as the organization's co-president, a lot of my work is having these conversations with not only people who are currently incarcerated, but people who were formerly incarcerated and don't see a clear pathway to going to a university or even to school in general. I want them to know that we have worked and we are working to make these resources available. I've seen how it transforms lives. Prison is one of the most dehumanizing processes, and education and learning are so humanizing by nature. It's this process of bringing people back to what should have been, because so many of the experiences that people are forced into in prison take away that element of curiosity that one naturally has for this world, and Underground Scholars focuses on creating a space where that curiosity can be brought back to the surface. All of the efforts made by Underground Scholars are brought to the table by students. They're supported by faculty advisors, but students are the ones called on to execute this work. I think it's so empowering because this is probably the only space I've ever been in where I've seen so many people who were formerly incarcerated who are about to be called "Doctor." It's not to say that this position or name is what makes a life of worth, but it's this idea that you can create a pathway for yourself despite having so much systematic disruption.

A lot of the work that I do is making myself available to people who are currently incarcerated and getting resources to folks, especially those who are about to get out or have just gotten out. I try to make sure current students are financially supported in every way possible. Sometimes this is asking departments, can you give us a scholarship? Sometimes it's asking the school, I have a student here who's needing X, Y, and Z. On what basis are you willing to help support this student through Underground Scholars? That's a lot of the work that I do, going and shaking some tables and asking some questions and asking for the support the university promised that it has for its students, keeping that pathway of accountability alive.

Abolitionist for my community now means abolishing prisons, and there really can be no way around this. A more just, more beautiful, and equitable world will exist without prisons, and this is really the focal point of so much of the work that we do. Creating this prison-to-school pipeline that USI [Underground Scholar Initiative] focuses on is very key to this idea of abolition, because we want people who have been in these prisons to be able to articulate in a way that can be understood and disseminated widely what was actually going on within these prisons. I think from there, we can better understand that these places should not exist. There is nothing rehabilitating about a prison. It's all about punishment, it's all about retribution. I believe that a better world has no space for prisons, and so much of the work around abolition isn't just, "I don't want this to exist." It's, "How can we create spaces that make sure this never exists again?"

I designed and taught a class, "Resistance Theory: Making the Personal Political in the United States." It's an R'Course, where students teach students. It's definitely been a labor of love. This course came from my work at KUCR. At the time, I was doing my show and I was getting a lot of calls from people asking, you discuss this movement, can you please share this with me, is there anything you can share, a resource, any links. Of course! I started to realize that people do care about this, and I also started to think about this idea of history and the way in which it's told. I was seeing so much storytelling again. Amazing teachers tell these histories and they say, "This is what was done to poor people. This is what was done to Black people. This is what was done, etc., etc." I thought the history of oppression was so important. But then, I wasn't seeing this equally important history of how people responded to that oppression. That's what this course is completely structured around: how people respond to all of these histories of oppression and suppression. We're talking about Audre Lorde and emotions as a form of resistance, spatial resistance and gentrification; we discuss boycott as a form of resistance; we discuss just being, clothing, music as forms of expression and resistance.

Inspiration

There's a woman who created an online archive of African stories from around the world, Amy Sall, and that's the SUNU Journal. I absolutely love it. I constantly go to it for inspiration, just even in images, looking at those images of people in their full and complete Blackness, anywhere around the world. It does inspire me so incredibly, but even more so someone taking the time to put it all together, because everybody loves history, everybody loves going to the library and being able to find whatever's on their mind, but so, so rarely do we say thank you to the archivists that make them available, and this preservation of the work and lives that we see value in is so critical. We would be nowhere without our archivists. Archivists inspire me so much, because my storytelling is not just, "Here's a story that I think is cool." I want this to live longer than just my eyes can see it now. I want a Precious two hundred years from now to be able to gain insight and see herself within whatever story is being preserved in this moment. Amy Sall is amazing.

Mariame Kaba is my inspiration for all things abolition. She really does live it. One of my favorite things about her is it's so hard to find a picture of her face. It's not about her, it's about these communities, so being able to take a step back and again put at the forefront the people who you are advocating alongside. Mariame Kaba really emphasizes that we're not advocating for people, we're advocating alongside people. She's one who has inspired me so much, she does so much critical abolition work, so much work to dismantle this prison industrial complex in which we live, and she just inspires me constantly.

My mom is the one who introduced me to storytelling itself. She's still the most animated storyteller I know. She's smiling bigger than the sun, and she makes you feel as though you're experiencing what she's describing right there and then. She's so full, yet so soft, and I think that I try to create a similar feeling with the stories that I tell, a fullness but also a softness that we all really need.

On the UCR campus, there's just so many. Dr. Anthonia Kalu in Comparative Literature, one of the people doing the amazing work of preserving the stories that we hold dear. She was like my auntie on campus, giving me the pushes and the love and also the tough love to make me do things in a way that's wholehearted. She said, "Don't just do this essay. Don't just take this class. Do the absolute best that you can, because you owe it to the people who wrote these books, the people who are gonna read your book one day." You could definitely see all the love that was coming from her. She's been an amazing mentor.

Advice

Do some documentation of your life and those around you. I wish that somebody had told me this more. Write down how you feel every day, how you feel the people around you may feel, take pictures, do the work of documentation. **Be the archivist of your own life and your own family**, and upon reflecting on that, you'll be able to see what is important to you, what you want to be sustained into this world. Once you start being the documentarian, the archivist of your own life and the lives of those who you love and you want to be preserved beyond this time and this breath today, you'll be able to see where you are needed in this world, in what capacity, and once you find that space, go into it wholeheartedly. Do that work for yourself, but also generations to come will thank you for it. I thank you right now for doing this work as we speak.

"Then pass the torch"

Rose Mayes

Roots

I was born in a little town called Melville, Louisiana in the deep, deep South. My mother and father Lucy Green and Roosevelt Green had a total of fourteen kids, seven boys and seven girls, and I was the eleventh child. It was a beautiful family growing up in the country. I migrated to Houston, Texas, in the late sixties, and then made my transition here to Riverside, California in 1979. My sister Katie Green was in the military at the time, and she was stationed at March Air Force Base. Katie and I were very, very close, and we always said after we completed high school, we'd go to college or university, and wherever she would go, I would follow her. She ended up in Riverside, California and March Air Force Base, and finally she said, "Well, when are you coming?" That is when I packed my bag and I moved to Riverside.

Call to activism

My mother and father taught us to be fair. If you see something that's wrong, ask questions about it—why is it done that way? They taught us all to have the courage to speak out against it. We were grounded in that. That's the thing that started me on my way. When I was in high school, I began to see the difference in how people were treated based upon certain aspects of their lives, whether or not they were rich, poor, middle class. And especially coming from the South, I saw the difference between how Blacks and whites treated one another. And I began to ask those questions. Why?

My parents worked so hard, so long, and always did an excellent job and whatever was asked of them. I remember when my mother worked as a maid in a white lady's kitchen and this white lady had a son who did not like to have people of color in his household. When he came home for lunch, we had to go outside because he did not let Black people in his house. However, I kept thinking about that as a child. She had her hands all over his lunch, but he's eating that. That was me as a child, asking those questions to myself, afraid to ask my mother because I knew what she would say: "Be quiet. We have to do what we have to do." She was always warning us of the danger. We could not walk into a restaurant through the front door.

When we moved to Houston, I was in high school and I worked in the restaurant at the school. I would feed all of the civil rights workers—the boss man hired me to make sure that they got free food, free drinks, and whatever they needed in order to go back on whatever line that they were on. I got their meals out on the table so they can eat so they can go back on the picket lines.

Contributions

It was a lonely feeling when I first got here in 1979 because I expected to find things that I saw in the South here, but I couldn't find the African American community when I first arrived. I saw some African American and Hispanic people in the Eastside of Riverside, but they were so scattered. I expected to see a cluster of the African American community working together, doing things together, and I just didn't see the organizing and the sheer number that I saw in Texas. Then I recognized that there was a low percentage of African Americans living in the city of Riverside. Even with the ones here, it was very difficult to break into getting involved. That is how I decided that you can't sit around and complain all the time. You have to do something, make it happen. I started getting involved in NAACP, the Urban League with Rose Oliver. A lot of the old timers here, June Foreman, we started doing things together. I wanted to make a difference.

I worked a lot of jobs here, I worked for various places, and I also had my own business. I had the print shop along with a post office out on Wood Road, Van Buren. I was doing some volunteer work as well. After I finished my shift at my dear printing and post office services, I would do volunteer work for the Fair Housing Council. I was a tester, finding out whether or not a person who wanted to rent a certain apartment was being discriminated against. I was the key African American tester. If they told me, "No, we have no vacancies," and if my white counterpart was given the paperwork or given something different, I would bring it back to Fair Housing, and they would do an analysis to see what was given to me as opposed to what was given to the white testers. Most of the time, I was denied and most of the time my white tester was given their unit and asked when she wanted to move in. One day a woman named Mildred Taylor—I'll never forget her—came to my business and told me I had to close my store down and come work for Fair Housing Council because they needed an executive director. That's how I got to the Fair Housing Council.

We are the boots. We are the people at the grassroots level that receive calls. With all of that data, we see trends, because one call after another, you hear some of the same issues coming up over and over again. We knew that they were giving low- to moderate-income clients nice homes with these flexible types of funding. We saw a trend there that a lot of people after two or three years were losing those homes. That's when the foreclosure crisis came. We had said this is the wrong thing to do.

I moved away to Seattle for a time. When I came back from Seattle, I met with the mayor of Riverside at that time, Mayor Loveridge. I started asking him, "Why can't we have statues like I saw in Seattle, Washington?" I said, "What if I recommend that we have a statue to Dr. Martin Luther King somewhere?" I just didn't see enough of history and of other nationalities within our city at all, and I was very, very frustrated about that. I got in touch with Norm Martin, Rose Oliver, Jennifer Vaughn-Blakely, Katie Green, Ola Faye Stephens. I said, "I'm thinking about putting up a statue of Dr. Martin Luther King here," and they said, "Good luck." Then Jack Clark told me, "Rose, you got to be out of your mind. Do you realize that you want a statue of Dr. Martin Luther King in downtown Riverside where there's nothing but mostly white folks?" I said "Jack, you can't give up just like that." Of course, Jack is real funny, he said, "Well, maybe you can't, but I can." We worked for ten years and we finally got that together.

We also got the street named for Dr. King, and then came the high school. It was so ugly. One lady called me at 2:30 in the morning. She said, "Do you recognize that my child grew up in Woodcrest and we're not moving out of Woodcrest, but I don't want her to go to no school named after a Black man." I said, "Well, I'm sorry. But I've got to go back to sleep because I've got to get up early in the morning, because I have a lot of questions to answer to you and others, then we have to make this a reality, because it's unfair to other students of color. As far as I'm concerned, we're going to fight for that." She said, "We'll see." And the rest is history.

Mayor Loveridge finally decided after all the controversy was coming in that we needed to get together and he got all of the business leaders together. Dr. Lulamae Clemons was there—she was treasurer of the MLK Visionaries Foundation—and she pulled out her index cards, and she said, "I've got every name of every individual who's given us every penny written here." And she said, "We still have not raised enough money. I'm going to pass some cards around and see whether or not you want to put your name, telephone number and address and how much money that you want to donate towards this monument." We raised over seventy thousand dollars that day.

When Tyisha Miller was killed, I had three months left as Human Relations chairperson, and the only thing that I could do was to keep praying. Rose Oliver, Norm Martin, Chani Beeman, a couple of other people kept on coming to the meetings, and the Human Relations Commission didn't want to touch that. I said, "Well, we have to do something." I got away from the Human Relations Commission and started meeting with the mayor by myself. I said, "We cannot just sit here and not do anything." We started looking to Chani Beeman and Deborah Wong, they were coming to some of those meetings. Then we started reaching out to the Black ministers here in the city, in Rubidoux, San Bernardino, and they started gathering as well. We started talking with the elected officials, with Ameal Moore and Chuck Beatty. That's when they appointed the Police Review Commission.

During that period of time, Rose Oliver called me and said, "Rose, what are you doing for Christmas?" I said, "Nothing really." Then she said, "Well, is it okay if we have a little potluck or something over at your house?" Rose Oliver came over and invited a lot of people, Dr. Lulamae Clemons, Sylvia Martin James, a lot of folks. I didn't realize it was going to be so many people, but it didn't cost me anything, and then it turned into a meeting! That's when The Group was formed. We started meeting, we started talking about issues and concerns, we recognized that we were identifying a lot of issues and concerns that people were afraid to speak out or speak up. Then we said, "Why don't we get these elected officials in our audience so that they can answer some of these questions?" That's how it all got started. We were most effective because we were able to speak out against some of the things going on in the community that no one would address. A lot of issues that were being covered up. There were people just as sick and tired of being sick and tired. They started coming to The Group.

I was looking at boards and commissions and I never could see a person of color there, and I asked, "Why not?" They kept telling us at City Hall, "We can't find people of color to serve on boards and commissions." I thought that was so interesting. I had one council member tell me, "A lot of them don't know about the boards and commissions." I said, "How do you make them aware of it?" It was then I talked with Jennifer Vaughn-Blakely, Ola Faye Stephens, Rose Oliver, Norm Martin, a lot of those people, and I just said, "Well, why aren't we doing anything? We don't have anybody on boards and commissions and it's just white folks up there, and yet we sit around and we go to these meetings and we're complaining, so let's get involved." They said, "Well, they don't seem to understand parliamentary procedures and they don't seem to even say that much even when they serve." That's how the Eleanor Jean Grier Leadership Academy got started. We decided we needed an academy here to start training people who want to serve on boards and commissions. Jennifer had been in that setting, and she had the talent and the skills to be able to put the curriculum together. Katie Green who had retired from the military, worked for the County of Riverside, and had a law degree, decided, "I'm going to teach it." A lot of wonderful people came out of that class. Some are now city council people. A lot of them are very engaged in the community.

Fair Housing was a community place where people would come. But the owner of the property sold it, and the rent increased. You can't remain stable if you're constantly moving from here to there as a nonprofit organization, changing addresses so that people can't find you. The city manager called me one day to introduce me to a couple that had this property on Mission Inn Avenue. It was a maintenance supply place and they wanted to sell the property to a nonprofit organization. The city manager told them, "If anybody can do something with your property that you will be proud of, it is this lady right here, Rose Mayes." It was an old house sitting on the corner with a parking lot. We did fundraisers and we put the down-payment on it and the rest is history. We cleaned it up, we made what we could make out of it, and we allowed nonprofit organizations to come in and have meetings.

We formed another nonprofit entity called the Civil Rights Institute. Everything we have done thus far has been so timely, because looking at the state of affairs that we're in now, we need something like this. Let's work together for the good of this city, this state, the country, because it's a lose-lose situation when you allow people to use you to fight against one another. Come in here with your untold stories. Come in here with issues that we have to address. Come in here when we see things that we know are not going right at City Hall, at the County Board of Supervisors. Let's discuss them. I'm leaving it to the next generation. The Walk of Fame should not just come from the Civil Rights Institute. It must go all the way down Mission Inn Avenue, make a right there on Main Street, all the way to City Hall, to the courthouse, for those people making an impact in our region, so that not only is it archived, but people can walk the Walk of Fame and young people can know what we did. They can continue to do it.

Inspiration

June Foreman and Dr. Lulamae Clemons. Dr. Lulamae Clemons was very quiet, but very powerful. She was there at ninety-five years old, encouraging young people. She was always there. She said, "Don't be afraid to speak the truth. The truth will set you free." I found that to be very close to my heart. Whenever I would speak the truth, it may hurt some people at the beginning, but by and by, they'll understand it.

Advice

What I'll say to young people is to learn very early on in life, find your mission. Find your passion, never, never, never give up. There are going to be ups and downs. Never give up and keep your eyes on the prize. And **once you have done all that you possibly can do, don't forget to pass the torch to the next generation.**

Women's History Timeline

1848 – Seneca Falls Convention, considered the first women's right convention, held in New York and organized by Elizabeth Cady Stanton, Lucretia Mott, and others

1851 – Sojourner Truth, a formerly enslaved woman, delivers"Ain't I A Woman" speech at a women's convention in Ohio

1869 – Elizabeth Cady Stanton and Susan B. Anthony found National Woman Suffrage Association

1873 – **Parent navel orange trees planted in Riverside by Eliza Tibbets**

1911 – **Ysabel Solorio Olvera and Margarita Salcedo Solorio petition the Riverside Board of Education for a school in Casa Blanca**

1917 – Jeannette Rankin elected to the U.S. House of Representatives, the first woman to hold that role

1920 – The 19th Amendment to the U.S. Constitution ratified, extending voting rights to women

1929 – **The Riverside YWCA (Young Women's Christian Association) built; designed by pioneering architect Julia Morgan, the building would later become the Riverside Art Museum**

1933 – Frances Perkins appointed Secretary of Labor by President Franklin D. Roosevelt and becomes the first women to serve as a cabinet member

1934 – **Vera L. Barger first woman to be elected to Riverside City Council**

1935 – The National Council of Negro Women founded, led by Mary McLeod Bethune

1946 – **Mine Okubo's *Citizen 13660* first published, described by her as "the first and only documentary story of the Japanese evacuation and relocation written and illustrated by one who was there." Okubo was born in Riverside and attended Poly High School and Riverside City College**

1961 – The President's Commission on the Status of Women established by President John F. Kennedy and chaired by Eleanor Roosevelt

1962 – Rachel Carson's *Silent Spring* published

1963 – Betty Friedan's *The Feminine Mystique* published

1964 – Civil Rights Act signed into law

1965 – **Lowell School is burned; Riverside Unified School District devises bussing plan to integrate Riverside schools; Art Alliance of the Riverside Art Museum founded by twelve women**

1966 – The National Organization for Women (NOW) founded; **Ruth Anderson Wilson, Martha McClean, and Kay Black found the Tri-County Conservation League**

1967 – The New York Radical Women and Chicago Women's Liberation Group founded

1968 – The First National Women's Liberation Conference held; New York Radical Women stage "No More Miss America!" demonstration at the Miss America Pageant; New York Radical Women begin holding consciousness-raising groups; Shirley Chisholm becomes the first Black woman elected to Congress

1969 – The Boston Women's Health Collective publishes a pamphlet that represents the first edition of *Our Bodies, Ourselves*

1970 – The North American Indian Women's Association founded; Robin Morgan's *Sisterhood Is Powerful* published; first Earth Day is celebrated

1971 – Bella Abzug, Shirley Chisholm, Betty Friedan, Gloria Steinem, and others form the National Women's Political Caucus to support more women candidates

1972 – *Ms.* Magazine begins publication; The Equal Rights Amendment passes both houses of Congress; Title IX of the Educational Amendments to the Civil Rights Act requires educational institutions to provide support for women's athletics

1973 – The Supreme Court decision *Roe v. Wade* establishes rights to abortion; first "battered women's shelters" open in U.S.; the Government Printing Office first accepts the prefix "Ms."

1973 – **Riverside Area Rape Crisis Center founded; Women's Resource Center founded at UC Riverside**

1974 – The Equal Credit Opportunity Act allows married women access to credit in their own name for the first time; the Mexican American Women's National Association formed; **Riverside County Commission on the Status of Women formed**

1975 – The First International Conference on Women held in Mexico City; the first National Women's Health Conference held in Boston

1976 – The Organization of Pan Asian American Women formed

1977 – The First National Women's Conference held in Houston, Texas; first women pilots graduate from the Air Force

1978 – **Glen Avon residents begin organizing to shut down the Stringfellow Acid Pit toxic waste site; Jane Block debuts the feminist radio program "Women's Space, Women's Place" on KUCR – it would run until 1982**

1981 – Sandra Day O'Connor becomes the first woman appointed to the U.S. Supreme Court.

1982 – **Melba Dunlap elected to the Riverside County Board of Supervisors, leading to a female majority on the Board of Supervisors**

1983 – Sally Ride becomes the first woman in space; **Inland AIDS Project incorporated**

1984 – Geraldine Ferraro becomes the first woman to serve as a vice presidential running mate on a major party ticket

1985 – **Political Action Coalition for Election (PACE) founded**

1986 – **Fair Housing Council founded**

1987 – Congress declares the month of March "Women's History Month"

1987 – **Riverside County Childcare Consortium founded**

1989 – **Riverside Land Conservancy founded**

1990 – **Teresa Frizzel elected Mayor of Riverside, the first woman to hold that office**

1992 – Barbara Boxer and Dianne Feinstein elected to the United States Senate as the two senators from California, the first state to be represented in the Senate by two women; **Nancy Willem, a local lesbian activist, raped and beaten to death; her murder led to the founding of Women Enraged! (WE!)**

1993 – **UCR LGBT Resource Center formed; Center for Community Action and Environmental Justice founded**

1998 – **Tyisha Miller killed by Riverside police**

1999 – **The Group is officially founded**

2000 – The Million Mom March is organized in Washington, D.C. to call for an end to gun violence; **Riverside African American Historical Society founded**

2002 – California becomes the first state to require employers provide partial pay for six weeks of parental leave

2006 – Nancy Pelosi becomes the first woman to serve as Speaker of the House of Representatives; **Inlandia Institute founded**

2012 – **The Center for Social Justice and Civil Liberties opens, housing a large collection of artwork and archives from Riverside-born artist and Riverside City College alumna Mine Okubo**

2016 – Hillary Rodham Clinton becomes the first woman to serve as the presidential nominee of a major political party

2017 – **The Women's March held in Riverside; Riverside Resistance Revival Chorus formed**

2018 – **March for Our Lives**

2019 – **Erin Edwards and Gabriela Plascencia elected to Riverside City Council; Riverside Women Creating Change meetings begin**

2020 – COVID-19 pandemic begins; Kamala Harris elected Vice President, the first woman to serve in that office; **Patricia Lock Dawson elected Mayor of Riverside**

2021 – **Clarissa Cervantes elected to Riverside City Council**

2022 – **Riverside's Chicago Avenue Post Office officially renamed in honor of late Riverside NAACP President Woodie Rucker-Hughes;** U.S. Supreme Court overturned *Roe v. Wade*

2024 – Kamala Harris becomes the first woman of color to serve as the presidential nominee of a major political party

Sources for timeline include: Ruth Rosen, *The World Split Open: How The Modern Women's Movement Changed America* (Penguin, 2006); City of Riverside LGBTQ+ Historic Context Statement (August 2023).

Acknowledgments

Riverside Women Creating Change would not exist were it not for the generous support of many individuals who gave of their time, talent, and treasure, including these early supporters: Judith and Phil Auth, Chani Beeman, Charles Block, Jane and Richard Block, Amy Conger, Catherine Daves, Cathy Gudis, Kris and Steve Lovekin, Roger and Connie Ransom, Ofelia Valdez-Yeager.

Financial support for this project was also provided by The City of Riverside through the City Sponsorship program and through a California Humanities Humanities for All Quick Grant.

All photographs courtesy of the interviewees with specific credit to:

John Briggs: Andrea Briggs
Andrea Decker: Judith Auth, Elizabeth Ayala, and Jane Block
Jennifer Cappuccio Maher, Southern California News Group: Lecia Elzig
Emma Donahue: Joan Donahue
Michael Dunn: Linda Dunn
David Fouts: Patricia Lock Dawson
Elisabeth Girke Photography: Selin Yildiz Nielsen
Jeffrey S. Laird: Marilyn Sequoia
Stan Lim: Precious Pipeloluwa Fasakin
Courtney Lindberg Photography: Clarissa Cervantes
Dr. Sofia Vizcarra: Carol Park
Michael J. Elderman: Connie Ransom plus group photo
Daniel T. Jester: Erin Edwards
JSK Journalism Fellowships @ Stanford University: Paulette Brown-Hinds
Kurt Miller: Riverside Resistance Revival Choir
Christine Racz: Rabbi Suzanne Singer
Carrie Rosema: Sarah Wright Garibay
Lori Stirling: Nancy Melendez
Community Settlement Association: Rose Y. Monge
Riverside Community College District: Mary Figueroa
Ofelia Valdez Yeager: Meredith Gradishar at ZoomTheory.
Marisa V. Yeager: Corinne McCurdy, CSUSB photographer

WITHOUT FREEDOM OF THOUGHT,
THERE CAN BE NO SUCH THING AS WISDOM;
AND NO SUCH THING AS PUBLIC LIBERTY

About Riverside Women Creating Change

Riverside Women Creating Change was founded by a coalition of women—Jane Block, Connie Ransom, Deborah Wong, Nicolette Rohr, Cati Porter, and Andrea Decker—working together to share methodologies, perspectives, and philosophies of grassroots community organizing in the City of Riverside. Our purpose is to distill that information into a highly digestible form to be used as a tool by current and future community organizers. These tools include a website & blog which will serve as a repository of data and information, occasional public forums, and this culminating book project.

Jane Catherine McMenamin Block has been an environmental and social activist in Riverside City and County since 1970. She has played a leading role in the establishment of nature preserves including Box Springs Mountain Park/Reserve, Sycamore Canyon Wilderness Park, the Santa Rosa Plateau, and Indian Canyon, as well as helping to preserve Riverside's Victoria Avenue and establish the City's bike-way system. In the mid-1970s she assisted in establishing the Riverside County Commission on the Status of Women, Alternatives to Domestic Violence with its shelters for battered women, and the Riverside County Child Care Consortium. Jane also interviewed active women on the KUCR radio program Women's Space, Women's Place and established the UCR Women's Resource Center.

Dr. Andrea Decker is an accomplished ethnomusicologist and librarian with a Ph.D. from UC Riverside and an M.S. in Library and Information Science from University of Illinois, Urbana Champaign. She specializes in Indonesian popular music and has extensive experience in library and archival settings. In addition to the Riverside Women Creating Change project, she has processed and archived oral histories at the Library of Congress and the Autry Museum of the American West. Currently, she serves as a Reference Librarian at the American Folklife Center.

Cati Porter has been executive director of Inlandia Institute since 2013. She is a poet and essayist and the recipient of an Individual Artist Fellowship from the California Arts Council. She received her MFA in Creative Writing with a concentration in poetry from Antioch University Los Angeles. Cati Porter has lived in Riverside for more than thirty years. Her activism focuses on championing the literary arts in all of its forms, particularly in K-12 education, and working behind the scenes in local, regional, and statewide arts advocacy. She would like you to know that language arts and literary arts are *not* equivalent.

Connie Ransom earned a BA from Reed College and an MFA from Claremont Graduate University. Using an artist's problem-solving tools plus her ability to connect people she fights for art and music in the schools and helped lead the 2017 Riverside Women's March. Connie uses her experience, her voice, her feet, and her financial resources to protect cultural, arts, educational, and environmental assets. Preserving and building a strong, safe, and attractive community where these assets thrive motivates Connie to action in Riverside and the Inland Empire. She is past President of both the Citizens University Committee and the Maloof Foundation. She strongly supports City, Regional and National leaders who share in her beliefs and goals.

Nicolette Rohr was born and raised in Riverside and grew up with a love for stories and songs. Her curiosity about what happened here led to her to the Public History Program at UC Riverside, where she earned her PhD in History. She has taught at UCR, Riverside City College, University of Redlands, and Pomona College. Her research on the history of the 1960s, popular music, and fandom have taken her many places, but her favorite projects are about Riverside. She strives to create change in this community through gun violence prevention advocacy, refugee support, faith, spirituality, and storytelling.

Deborah Wong is an ethnomusicologist and Professor Emerita at the University of California, Riverside. She has written three books: *Louder and Faster: Pain, Joy, and the Body Politic in Asian American Taiko* (2019), *Speak It Louder: Asian Americans Making Music* (2004), and *Sounding the Center: History and Aesthetics in Thai Buddhist Ritual* (2001). She served as editor for Nobuko Miyamoto's extraordinary memoir, *Not Yo' Butterfly: My Long Song of Relocation, Race, Love, and Revolution* (2021). Her happiest hours of the week are spent going on air with her weekly radio show *Gold Mountain* for KUCR 88.3 FM in Riverside. She was a member of the Taiko Center of Los Angeles for many years and still dances *bon-odori* every summer in Southern California Obon gatherings.

About Inlandia Institute

Inlandia Institute is a regional literary non-profit and publishing house. We seek to bring focus to the richness of the literary enterprise that has existed in this region for ages. The mission of the Inlandia Institute is to recognize, support, and expand literary activity in all of its forms in Inland Southern California by publishing books and sponsoring programs that deepen people's awareness, understanding, and appreciation of this unique, complex and creatively vibrant region.

The Institute publishes books, presents free public literary and cultural programming, provides in-school and after school enrichment programs for children and youth, holds free creative writing workshops for teens and adults, and boot camp intensives. In addition, every two years, the Inlandia Institute appoints a distinguished jury panel from outside of the region to name an Inlandia Literary Laureate who serves as an ambassador for the Inlandia Institute, promoting literature, creative literacy, and community. Laureates to date include Susan Straight (2010-2012), Gayle Brandeis (2012-2014), Juan Delgado (2014-2016), Nikia Chaney (2016-2018), and Rachelle Cruz (2018-2020).

To learn more about the Inlandia Institute, please visit our website at www.InlandiaInstitute.org.

Inlandia Books

Writing from Inlandia annual anthology series

Guajira, the Cuba girl by Zita Arocha

Breaking Pattern by Tisha Marie Reichle-Aguilera

Exit Prohibited by Ellen Estilai

These Black Bodies Are…, edited by Romaine Washington

Vermillion Speedateer by Sebraé Harris

Pretend Plumber by Stephanie Barbé Hammer

Ladybug by Nikia Chaney

Vital: The Future of Healthcare, edited by RM Ambrose

Güero-Güero: The White Mexican and Other Published and Unpublished Stories by Dr. Eliud Martínez

A Short Guide to Finding Your First Home in the United States: An Inlandia anthology on the immigrant experience

Care: Stories by Christopher Records

San Bernardino, Singing, edited by Nikia Chaney

Facing Fire: Art, Wildfire, and the End of Nature in the New West by Douglas McCulloh

In the Sunshine of Neglect: Defining Photographs and Radical Experiments in Inland Southern California, 1950 to the Present by Douglas McCulloh

Henry L. A. Jekel: Architect of Eastern Skyscrapers and the California Style by Dr. Vincent Moses and Catherine Whitmore

Orangelandia: The Literature of Inland Citrus edited by Gayle Brandeis

While We're Here We Should Sing by The Why Nots

Go to the Living by Micah Chatterton

No Easy Way: Integrating Riverside Schools - A Victory for Community by Arthur L. Littleworth